# The Mitchell Beazley
## pocket guide to
# *Italian Wines*

# Burton Anderson

## *Third Edition*

Mitchell Beazley

## Key to symbols

| | |
|---|---|
| r. | red |
| p. | rosé |
| w. | white |
| am. | amber |
| dr. | dry |
| s/sw. | semisweet |
| sw. | sweet |
| fz. | *frizzante* |
| sp. | sparkling |

In parentheses means relatively unimportant

| | |
|---|---|
| ★ | everyday wine |
| ★★ | above average |
| ★★★ | superior in its category |
| ★★★★ | outstanding |
| ★★ (boxed) | usually good value in its class |

| | |
|---|---|
| DOC | name and origin controlled |
| DOCG | name and origin controlled and guaranteed |
| Ag. 1 yr. etc. | aging required under DOC |
| 74 75 etc. | recommended years. Where red, rosé and white are indicated the red is intended unless otherwise stated. |
| DYA | drink the youngest available |
| NV | vintage not normally shown on label |

See p. 5 for more information.

## Key to maps

200 meters
500 meters

Edited and designed by
Mitchell Beazley International Ltd
Artists House, 14-15 Manette Street, London W1V 5LB
© Mitchell Beazley Publishers 1982, 1984, 1987
First edition 1982
Revised editions 1984, 1987
Reprinted 1988
Text © Burton Anderson 1982, 1984, 1986

ISBN 0 85533 678 1

The author and publishers will be grateful for any information which will assist them in keeping future editions up to date. Although all reasonable care has been taken in the preparation of this book, neither the publishers nor the author can accept any liability for any consequences arising from the use thereof, or from the information contained herein.

Typeset by Servis Filmsetting Ltd., Manchester
Printed in Hong Kong by Mandarin Offset

*Editor* Alison Franks
*Production* Androulla Wakefield
*Senior Executive Editor* Chris Foulkes
*Senior Executive Art Editor* Roger Walton

Maps by Illustra Design Ltd., Reading

# Contents

# Foreword

Italy has always stood in the central piazza of civilization like a great baroque fountain, rather battered by time and small boys, spewing forth a torrent of wine of all colours and kinds. The Italians were happy to fill their pitchers at it and relatively unconcerned about whether the tourists joined them. To post notices round the fountain explaining the contributions of myriad farmers in scores of regions seemed absurd. Besides it would spoil the view.

But now things are different. The public, and particularly the public abroad, is intensely interested in precisely who makes what wine where. It wants to identify the wine of each region, to enjoy it with the region's food. It wants to celebrate the individual winemakers and get the feel of their land – and to understand why some wines are inherently better than others.

Italy is so vast and various that it takes a certain kind of mind to plot its ramifications. It must be methodical – but not Germanically so. It needs patience – oh what patience! Dedication is essential and a sense of humour a *sine qua non*. It must be someone who cares about people – because that, emphatically, is what Italians do.

The model guide, in fact, turned out to be a reformed American newspaperman who lives in Tuscany. He broke cover with his book *Vino* in 1980. My first reading convinced me that this author knew what he was talking about. When I met him I realized that he judges wine as well as he describes it and the men who make it. I was delighted to have found a kindred spirit, and I am delighted to introduce him, and the fruit of his Herculean labours, to you.

The toast is – Burton Anderson.

Hugh Johnson
*April, 1982*

# Introduction

In a world of increasingly standardized styles and tastes, Italy stands unrivaled as wine's champion of diversity. The nation produces, consumes and exports more wine than any other, but even more remarkable than the scope is the intricacy of it all.

It might be conjectured that Italy has 1,605,785 wines, allowing one for each registered vineyard. Well, maybe, though my aim in this compact volume was not to count them all but to single out as many as possible of those wines that count.

Since enactment of the laws of controlled name and origin (DOC) in the mid-1960s, winemaking in Italy has evolved from an antiquated, often makeshift trade, to a growingly disciplined high-tech industry. Yet the science is enhanced by enough artistry to draw references to the movement as a renaissance. The methanol tragedy of 1986, though the work of a few criminals, smeared the good name of Italian wine, but it also heightened the resolve of honest producers whose quest for quality has never been more vital.

Consumers seem to agree that Italian wine is generally the best value on the world market. Yet only about a quarter of an annual production of 7.2 billion liters is exported, meaning that most Italian wine is drunk at home. This is not because Italians are reluctant to share the wealth, but rather because non-Italians have been slow to recognize that there is so much there. Only recently have foreigners lifted the lid off Italy's enological treasure chest after overcoming fears that they might be opening another Pandora's box of cheap wine in straw flasks, painted crockery and fishy amphorae.

Now that the lid has been lifted, the challenge is picking the gems. The profusion of colors, scents and flavors that make modern Italian wine so alluring is partly screened by the jumble of names – of grape varieties, wine types, places, people, trademarks – which can, even if inadvertently, create confusion and inhibit sales. For example, the more than 220 DOC zones take in more than 800 distinct wines. Yet DOC represents only 10–12% of total production – supposedly the cream of the crop, but not always. Some of Italy's finest wines fly their own colors.

Despite a gradual decline in production in Italy, the ranks of qualified wines and winemakers continue to expand. Dramatic progress has been achieved with both native and foreign varieties in regions where natural conditions for vines are unsurpassed and the potential for great wines is being increasingly fulfilled.

Most Italian wines of importance are described in the A–Z section, which surveys all 20 regions in alphabetical order. An encyclopedic listing may have seemed handier, but it would have put the subject out of focus. Italian wines come into context only when related to their habitats – to the soil, climate, customs, foods and people of their own regions.

This pocket book is a buyer's guide, compact enough to take along for reference to a shop or restaurant anywhere. It is also designed to be a tour guide with maps, travel tips, local food specialities and recommended restaurants, an ideal companion for discovering the intricacies of Italian wine at first hand.

# How to read an entry

The top line of each entry indicates in abbreviated form:

1. If the wine is DOC or DOCG. If not, whatever its class, its authenticity is not officially controlled.
2. Whether it is red, rosé, white, amber, dry, semisweet, sweet, *frizzante* (lightly bubbly), sparkling, or several of these.
3. Rating of general quality:

   * everyday wine
   ** above average
   *** superior in its category
   **** outstanding

   These rankings weigh personal experience against status consigned by recognized critics and experts. The context is strictly Italian. Four stars (applied cautiously) indicate wine of the top echelon in Italy without hypothesizing international status. One reason for this is that some exceptional Italian wines are hardly known elsewhere. One star indicates the ordinary, but bear in mind that what some Italians drink daily would be prized in other nations. Because so many Italian wine names cover various colors and types and represent a multitude of producers, quality may vary considerably within a single denomination, indeed by as much as *→****. A box ☐ signals generally good value, though prices, too, may fluctuate among wines of the same name.
4. Recommended recent vintages. Each description mentions in principle when the wine should be at prime. If, for example, 82 is recommended and prime is in 5–8 years, ideal drinking should be from 1987 to 1990. Remember, though, that vintage information is relative. Some producers make good wine in off years, and wine from certain vintages and winemakers may age better than wine from others. No matter what the charts say, your taste and experience of a wine are the final arbiters in deciding when to drink it. The abbreviation DYA suggests that the wine should be drunk within months or, at the most, a couple of years, but that doesn't exclude the possibility that it could hold up well for longer. The term NV usually applies to non-vintage sparkling or fortified wines.

If a wine is subjected to aging under DOC, the required time is mentioned, as is specified barrel aging, where it applies. Special designations, such as *vecchio* and *riserva*, signify further aging; these, too, are indicated.

Producers (listed after each entry) have been screened for reliability against every source I could find. Single listings of producers are given in zones with more than one wine because it would be beyond the limits of a pocket book to cite each producer with each type of wine. (Of 19 types in the Alto-Adige appellation, for instance, some producers make a dozen or more.)

Some Italian wines sold on foreign markets carry bottler, shipper or importer brands or names used only in countries where sold. Most such wines, however qualified they might be, are not considered. The focus is on wines whose grape compositions and origins are verifiable in Italy.

The information under *Wine & Food* at the end of each regional section is intended mainly to aid travelers in Italy, though home cooks and diners in Italian restaurants in other lands may also find it useful. Wine suggestions with each speciality are intended to be indicators, not requisites. Others will prefer to make their own choice, based on the selection of wines available.

# Glossary

These terms may help you to read a label or be of use while traveling through a wine zone.

**Abboccato** Lightly sweet, literally "mouth-filling."
**Acidità** Acidity.
**Acidulo** Acidulous, acidic.
**Alcool** Alcohol.
**Amabile** Semisweet, literally "amiable," a shade sweeter than *abboccato* or *pastoso*.
**Amaro** Bitter.
**Amarognolo** The almond-like bitter undertone detectable in many Italian wines.
**Ambrato** The amber hue noted in many dessert or aperitif wines.
**Annata** Year of vintage.
**Aroma** The ample scent of young, fruity (*aromatico*) whites, such as Moscato or Traminer.
**Asciutto** Bone dry.
**Azienda agricola, azienda agraria, azienda vitivinicola** Terms for farm or estate winery.
**Barrique** Small barrel often of French origin increasingly used for aging in Italy. Also *carato*.
**Bianco** White.
**Bicchiere** Drinking glass.
**Blanc de blancs** French term for white wine from light grapes only, sometimes used on labels of Italian sparkling wine.
**Botte** Cask.
**Bottiglia** Bottle.
**Brut** French term for dry sparkling wine, also used in Italy.
**Cantina** Wine cellar or winery.
**Cantina sociale** or **cooperativa** Cooperative winery (abbreviated to C.S. in producer listings).
**Casa vinicola** Wine house, usually in reference to one that processes purchased grapes.
**Cascina** Farm or estate, usually in northern Italy.
**Cerasuolo** Cherry red, used to describe certain rosés.
**Charmat** The French-originated method of refermenting sparkling wines in sealed vats.
**Chiaretto** Though it means *claret*, it describes certain dark rosés.
**Classico** Classic, used to define zones of long-standing tradition within a DOC (i.e. Chianti Classico, Orvieto Classico) and the wine from grapes grown there.
**Consorzio** Voluntary consortium of growers and producers set up to supervise and control production and to promote wine.
**Degustazione** Wine tasting.
**Dolce** Sweet, technically in reference to wines with 5–10% residual sugar.
**Enologia** Enology, the study of wine.
**Enologo** Enologist. Italian graduate enologists are known as *enotecnici* or wine technicians.
**Enoteca** Literally wine library, applied to both public and commercial establishments with wines on display.
**Etichetta** Label.
**Ettaro** Hectare, or 2.471 acres, the standard measure of vineyard surface in Europe.
**Ettolitro** Hectoliter, or 100 liters, equivalent to a *quintale*, or 100 kilograms, the standard measure of wine volume in Europe.
**Fattoria** Farm or estate, usually in central Italy.
**Fermentazione** Fermentation. Wine made bubbly through natural processes is often labeled as *fermentazione naturale*.
**Fiasco** Flask, i.e. the straw-based, bulbous Chianti container.
**Frizzante** Lightly bubbly, *pétillant*, but not with enough pressure to qualify as sparkling.
**Frizzantino** refers to wine with a barely noticeable prickle.
**Fusto** Cask, barrel.
**Gradazione alcoolica** Alcohol grade (%) by volume.
**Gusto** Flavor (not in the English-language sense of "gusto," however).
**Imbottigliato da** Bottled by.
**Invecchiato** Aged.
**Liquoroso** Wine of high-alcohol grade, usually, though not always fortified.
**Litro** Liter, equivalent to 1.056 U.S. quarts or 0.908 British quart.
**Marchio depositato** Registered brand name or trademark.
**Marsalato** or **maderizzato** Refers to wines which through oxidation take on flavors reminiscent of Marsala or Madeira, favorable when

controlled in certain dessert wines, undesirable in most table wines.
**Metodo champenois** or **metodo classico** Italian ways of referring to the classical Champagne method (*méthode champenoise*) of bottle-fermenting sparkling wines.
**Passito** Strong, usually sweet wine from the concentrated musts of semidried, or *passito*, grapes.
**Pastoso** Mellow, off-dry.
**Podere** Small farm or estate.
**Produttore** Producer.
**Profumo** Odor or scent.
**Riserva** Reserve, applied only to DOC or DOCG wines that have undergone specified aging. *Riserva speciale* denotes even longer required aging.
**Rosato** Rosé.
**Rosso** Red.
**Rubino** Ruby color.
**Sapore** Flavor.
**Secco** Dry.
**Semisecco** Medium sweet, *demisec*, usually used to describe sparkling wine.
**Spumante** Sparkling wine. The term applies to dry as well as sweet wine.
**Stravecchio** Very old, a term permitted for few DOC wines.
**Superiore** Denotes DOC wine

that meets standards above the norm (higher alcohol, longer aging, a special subzone, etc.), though conditions vary.
**Tappo di sughero** Cork top.
**Tenuta** Farm or estate.
**Uva** Grape.
**Uvaggio** Mixture of grapes, as in a composite wine like Chianti or Valpolicella.
**Vecchio** Old. Certain DOC wines may carry the term after a set amount of aging.
**Vendemmia** The grape harvest, sometimes also used for vintage.
**Vigna, vigneto** Vineyard.
**Vignaiolo, viticoltore, coltivatore** Grape grower.
**Vino da arrosto** Robust, aged red wines that go with roast meats, e.g. Barolo, Brunello.
**Vino da pasto** Everyday table wine.
**Vino da taglio** Blending wine, usually produced in southern Italy and shipped north.
**Vino da tavola** Table wine. See explanation under *Laws & Labels* on p. 8.
**Vino novello** New wine, usually red, in the *Beaujolais nouveau* style.
**Vite** Vine.
**Vitigno** Vine or grape variety.

# Temperature

Wine expresses its best only when at the right temperature. All other arguments about serving – breathing, decanting, proper glass, etc. – are secondary. The chart indicates, with some leeway for personal preference, the best serving temperature for each type of wine.

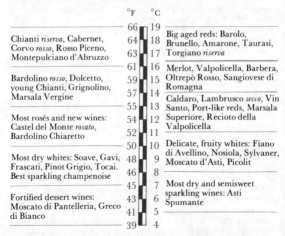

| | °F | °C | |
|---|---|---|---|
| Chianti *riserva*, Cabernet, Corvo *rosso*, Rosso Piceno, Montepulciano d'Abruzzo | 66 64 63 | 19 18 17 | Big aged reds: Barolo, Brunello, Amarone, Taurasi, Torgiano *riserva* |
| Bardolino *rosso*, Dolcetto, young Chianti, Grignolino, Marsala Vergine | 61 59 57 55 | 16 15 14 13 | Merlot, Valpolicella, Barbera, Oltrepò Rosso, Sangiovese di Romagna |
| | | | Caldaro, Lambrusco *secco*, Vin Santo, Port-like reds, Marsala Superiore, Recioto della Valpolicella |
| Most rosés and new wines: Castel del Monte *rosato*, Bardolino Chiaretto | 54 52 | 12 11 | |
| Most dry whites: Soave, Gavi, Frascati, Pinot Grigio, Tocai. Best sparkling champenoise | 50 48 46 | 10 9 8 | Delicate, fruity whites: Fiano di Avellino, Nosiola, Sylvaner, Moscato d'Asti, Picolit |
| Fortified dessert wines: Moscato di Pantelleria, Greco di Bianco | 45 43 41 39 | 7 6 5 4 | Most dry and semisweet sparkling wines: Asti Spumante |

# Laws & Labels

Italian wine production is governed by national and regional authorities in compliance with European Economic Community policy. If exported, the wine must be certified by chemical analysis and labeled to meet standards of the importing nation. The legal steps involved, from planting only officially approved vines to making wine and selling it, are increasingly restrictive. Yet the rules, though burdensome and sometimes seemingly contradictory to producers, are being enforced with new severity since the methanol scandal of 1986. Despite appearances to the contrary, wine production in Italy works with a reasonable degree of discipline.

Though four official categories have been approved for Italian wines, only the highest two classifications are definitive: *denominazione di origine controllata* (DOC) and *garantita* (DOCG), which apply to only about 10% of production. Most other still, dry wines, no matter what their class or style, must be called *vino da tavola* (table wine), though lightly bubbly (*frizzante*), sparkling (*spumante*), sweet (*abboccato*, *amabile* or *dolce*), and fortified (*liquoroso*) wines may be thus labeled.

In its simplest form, *vino da tavola* applies to wines of unspecified type or origin with imaginative names like Lacrima di Paradiso and have no right to a vintage date. Gradually, some table wines with specific references to color and place (Rosso di Toscana) or grape variety and place (Moscato di Strevi) should qualify as *vini tipici*. But since more than 800 candidates have applied for this classification equivalent to France's *vin de pays* or Germany's *Landwein*, recognition will take time.

For the moment, *vino da tavola* and non-DOC *frizzante*, *spumante*, *dolce*, or *liquoroso* can be no more reliable than the producer's reputation. The bottle may contain something strictly mediocre or, indeed, one of Italy's best wines. More than a few wines labeled *vino da tavola* rate three or four stars here.

The category DOC applies to wines from specified grape varieties grown in delimited zones and processed and aged following set methods in order to meet prescribed standards of color, odor, flavor, alcohol content, acidity, etc. All of these processes favor quality but do not guarantee it. More than 800 distinct varieties or types of wine are produced in some 220 DOC zones. Details of each DOC are determined by producers in the zone (often grouped in a *consorzio* that helps supervise production) guided by the national DOC committee, whose approval must be confirmed by presidential decree. The program is relatively new (the first DOC was instituted in 1966), but reforms are being made constantly to improve quality and bring winemaking up to date. Overall, despite some dubious choices and questionable standards, DOC has done more than anything else to improve the status of Italian wine worldwide.

DOCG, which guarantees the authenticity of a chosen few wines, has gone into effect after years of delay. The original four – Barbaresco, Barolo, Brunello di Montalcino and Vino Nobile di Montepulciano – are truly elite. But the fifth, Chianti, is Italy's most heavily produced classified wine, and the newly tapped Albana di Romagna, a white of similar variability in style and quality, have raised questions about the reliability of a guarantee.

Italian DOC and DOCG wines rate the Common Market designation VQPRD (for quality wine produced in determined regions) or, for sparkling wine, VSQPRD. Such wines now must pass chemical and taste analysis before being sold.

Labeling of all wines, DOC and otherwise, has been restricted by the EEC to pertinent data presented in a set order in which the wording and even the type sizes are controlled. Obligatory on all labels are: the wine name; its category (DOC, VQPRD, *vino da tavola*, etc); the producer or bottler's name and place of bottling; volume (a standard 750ml bottle must carry the letter **e**); the alcohol by volume. Labels may also carry the producer's trademark, coat of arms or other illustration and a vintage date (obligatory on all DOCG and most DOC wines). Also allowed are mention of awards (but only for the wine and vintage contained), a *consorzio* symbol and number, data on vineyards and (for DOC and DOCG only) the number of bottles produced.

Further information may be given on a back label or an attached card or scroll, though this must be verifiable and cannot include such terms as *speciale, riserva, extra*, and *vecchio* unless the wine qualifies for them under DOC and DOCG. Most Italian terms found on labels are defined in the *Glossary*.

Wines exported to the United States must have the official INE mark either on the cork or a neck label and must be described in English (e.g. Red Table Wine, Product of Italy). Net contents, alcohol percentage by volume and importer must also be given.

# *Anatomy of Italian wine*

Italy produces about a fifth of the world's wine. Its average of 7.2 billion liters a year surpasses the combined output of all nations outside Europe. Only France rivals it in volume, but in recent years Italy has usually outproduced its neighbor.

Why this mass of vines in a relatively small country somewhat cramped for space? Vines and wines obviously suit the nature of the land and its people, even though that nature varies to extremes. As for space, there's plenty: Italy's endless hillsides are better suited to vines than any other type of agriculture.

Mountains play a decisive role in Italian viticulture. The Alps shield the temperate climate from the damp cold of central Europe and the Apennines shape weather patterns from Piedmont to Calabria. Sicily and Sardinia also have snowy peaks. What makes it all so complex is the way in which the myriad microclimates correlate with the different types of soil.

Although generalizations can be made about growing conditions in various sections of the country, exceptions abound. For instance, low-lying zones in the Veneto and Friuli-Venezia Giulia in the far north have longer, hotter seasons than do Sicily's Etna or Calabria's Donnici in the mountains of the deep south. In short, in this land that is 39.7% hills and 38.7% mountains, altitude is often more significant than latitude.

Still, the north is well ahead of the rest of Italy in premium wine production. The eight northern regions produce more than half the nation's DOC wine in the vast arc formed by the Alps and Apennines around the broad valley of the Po. The cool climate in hills of glacial moraine, limestone, and clay, favors slow ripening for perfumed young wines and aged reds of rarefied bouquet.

Native varieties – Nebbiolo, Barbera, Dolcetto, Tocai, Albana and Cortese, among many – vie for space with the so-called international varieties. Much new planting is in vines for dry white and bubbly wines, including fine *méthode champenoise* from Pinots and Chardonnay. Commercial-scale red wines have been lightened, influenced by the vogue for the *nouveau*-style *vini novelli*.

Viticulture and enology have been upgraded at the major wine schools to levels comparable with those of France, Germany or California. As winemakers in privileged zones of northern Italy (the Apennine foothills around Alba, Asti and the Oltrepò Pavese, for example, and the Alpine foothills of northern Lombardy and the Tre Venezie) heighten their commitment to excellence, their wines are becoming more prominent in the world hierarchy. Yet, whether they are devoted to tried-and-true Barolo or new-wave Chardonnay, few among them would pretend to have reached the pinnacle as a winemaker. Many are striving for better balance in red wines and more character in whites, while modifying the medium from weathered wooden casks to stainless steel tanks and small oak barrels.

Change seems even more dramatic in central Italy. The six regions from Tuscany south to Latium and Molise produce about a third of Italy's DOC–DOCG wine and roughly half of that has been Chianti. But the spirit of renaissance there seems best expressed in the new-style wines, mainly red but also white, the most inspired of which carry no official appellations.

Winemakers in central Italy have revised not only their styles but, equally important, their grape varieties to take better advantage of the temperate climate in their sunny hills. They are proving that the traditional Sangiovese and Montepulciano respond accordingly when treated as nobles, while increasing their options with new plantings of Cabernet, Merlot and Pinot Noir. Among whites, the usefully prolific Trebbiano and Malvasia have begun to lose ground to Chardonnay, Sauvignon and the Pinots, while growers in the Marches and Umbria have gained new respect for their native Verdicchio and Grechetto.

Southern Italy (six regions including Sicily and Sardinia) makes about 40% of the nation's wine, but only about 9% of the DOC. Cooperatives dominate production, particularly in Sicily, Apulia, and Sardinia, where surpluses are most severe in the blending wine field. Renovation has been more sweeping in the Mezzogirono (south) than elsewhere, but, ironically, southern wines have been neglected by consumers despite low price and improved quality. Some examples of how good southern wines can be provided by Basilicata's Aglianico del Vulture; Campania's Fiano, Greco, and Taurasi; Apulia's Favonio, Torre Quarto, Rosa del Golfo, and several DOC reds; Sicily's Regaleali, Corvo, Etna, and Marsala; Calabria's Cirò and Greco di Bianco; and Sardinia's Cannonau, Vermentino, and non-DOC wines of Alghero.

The surplus, aggravated by declining domestic consumption (from 110 liters a head to 90 in a decade) and a slowdown in exports in the mid-1980s, had engendered a crisis in Italian wine that was causing radical change. The methanol scandal of 1986 made it tragically clear that the emphasis could no longer be on uncontrolled quantity but on authentic quality. Italy has stepped up law enforcement against fraud and manipulation while the Common Market, drained by the high cost of distilling the "wine lake" into industrial alcohol, was offering premiums to growers to uproot vines.

But Italian wine has weathered crises before. Despite rising production costs, middle range bottlings have retained a competitive edge over wines from most other nations. Steady improvements have increased prices at the top level, but in the long run Italians expect to capitalize on natural advantages to keep their premium wines on the world market as exceptional values.

# Grape varieties

Before the scourges from America struck Italian vineyards around the turn of the century, Italy grew thousands of types of vines, some universally recognized, but most so localized that their features, like their names, varied from one village to the next. For example, in Lombardy's Oltrepò Pavese in the mid-19th century, some 260 different varieties were recorded growing in an area smaller than Burgundy's Côte d'Or. Phylloxera reduced the numbers, though the ensuing tendency in much of Italy to plant heavy-bearing varieties did little for quality. In the last two decades, the steady conversion from mixed crops to uniform vineyards has brought new order and increased plantings of outstanding varieties, both native and imports (most of which were present in Italy in the last century). Still, the numbers and names of Italian grape varieties remain staggering. Listed are 89 of more than local interest.

## Dark-skinned Grapes

**Aglianico** An aristocrat of Greek origin, epitomized in Campania's Taurasi and Basilicata's Aglianico del Vulture.

**Aleatico** Makes attractive dark dessert wines in Latium (Aleatico di Gradoli), Apulia (Aleatico di Puglia), Tuscany, and Umbria.

**Barbera** Hearty Piedmont native, most prominent in varietals and blends in NW Italy. Vies with Sangiovese as the nation's most widely planted vine for red wine.

**Bombino Nero** Source of Apulia's Castel del Monte *rosato*.

**Bonarda** Strain of Croatina used for varietals and blends in Lombardy, Piedmont, and Emilia.

**Brachetto** Makes bubbly, usually sweet red wines in Piedmont.

**Brunello di Montalcino** The special clone of Sangiovese that carries the same name as Tuscany's vaunted red wine.

**Cabernet** Bordeaux native most prominent in NE Italy, where Cabernet Franc has been favored, though Cabernet Sauvignon is gaining in many places in Italy both as a varietal and in composites.

**Calabrese** or **Nero d'Avola** Noted in Sicily as a source of both DOC Cerasuolo di Vittoria and table wines.

**Cannonau** Sardinia's main dark variety – apparently France's Grenache introduced via Spain – is used for dry and sweet wines.

**Carignano** The Carignan of France and Spain is grown in Sardinia.

**Cesanese** Most respectable native of Latium.

**Corvina Veronese** Chief component of Veronese reds (Valpolicella, Recioto, and Bardolino) along with Rondinella, Molinara, Negrara, and Rossignola.

**Croatina** Used heavily in Lombardy's Oltrepò Pavese, mainly in composites with Barbera and Uva Rara. See Bonarda.

**Dolcetto** Treasured in S Piedmont, where it makes supple, mouth-filling varietals in seven DOC zones.

**Freisa** Makes unique wines, often bubbly, in its native Piedmont.

**Gaglioppo** Source of most Calabrian reds, including Cirò.

**Gamay** Beaujolais grape makes DOC wine in Valle d'Aosta, sometimes found elsewhere.

**Grignolino** Once prominent, this Piedmontese variety is still admired in light red wines around Asti.

**Groppello** Worthy base of Lombardian reds, chiefly Riviera del Garda.

**Guarnaccia** Chief grape of Ischia *rosso*, known elsewhere as Alicante.

**Lagrein** Source of distinctive reds and rosés in Trentino-Alto Adige.

**Lambrusco** Abounds in Emilia's plains, where its several subvarieties make bubbly wines – red, pink, even white – DOC and otherwise.

**Malbec** or **Malbeck** Usually secondary in Bordeaux composites, it is sometimes a protagonist in the Veneto and Apulia.

**Malvasia Nera** Dark versions of the wide-ranging Malvasia family make DOC reds in Piedmont and Alto Adige. Prominent in Apulia.

**Marzemino** Popular variety in Trentino and Lombardy.

**Merlot** The Bordeaux native is extremely popular in NE Italy as a source of varietals. One of the nation's most heavily planted vines, it is used both alone and in mixes in many regions.

**Monica** Of Spanish origin, it makes sweet and dry wines in Sardinia.

**Montepulciano d'Abruzzo** Dominant dark variety of the Abruzzi, gaining favor in other regions for fine varietals and blends.

**Moscato Nero** Dark Muscat used for sweet red wines in Piedmont. Moscato Rosa makes fragrant pink wines in the Venezie.

**Nebbiolo** Noble progenitor of Piedmont's greatest red wines – Barolo, Barbaresco, and Gattinara – and a host of others elsewhere in Piedmont, Lombardy, and Valle d'Aosta. Among many synonyms are Spanna, Chiavennasca, and Picutener.

**Negroamaro** Apulian variety that dominates the big reds of Salento.

**Nerello Mascalese** Worthy Sicilian, most noted as source of Etna *rosso*.

**Petit Rouge** Used in some of Valle d'Aosta's distinguished reds, including Enfer d'Arvier and Torrette.

**Piedirosso** or **Per'e Palommo** Prominent in Campanian reds, notably of Ischia.

**Pinot Nero** Burgundy's Pinot Noir is used for red wines, especially in N Italy, with mixed results. It has been more successful in white and pink sparkling wines. Known as Blauburgunder in Alto Adige.

**Primitivo** or **Primativo** Apulian source of powerful table, dessert, and blending wines. Possibly related to California's Zinfandel.

**Raboso** Makes interesting reds in its native Veneto.

**Refosco** Makes fine varietals in Friuli. Known as Mondeuse in France.

**Rossese** Source of Rossese di Dolceacqua and other good Ligurian reds.

**Sangiovese** Mainstay of all Tuscan DOC reds (Chianti, Brunello di Montalcino, Vino Nobile di Montepulciano, and more), it is one of Italy's most widely planted vines, though in various strains, including Brunello, Prugnolo, Sangiovese di Romagna, and Chianti's Sangioreto.

**Schiava** Important vine of Trentino-Alto Adige, its various clones account for such wines as Santa Maddalena and Caldaro. Known as Vernatsch in German.

**Schioppettino** Rare Friulian used for an exquisite red.

**Teroldego** Grown only in Trentino, where it makes the admired Teroldego Rotaliano.

**Tocai Rosso** or **Nero** Dark version of the Friulian vine.

**Uva di Troia** Fine variety from N Apulia, where it dominates DOCs.

**Vespolina** Often blended with Nebbiolo in Piedmont's Novara-Vercelli hills.

## Light-skinned Grapes

**Albana** Native of Romagna's hills, where it makes both dry and semisweet wines, still or bubbly.

**Arneis** Gaining stature in the Alba area of Piedmont after it almost disappeared.

**Biancolella** Campanian vine prominent on Ischia as a varietal and a partner of Forastera in Ischia DOC *bianco*.

**Blanc de Valdigne** Source of Blanc de Morgex and Blanc de La Salle, grown in Italy's highest vineyards in Valle d'Aosta.

**Bombino Bianco** Main grape of Apulia's San Severo *bianco*; grown in Abruzzi as Trebbiano d'Abruzzo.

**Bosco** Prime ingredient of Cinqueterre in Liguria.

**Carricante** Chief grape of Etna *bianco* in Sicily.

**Catarratto** Prevalent in W Sicily, where it figures in Marsala, Bianco Alcamo, and in many other wines.

**Chardonnay** Aristocratic Burgundian, often confused with Pinot Bianco and incorrectly called Pinot Chardonnay, is more widely planted in Trentino-Alto Adige, Veneto and Friuli than previously estimated. Increasing source of varietal wine in many regions.

**Cortese** Piedmont's popular whites, including Gavi, derive from this native variety also found in Lombardy's Oltrepò Pavese.

**Durello** Source of good, sturdy whites between Verona and Vicenza.

**Fiano** Known as Apianum to the ancient Romans, it makes Campania's fine Fiano di Avellino.

**Forastera** Campanian variety mixed with Biancolella in Ischia *bianco*.

**Garganega** Mainstay of Soave is grown mostly in the Veneto.

**Gewürztraminer** A superior clone of Traminer, developed in Alsace, is widely planted in NE Italy. Often confused with its common cousin.

**Greco** Vines of this name, probably of Greek origin, are grown in several parts of Italy, notably Campania (Greco di Tufo) and Calabria (Greco di Bianco). Vines known as Grechetto (which gives impressive results in Umbria) and Grecanico may be related.

**Grillo** Once the chief grape of Marsala (still considered the best), it now usually supplements Catarratto.

**Inzolia** Grown throughout Sicily for use in white wine, including Marsala and Corvo *bianco*.

**Malvasia** Name applied to a vast range of S European vines, also known as Malvoisie and Malmsey. Light varieties are grown throughout Italy, conspicuously in Latium (for Frascati, Est! Est!! Est!!!, etc.), though something of the name can be found in nearly every region, used for both dry and sweet, and still and bubbly wines.

**Moscato** Muscat vines are found throughout Italy and usually used for white or golden wines, generally with some degree of sweetness and distinct aroma. Basic styles are sparkling and *frizzante* – as in Piedmont's Asti Spumante and Moscato d'Asti – and richly sweet, as in Sicilian Moscato.

**Müller Thurgau** The Riesling-Sylvaner cross is catching on in Italy, making wines of unexpected class in Trentino-Alto Adige and Friuli.

**Nosiola** Worthy native of Trentino used in dry wines and Vin Santo.

**Nuragus** Ancient Sardinian vine, source of Nuragus di Cagliari.

**Picolit** Native of Friuli long rendered Italy's most prized dessert wine. It is now coming back after decades of decline.

**Pigato** Grown only in SW Liguria, where it makes fine dry wines.

**Pinot Bianco** Burgundy's Pinot Blanc is grown throughout N Italy, where it is sometimes confused with Chardonnay. It makes both still and sparkling wines, often DOC, in Friuli, Veneto, Trentino-Alto Adige, and Lombardy. Known as Weissburgunder in Alto Adige.

**Pinot Grigio** France's Pinot Gris is increasingly popular in Italy, especially in the Tre Venezie and Lombardy, where it is often DOC, though much Pinot Grigio is not. Known as Ruländer in Alto Adige.

**Prosecco** Prominent in E Veneto for sparkling, *frizzante*, and some still wines, usually a touch sweet. The most respected is Cartizze.

**Ribolla Gialla** Ancient Fruilian vine used in varietals and blends.

**Riesling Italico** Not a true Riesling and not even native to Italy. It sometimes stands alone and occasionally alternates with Riesling Renano in DOCs. Known as Welschriesling in Alto Adige.

**Riesling Renano** The Johannisberg or White Riesling of the Rhine, increasingly respected in N Italy, where it is often interchanged with Riesling Italico. Known as Rheinriesling in Alto Adige.

**Sauvignon** The outstanding promise of Sauvignon Blanc of Bordeaux has begun to be realized in certain parts of N Italy, where it makes DOC varietals. It is also blended with Semillon in places.

**Sylvaner** Limited, but it makes remarkable wines in Alto Adige's heights.

**Tocai Friulano** Friuli's beloved vine also makes DOC whites in the Veneto and Lombardy. Gaining interest elsewhere.

**Traminer** Native of Asia but developed at Tramin in Alto Adige, this progenitor of Gewürztraminer is more productive but less distinguished.

**Trebbiano** Vines of the name abound through Italy, though they may vary markedly in character. Trebbiano Toscano is most diffused; the Romagnan strain is also widespread.

**Verdeca** Important Apulian variety, used with Bianco d'Alessano in Locorotondo, Martina Franca, and other whites.

**Verdicchio** Predominant light grape of the Marches.

**Verduzzo** Friuli grape, also used in Veneto for dry and dessert wines.

**Vermentino** Makes DOC white in Sardinia and Liguria.

**Vernaccia di Oristano** Used exclusively around Oristano in Sardinia for a Sherry-like dessert wine.

**Vernaccia di San Gimignano** Ancient vine used for the white of Tuscany's famous towered town.

# Abruzzi

Abruzzo

*Bacchus amat colles*, as the Romans observed, so the wine god must adore the Abruzzi. Between the Adriatic Sea and the Apennines, which reach their highest point in the snow-capped Gran Sasso range above the regional capital of L'Aquila, there is little else but hills. The microclimates of these sun-drenched slopes vary from warm maritime to alpine, so if you pick your spot carefully, you can find conditions suited to nearly any type of vine. But growers in the Abruzzi have chosen to work almost exclusively with grapes for two regional DOCs: Montepulciano d'Abruzzo, which comprises both a red and a pink Cerasuolo, and the white Trebbiano d'Abruzzo. Montepulciano d'Abruzzo *rosso* (not to be confused with Vino Nobile di Montepulciano of Tuscany) has been drawing praise in Italy and abroad for the way it combines power with *souplesse*. Trebbiano d'Abruzzo, usually neutral as Trebbianos tend to be, has less to offer, though it is capable of inspiring a surprise or two.

**Wine Zones**
1 Montepulciano d'Abruzzo
2 Trebbiano d'Abruzzo

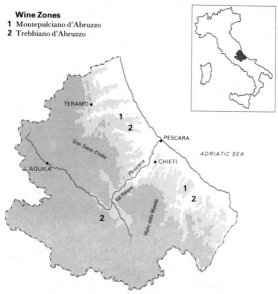

The Abruzzi, easily accessible from Rome via the *autostrada* to L'Aquila and the Adriatic port of Pescara, has fine beaches and some of Italy's grandest mountain scenery, including the wilderness area known as the Abruzzi National Park. Wine tourism has not been explicitly introduced in the region, but the coastal hills between Teramo and Chieti have numerous wineries and country inns where local wines can be tasted. In Pescara, the *Enoteca Europa* provides a good choice of the region's wines.

### Recent vintages

Red Montepulciano d'Abruzzo improves with moderate aging, usually 3–6 years, occasionally more. Some producers also age Trebbiano d'Abruzzo for 5 years or more.

1986   Fine harvest for smooth, balanced Montepulciano.
1985   Heat reduced quantities, but wines are rich and durable.
1984   Wet and cool; lightweight wines.
1983   Abundant crop of satisfactory quality or better.
1982   Heat and drought took toll, but select wines good to excellent.
1981   Reduced; fine, perfumed wines from select grapes only.
1980   Big crop, satisfactory quality.
1979   Generally very good wines.
1978   Uneven harvest, middling quality.
1977   Meager harvest, but some outstanding wines.

**Abruzzo** r. p. w. dr. ★ DYA
Simple table wines made in many parts of the region, the red and rosé from Montepulciano and Sangiovese, the white from Trebbiano.

**Cerasuolo d'Abruzzo**
See Montepulciano d'Abruzzo Cerasuolo.

**Montepulciano d'Abruzzo** DOC
Red and rosé from Montepulciano d'Abruzzo with up to 15% Sangiovese grown in choice vineyards through the coastal hills and in valleys in the uplands around L'Aquila.

– **Cerasuolo** p. dr. ★→★★★ 85 86
The rosé version is vinified only briefly with the skins. Cherry pink, fresh and tasty, it is a good, all-purpose wine, if rarely distinguished. Drink in 1–3 years.

– **Rosso** r. dr. ★★→★★★ 77 79 80 81 82 83 85 86
Deep ruby, robust, round, lightly tannic, with 3–6 years of age – and from certain producers – it can be one of central Italy's smoothest and most attractive red wines. Made in significant quantity (about 18 million liters a year), it seems to have a highly promising future.
Ag. *vecchio* 2 yrs.

| | |
|---|---|
| Barone Cornacchia | Paolo Mezzanotte |
| Nestore Bosco | Antonio Monti |
| Cantalupo (Di Giulio) | Camillo Montori |
| C.S. di Tollo | Bruno Nicodemi |
| Casal Thaulero | Emidio Pepe |
| Santoro Colella | Italo Pietrantori |
| Duchi di Castelluccio | Gaetano Petrosemolo |
| Dario D'Angelo | Rosso della Quercia |
| Dino Illuminati | Scialletti |
| Vittorio Janni | Edoardo Valentini |

**Moscato** w. sw. fz. sp. ★ DYA
Dessert wine, often sparkling or *frizzante*, made from Moscato Bianco grapes in various places. The best Moscato, noted for its fruity Muscat aroma, is from Torre de' Passeri, near Pescara.

**Rubino** r. dr. ★★→★★★ 82 83 85 86
Like Montepulciano DOC, except that it contains 20% Sangiovese. Bright ruby, finely scented, generous, and warm, it is best in 2–4 years.
Tenuta S. Agnese (Acciavatti)

**Rustico** r. dr. ★ DYA
Thick mountain wine, in keeping with its name, made from Montepulciano and Sangiovese in the high Val Peligna.

**Spinello** w. dr. ★★ DYA
Fine, light table wine from Trebbiano grapes, made at Città Sant'Angelo, near Pescara.
Tenuta S. Agnese (Acciavatti)

**Trebbiano d'Abruzzo** DOC w. dr. (fz.) ★→★★ DYA
White from Trebbiano d'Abruzzo and/or Trebbiano Toscano grown in designated vineyards in coastal hills and upland valleys. Usually bland in odor and flavor, bone dry, and pale straw in color, it may also be

*frizzante*. From one producer, Edoardo Valentini, from certain vintages, it can attain a luxuriant (\*\*\*\*) tone of fine white Burgundy while retaining appealing full ripe fruit flavors for 5–6 years or more.

| | |
|---|---|
| Casal Thaulero | Camillo Montori |
| Barone Cornacchia | Bruno Nicodemi |
| Dario D'Angelo | Emidio Pepe |
| Duchi di Castelluccio | Scialletti |
| Dino Illuminati | Edoardo Valentini |

**Val Peligna** r. w. dr. \*→\*\* DYA

Besides the standard varieties in this mountain valley, one winemaker has been experimenting with such unfamiliar vines as Pinot Grigio, Riesling Renano, Traminer, Veltliner, and the hybrid Sejve Villard in limited quantities.

Santoro Colella

**Vin Cotto** am. dr. or sw. \*\*

Rare fortified wine made by cooking down musts of light grapes and fermenting them with freshly pressed grapes. This "cooked wine," with its burnished color, syrupy texture and bitter or bittersweet prune-like flavor is reputed to aid digestion (18–20% alcohol). But you'll have to try it privately because it's banned from commerce.

## Wine & Food

When it comes to eating, the people of the Abruzzi don't mince matters; they like strongly flavored food and lots of it. Though the Adriatic is full of fish, even coastal dwellers look to the land for sustenance. Historically an abode of shepherds, the Abruzzi's favored meats are lamb and mutton. Ewe's milk is the source of *pecorino* cheese. Pork is popular, too, either fresh or in preserved *salame*, sausages, and *prosciutto*. The seasoning is often hot, peaking in the chili-flavored *diavolino*. The Abruzzi's "national dish" is pasta: *maccheroni alla chitarra*. Once, before girth went out of style, the Abruzzesi celebrated with *la panarda*, a feast that ranged upward from 30 courses. Today, most young people have never heard of it, let alone eaten their way through one.

**Agnello alla diavola** Lamb sautéed with chili peppers and white wine.
  \*\* Cerasuolo.

**Brodetto pescarese** The Pescara version of Adriatic fish soup, this one cooked with green peppers.
  \*→\*\* Trebbiano.

**Maccheroni alla chitarra** Pasta noodles cut into quadrangular sticks on a stringed instrument (the "guitar") and served with either tomato sauce or meat *ragù*.
  \*\* Cerasuolo (with tomato sauce), \*\* Montepulciano (with *ragù*).

**'Ndocca 'ndocca** Pungent stew of pig's innards, ribs, feet, and head with peppers, rosemary, and vinegar, a speciality of Teramo.
  \*\* Montepulciano *rosso*.

**Rosticini** Lamb or pork grilled on skewers and served at street stalls.
  \*\* Montepulciano *rosso*.

**Scrippelle 'nfuss** or **'mbusse** Pancake-like fritters or crêpes served in broth.
  \*\* Cerasuolo.

**Stracci** Baked timbals of meat, béchamel, cheese, and vegetables, a speciality of L'Aquila. Known as *fregnacce* around Teramo.
  \*\*→\*\*\* Montepulciano *rosso* (fairly young).

**Virtù** or **le sette virtù** Legendary soup of Teramo that once took seven damsels each using seven different ingredients seven days to put together. Today the "seven virtues" soup is less romantic, but still good.
  \*\* Cerasuolo.

### Restaurants

Recommended in or near wine zones: *Le Salette Aquilane* at Coppito near L'Aquila; *Beccaceci* at Giulianova Lido; *Le Tre Marie* at L'Aquila; *Ranieri* at Lanciano; *La Bilancia* near Loreto Aprutino; *Tatobbe* at Penne; *Guerino* and *Da Duilio* at Pescara; *Onofrietto* at Popoli; *Golfo di Venere* at San Giovanni in Venere; *Vecchia Silvi* at Silvi Alta; *Il Duomo* at Teramo; *Il Corsaro* at Vasto.

# Apulia

## Puglia

Apulia, a relatively level region at the heel of the Italian boot, rivals Sicily as the most abundant producer of grapes and wine. Though leading producers have switched the focus from blending wines to dry table wines of moderate strength, the rust-colored soil of Apulia's plains and low plateaus seems to favor natural abundance.

Though the region's wines are better than ever, they have not realized merited success in bottle. Of 23 DOCs, only a handful of names are recognizable to outsiders and less than 2% of an average output of more than a billion liters a year is officially classified. Several of Apulia's superior modern wines are not DOC.

Production follows two basic patterns divided geographically by a line drawn across the region from the port of Taranto, on the Ionian Sea, to Brindisi, on the Adriatic. Southeastwards lies the hot Salento peninsula with Italy's easternmost point at Capo d'Otranto, long the source of strong, dark blending wines based on Negroamaro and Primitivo grapes (the latter possibly related to California's Zinfandel). New techniques have reduced the strength but retained the remarkable robust character in red table wines. Rosés here show elegance rarely equaled elsewhere. Made by the *lacrima* or teardrop system using only about half the juice of uncrushed grapes, they are delicately dry and pale roseate in color – comparable to what Americans call "blush wines".

North of the Taranto–Brindisi line, the climate is warm and dry along the coast near the regional capital of Bari, becoming relatively cool in the interior. The whites, noted for their neutral nature that makes them ideal for vermouth, are beginning to show some fruitiness when processed at low temperature. Some reds and rosés from Uva di Troia, Montepulciano, and Bombino

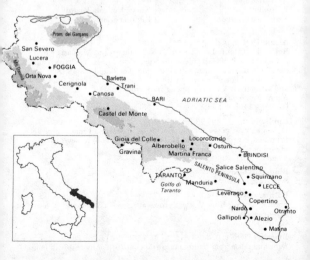

Nero have the delicately perfumed qualities of northerly wines. Such outside varieties as Malbec, Cabernet Franc, Pinot Bianco, Chardonnay and Sauvignon have been introduced with success.

As Italy's perennial gateway to Greece, Apulia has remnants of Hellas along with reminders of innumerable other peoples. Of particular interest are the *trulli* dwellings in the Itria valley. The octagonal Swabian structure that gave Castel del Monte its name is well worth a visit, as is the Salento peninsula with its ancient Greek cities of Lecce and Gallipoli.

Select Apulian wines are on display at the *Enoteca Puglia* in Alberobello and the *Enoteca De Pasquale* in Bari.

### Recent vintages

Apulian reds are noted for longevity, as are certain rosés of Salento, though as a rule pink and white wines should be drunk young. The hot Salento peninsula tends to have more consistent harvests than do more temperate northern zones.

1986  Excellent in the north, but scirocco caused rot in Salento.
1985  Though volume was down, an outstanding year for reds.
1984  Generally weak for reds, but rosés and whites fared better.
1983  Despite heat and drought, Castel del Monte and Salento recorded a good harvest.
1982  Reduced crop due to drought and hail, and heat caused problems with acidity. Where irrigation was possible good wines made.
1981  Meager harvest; excellent quality in Castel del Monte, generally satisfactory elsewhere.
1980  A good crop, bountiful in Salento, reduced in the north.
1979  The best in a series of fine vintages in Salento, good to excellent in the north. Red wines to keep.
1978  Good to excellent year in Salento; above average if light in north.
1977  Generally very good harvest of wines to lay down.
1976  Subpar vintage.
1975  Excellent, except in isolated sections of the north.

**Aleatico di Puglia** DOC r. sw.  ★★  77 78 79 80 81 82 83 85 86
Smooth, warm, garnet-violet dessert wine from Aleatico di Puglia grapes in two types: *dolce naturale* (of 15%) and the fortified *liquoroso dolce naturale* (of 18.5%). Produced throughout Apulia, but only a little is made. Ag. *riserva* 3 yrs.

| | |
|---|---|
| Felice Botta | Nuova Vinicola Picardi |
| Francesco Candido | Riforma Fondiaria |
| Lippolis | |

**Alezio** DOC r. p. dr.  ★★→★★★  83 85 86
Recent DOC for red and rosé from Negroamaro and Malvasia Rossa grapes grown E of Gallipoli on the Salento peninsula. The *rosso* is ample in color and body, warm, suited to aging. The brand names Doxi Vecchio and Portulano will qualify. The *rosato* is coral pink, fragrant and attractively flavored, among Italy's finest rosés. Ag. *riserva (rosso)* 2 yrs.

| | |
|---|---|
| Giuseppe Calò & Figlio | Niccolò Coppola |

**Apulia** r. dr.  ★★  77 78 79 81 83 85 86
Dynamically robust red table wine made at Martina Franca from Primitivo, Negroamaro, and Malvasia Nera. It tends to develop smoothness and bouquet after about 6 years.
Vinicola Miali

**Bianco di Gravina**
See Gravina.

**Bolina** w. dr.  ★★  DYA
Fresh new white from Verdeca grown at Alezio in Salento, ideal for seaside sipping.
Giuseppe Calò & Figlio

**Brindisi** DOC r. p. dr.  ★→★★★  75 77 78 79 81 83 85 86
*Rosso* and *rosato* from Negroamaro grapes at 70% or more grown inland

from the port of Brindisi towards Mesagne. The rosé can be pleasant. The red, though powerful, can be smooth and elegant at 5–10 years old or more. Cosimo Taurino's Patriglione stands out.
Ag. *riserva (rosso)* 2 yrs.
Santachiara (Medico)                    Cosimo Taurino

**Cabernet Franc**
See Favonio.

**Cacc'e Mmitte di Lucera** DOC r. dr.  ★ DYA
The dialect name – one interpretation is "toss it down and fill it up" (your glass presumably) – is more colorful than the wine. It derives from a staggering mix of grapes: the dark Uva di Troia, Montepulciano, Sangiovese, and Malvasia Nera, and the light Trebbiano Toscano, Bombino Bianco, and Malvasia Bianca grown around Lucera in N Apulia. Results fall somewhere between unusual and nondescript.
Lorenzo Carapelle                    Riforma Fondiaria
Federico II

**Castel del Monte** DOC r. p. w. dr.  ★→★★★  73 75 77 79 81 83 85 86
Apulia's best-known DOC is named after the octagonal castle of Emperor Friedrich II von Hohenstaufen. The general good quality is due to relatively cool climate and grower discipline. The *rosso* from Uva di Troia with some Bombino Nero and Montepulciano is well-rounded with deep ruby-garnet color and a capacity to improve, as *riserva*, with 5–10 years of aging, sometimes more. The *rosato* is the trio's bestseller, understandably, with its pretty roseate color and finesse in scent and flavor. It comes mainly from Bombino Nero. The *bianco*, from Pampanuto and other grapes, has little to say. See also Il Falcone.
Ag. *riserva (rosso)* 3 yrs. (1 in wood).

| | |
|---|---|
| Felice Botta | Riforma Fondiaria |
| Bruno | Rivera |
| Fattoria Torricciola | Giuseppe Strippoli |
| Vittorio Jatta | Torre Sveva |
| Gennaro Marasciuolo | Vini Chiddo |
| Nuova Vinicola Picardi | Vinicola Palumbo |

**Castel Mitrano** r. dr.  ★★→★★★  77 79 80 81 83 85 86
Elegant red table wine from Negroamaro and Malvasia Nera grown at Mitrano near Brindisi. Dry, tannic, and warm, it needs 4–5 years before starting to show its impressive bouquet.
Tenuta di Mitrano

**Chardonnay**
See Favonio.

**Copertino** DOC r. p. dr.  ★★→★★★  77 78 79 80 81 83 85 86
Red and rosé from Negroamaro primarily grown at Copertino. The *rosso* can be one of Salento's finest reds, especially the *riserva*. Deep ruby, velvety, rich in aroma and flavor, it has a nicely bitter undertone and improves with 4–10 years. The *rosato* is salmon pink and finely scented.
Ag. *riserva (rosso)* 2 yrs.
Barone Bacile di Castiglione

**Donna Marzia** r. p. w. dr.  ★★→★★★  77 78 79 80 81 83
Impressive red and white table wines made at Leverano on the Salento peninsula. The *rosso*, based on Negroamaro, is rich and warm, developing a smooth bouquet over 5–8 years, sometimes more. The *bianco*, from Malvasia Bianca, has a fine aroma and more suavity than you'd expect in a hot-climate dry white. Its straw-yellow color deepens as it develops character over 2–3 years or more.
Conti Zecca

**Doxi Vecchio**
See Alezio.

**Favonio** r. w. dr.  ★★→★★★  79 80 81 82 83 85 86
The wines called Favonio made by Attilio Simonini defy (with astonishing success) Apulian viticultural traditions. Though grown in vineyards irrigated by a drip system on the hot, dry plain E of Foggia, the white Pinot Bianco and Chardonnay can be as crisp and as fruity as northern wines of those names. The full-blooded Cabernet Franc, with its distinct bell pepper scent and flavor, equals nearly anything from the Tre Venezie. The Pinot Nero and Trebbiano are less convincing.
Attilio Simonini

**Five Roses** p. dr. ★★ 77 78 79 80 81 83 85 86
Italy's first bottled rosé (in the 1930s), the name was given by U.S.
officers in Salento during World War II, a translation of the place it is
grown: Cinque Rose. Another curiosity is its longevity: after 5–6 years in
cask, it can hold up that long in bottle. Light cherry red, delicately
scented, its uniquely dry flavor doesn't betray its years – or strength of
13.5%
Leone De Castris

**Gioia del Colle** DOC
New DOC for types of wine grown around Gioia del Colle, S of Bari.
– **Aleatico** r. sw.
This will be similar to Aleatico di Puglia, whether naturally sweet or
fortified.
Ag. *riserva* 2 yrs.
– **Bianco** w. dr. DYA
Unproven dry white based on Trebbiano Toscano.
– **Primitivo** r. dr. (s/sw) ★→★★ 85 86
From Primitivo, the only known wine of the zone, this is big and strong,
sometimes *amabile*. May be called Primitivo di Gioia.
Ag. *riserva* 2 yrs.
– **Rosato** p. dr. DYA
From Primitivo with Montepulciano, Sangiovese and others, this could
be a good rosé.
– **Rosso** r. dr.
From the same base as the *rosato*, this would seem to promise class.
Giuseppe Strippoli

**Gravina** DOC w. dr. (sp.) ★ DYA
Dry white from Malvasia, Greco di Tufo, and Bianco d'Alessano grown
around Gravina near the border of Basilicata, SE of Bari. A *spumante* is
also permitted.

**Il Falcone** r. dr. ★★★→★★★★ 73 75 77 79 81 83 85 86
Though sold as Castel del Monte *riserva*, this luxuriant red contains
more than the 35% Montepulciano specified by DOC. Needs 7–8 years.
Rivera

**Leverano** DOC r. p. w. dr. ★→★★ 79 81 83 85 86
Recent DOC of Salento, the *rosso* and *rosato* come from Negroamaro.
The red, warm and smooth, is capable of aging. The rosé, fresh and
fruity, is to drink young. The *bianco*, from Malvasia, can be interesting.
Ag. *riserva* (*rosso*) 2 yrs.
C.S. Leverano                         Conti Zecca

**Locorotondo** DOC w. dr. (sp.) ★→★★★ DYA
Made from Verdeca and Bianco d'Alessano grapes grown around the
whitewashed town of Locorotondo in the Itria valley. As made by the
local cooperative this may be the best DOC white of Apulia. Pale straw
green, subtly fruity, it is a briskly satisfying fish wine. However, some
look and taste almost bleached. A *spumante* version is permitted.

| Borgo Canale | Leone De Castris | Rivera |
| C.S. di Locorotondo | Renna | Giuseppe Strippoli |
| Distante Vini | Riforma Fondiaria | |

**Lupinello** w. dr. fz. ★★ DYA
Snappy pale yellow wine from grapes grown in N Apulia – in the new
style of light (10.5%), dry and fizzy.
Federico II

**Martina Franca** or **Martina** DOC w. dr. (sp.) ★→★★ DYA
Almost identical to Locorotondo in grapes and personality, from around
one of Apulia's prettiest towns. The zone extends along the Itria to
Alberobello, capital of the conical *trulli* dwellings. A *spumante* is
permitted.

| C.S. di Alberobello | Lippolis | Giuseppe Strippoli |
| De Felice | Miali | Villa Valletta |
| Di Gregorio | Riforma Fondiaria | |

**Matino** DOC r. p. dr. ★ 79 80 81 83 85 86
The southernmost DOC of Salento, Matino's *rosso* and *rosato* are based
on Negroamaro. Similar to other Salento wines, they are rarely seen.

**Mitrano** p. dr. ★→★★ DYA
Tasty, light rosé based on Negroamaro grapes grown near Brindisi.
C.S. Mitrano                                   Tenuta di Mitrano

**Moscato di Trani** DOC w. sw. ★★ 81 82 83 85 86
Rich, golden dessert wine from Moscato Reale grapes grown inland
from the port of Trani as far as Cerignola. Luscious and velvety, it rates
as one of the better southern Italian Moscatos in two versions: *dolce
naturale* (15%) and *liquoroso* (18%).
Ag. *liquoroso* 1 yr.
Felice Botta                                   Nuova Vinicola Picardi
Mauro De Cillis                                Rivera
Gennaro Marasciuolo

**Nardò** DOC r. p. dr. ★→★★ 85 86
Good red and typical rosé from Negroamaro and Malvasia Nera grown
at Nardò in Salento. The red, robust and warm with a grapy aroma, is
best in 3–6 years.
Ag. *riserva (rosso)* 2 yrs.

**Negrino** r. sw. ★★★ 67 70 75
Port-like red dessert wine made from semidried Malvasia Nera and
Negroamaro grapes and aged in barrels for at least a decade. Warm,
alcoholic (16%), and moderately sweet with bitter undertone, it
becomes velvety with great age. Recommended for convalescents.
Leone De Castris.

**Orta Nova** DOC r. p. dr. ★ DYA
New DOC for obscure red and rosé from Sangiovese and other varieties
grown at Orta Nova near Foggia.

**Ostuni** DOC
The ancient town of Ostuni NW of Brindisi makes two distinct wines:
– **Bianco** w. dr. ★ DYA
Straw-yellow, delicate fish wine from Impigno and Francavilla grapes.
– **Ottavianello** r. dr. ★ 85 86
Light ruby, almost rosé, this subtly flavored wine from the Ottavianello
grape adapts to a range of foods. Drink in 2–3 years.
C.S. di Ostuni

**Pinot Bianco di Puglia** w. dr. ★★ DYA
Made experimentally from Pinot Bianco grown in the Castel del Monte
zone, early examples were fruity, balanced and well-scented, promising
an interesting future. See Favonio.
Rivera

**Portulano** r. dr. ★★→★★★ 77 80 82 83 85 86
Fine dry table wine from Negroamaro and Malvasia Nera grown near
the Salento town of Alezio. Bright ruby with ample body, it develops a
generous bouquet and elegant tone with long finish after 5–6 years of
aging. It could qualify as Alezio DOC.
Giuseppe Calò

**Primitivo di Gioia**
See Gioia del Colle.

**Primitivo di Manduria** DOC r. dr. sw. ★→★★ 78 79 80 81 83 85 86
Once used almost entirely for blending, Primitivo from around
Manduria E of Taranto is now occasionally made into varietal DOC
wine. It may be either dry or sweet, always big in body and strong with
deep purple color and blackberry-like flavor. The normal version may
be either dry or slightly *amabile*, a wine suited for heroic dishes. The
sweet versions are somewhat reminiscent of California Port. *Dolce
naturale* must have 16% alcohol, *liquoroso dolce naturale* 17.5%, and
*liquoroso secco* 18% (all with residual sugars). The normal and *dolce
naturale* age from 3 years to well over a decade. The *liquoroso*, which may
not be sold for 2 years after being fortified with alcohol, can last almost
indefinitely. See also Rosso di Sava.
Romano Luccarelli      Giovanni Soloperto      Vinicola Amanda

**Rosa del Golfo** p. dr. ★★★ DYA
One of Apulia's (and Italy's) best rosés; a table wine from Negroamaro

and Malvasia Nera grown near Alezio in Salento. Made by the ancient "teardrop" system, it is bright cherry pink with flowery scent and dry, harmonious, exquisite flavor.
Giuseppe Calò

**Rosato del Salento**
See Salento.

**Rosso Barletta** DOC r. dr. *→** 83 85 86
Made from Uva di Troia grown around the N Apulian port of Barletta, this ruby-garnet wine is usually refreshing if unremarkable young, though it can develop something resembling style within 3–4 years.
Ag. *invecchiato* 2 yrs (1 in wood).
C.S. di Barletta                          Nuova Vinicola Picardi
Fattoria Torricciola                      Giuseppe Strippoli

**Rosso Canosa** DOC r. dr. ★→★★ 81 83 85 86
Red of sturdy structure from Uva di Troia and other varieties grown around Canosa in N Apulia. Fresh and fruity when young, it shows some finesse with age. It may also be called Canusium after the Roman name.
Ag. *riserva* 2 yrs (1 in wood).
C.S. Nicola Rossi                         Giuseppe Strippoli

**Rosso del Salento**
See Salento.

**Rosso di Cerignola** DOC r. dr. ★★ 79 81 83 85 86
One of N Apulia's better reds, it is based on Uva di Troia and Negroamaro grown around Cerignola. Ruby turning to brick red with age, its fine bouquet and robust flavor support 4–8 years admirably.
Ag. *riserva* 2 yrs in wood.
Cirillo-Farrusi

**Rosso di Sava** r. dr. or sw. ★★→★★★ 79 80 83 85 86
Name used by Librale Amanda for red wines from Primitivo grown at the town of Sava. Dry or sweet, they qualify as Primitivo di Manduria DOC and are regularly the best wines of that name.
Vinicola Amanda

**Salento** r. p. w. ★→★★★ 80 81 82 83 85 86
Table wines from the Salento peninsula. The Rosso del Salento and Rosato del Salento, both based on Negroamaro and Malvasia grapes, are widely noted. The strong red can age well, the rosé can be attractively fragrant and tasty. The white is rarely as good.
Francesco Candido                         Notarpanaro (Taurino)
Cantine Riunite del Salento               Santachiara (Medico)
Distante Vini                             Giovanni Soloperto
Leone De Castris                          Vinicola Venturi
Baroni Malfatti                           Ubaldo Zanzarella

**Salice Salentino** DOC r. p. dr. ★★→★★★ 77 78 79 80 81 83 85 86
Fine red and rosé from Negroamaro primarily grown around Salice Salentino W of Lecce. The *rosso*, rich and velvety with bitter undertone and impressive durability, stands out among Salento wines. The *rosato* also has depth and, following tradition, is sometimes aged.
Ag. *prodotto invecchiato* (*rosato*) 1 yr; *riserva* (*rosso*) 2 yrs (1 in wood).
Leone De Castris                          Cosimo Taurino
Baroni Malfatti

**San Severo** DOC r. p. w. dr. (sp.) ★→★★ 83 85 86
Good if rarely distinguished wines from the Capitanata plain take this name, the red and rosé from Montepulciano and Sangiovese, the red from Bombino Bianco and Trebbiano.
D'Alfonso Del Sordo                        Aldo Pugliese
Federico II                               Riforma Fondiaria

**Spumante** p. w. (sw.) sp. ★→★★ DYA
The mania for sparkling wines is spreading south, though Apulia so far uses the *charmat* method. The leader was Leone De Castris with white Don Piero and pink Donna Lisetta. Rivera has a pink Rivera Brut.
Leone De Castris                          Rivera

**Squinzano** DOC r. p. dr. ★→★★★ 77 78 79 80 81 82 83 85 86
Sound wines from Negroamaro grown at the Salento town of Squinzano. The *rosso* needs a couple of years to develop robust goodness,

the *riserva* about 5 years. The *rosato* is bright coral pink, fresh, and tasty.
Ag. *riserva* 2 yrs (*rosso*).
Renna                                     Villa Valletta
Giuseppe Strippoli

**Torre Alemanna** r. dr.  ☐ ✭✭ ☐  81 83 85 86
Red table wine of character from Malbec, Negroamaro, and Uva di
Troia grown near Cerignola. Deep garnet, dry, and balanced, will age.
Riforma Fondiaria

**Torre Quarto** r. p. w. dr.  ✭→✭✭✭  71 73 74 75 77 79 81 83 85
The vast estate of the Cirillo-Farrusi family near Cerignola makes some
of Apulia's finest red wine for aging. From Malbec, Uva di Troia, and
Negroamaro, it has a ruby-violet color taking on *pelure d'oignon* with age
as it develops a warm bouquet on a sturdy structure that can hold up
well over a decade from some vintages. *Rosato* and *bianco* are modest.
Cirillo-Farrusi

**Torre Saracena** r. dr.  ✭✭  79 81 83 85 86
Fleshy red table wine of sound character made from Malvasia Nera and
Negroamaro just outside Taranto. Deep ruby, it has a hint of sweetness
in its otherwise dry flavor. Ages 5–8 years.
Teodoro Caiulo

Balance seems built in to the Apulian diet, probably because the
region, if not perennially rich, has never lacked for nutritive
elements. The northern plains provide grain for pasta and bread;
the plateaus lamb, sausages, and cheese; the Adriatic and Ionian
seas fish. Everywhere there are vegetables, herbs, fruit, olive oil.

**Agnello al cartoccio** Lamb chops
baked in paper with green olives
and *lampasciuoli*, a wild, bitter-
tasting bulb similar to onion.
  ✭✭→✭✭✭  Torre Quarto *rosso* or
  ✭✭  Rosso di Cerignola.
**Burrata** Soft, buttery cheese from
the town of Andria.
  ✭✭  young Castel del Monte *rosso*.
**Cavatieddi con la ruca** Conch-
shaped pasta served with *ruca*
(rue), tomato sauce and *pecorino*.
  ✭✭  Copertino *rosato*.
**Cozze alla leccese** Mussels
cooked with oil, lemon, and
parsley, one of dozens of ways of
preparing this favored shellfish.
  ✭✭  Martina Franca.
**Frisedde** Hard rolls softened with
water and served with fresh
tomato, oregano, and olive oil.
  ✭✭  Five Roses.
**Gniumerieddi** Lamb innards

flavored with *pecorino*, lard, lemon,
and parsley, rolled, skewered, and
cooked over coals.
  ✭✭  Primitivo di Manduria *secco*.
**'Ncapriata** Dried fava beans
boiled, peeled, and mashed with
chicory, pimentos, onion, tomato,
and lots of olive oil.
  ✭✭  Squinzano *rosato*.
**Orecchiette con cime di rapa**
Small, ear-shaped pasta served
with boiled turnip greens and chili.
  ✭  Brindisi *rosato*.
**Ostriche alla tarantina** Fresh
oysters cooked with oil, parsley,
and breadcrumbs.
  ✭✭  Locorotondo.
**Tiella** Versatile baked layer
concoction, always containing
potatoes, usually rice, and
vegetables, with meat, cheese, or
seafood, a heritage of Spain.
  ✭✭  Castel del Monte *rosato*.

### Restaurants
Recommended in or near wine zones: **North** *Bacco* at Barletta; *Ostello di
Federico* at Castel del Monte; *Cicolella* in Foggia (two restaurants).
**Center** *Il Poeta Contadino* at Alberobello; *Del Corso* at Altamura; *Ancora,
La Pignata* and *Vecchia Bari* in Bari; *Fagiano* at Fasano; *L'Aragosta* at
Santo Spirito; *Cristoforo Colombo* at Trani. **South** *Al Fornello-Da Ricci* at
Ceglie Messapico; *Marechiaro* at Gallipoli; *Al Gambero* at Taranto.

# Basilicata

Basilicata lacks nearly every benefit that could rate it some sorely needed attention. It has no major monuments to its Greek and Roman past; two meager strips of seacoast; few exploitable natural resources; pleasant but hardly spectacular upland scenery; and not so much as a restaurant of renown.

That the region has only one DOC would seem to fit the pattern of deprivation, except that Aglianico del Vulture is one thing about Basilicata that isn't innately underprivileged. Had the fates been a little kinder, it might be universally recognized for what it is – one of Italy's great red wines. The Aglianico vine was brought to Monte Vulture by the Greeks; its name is a corruption of Hellenico. This late-maturing variety performs best in the heights of Basilicata and Campania.

Basilicata, whose alternative name is Lucania and whose capital is Potenza, is not a tourist paradise. But these days obscurity in itself is worth something. The ancient city of Matera has Greek-like charm, and wine lovers looking for out-of-the-way places will find them on Monte Vulture near the Naples-Bari *autostrada*.

## Recent vintages

Though Aglianico del Vulture has extraordinary aging potential, only in the last decade have producers in the zone improved vinification and aging techniques to realize the optimum.

1986   Fine harvest that almost rivals '85 in class.
1985   Big, balanced wines, probably the best vintage of recent times.
1984   Generally poor due to damp and cold.
1983   Rain marred the harvest, bringing uneven results.
1982   Drought, then rain and hail resulted in a spotty crop of average to very good wines.
1981   Down by 40% but exceptional, certainly the best since '73. Wines to lay down.
1980   Fair to good, though earthquakes ruined the late harvest.
1979   Good, abundant vintage of wines of medium life spans.
1978   Uniformly good year.
1977   Fine crop of long-lived wines.
1976   Poor.
1975   Very good wines for medium-long aging.
1974   Average quality; not wines to keep.
1973   Some exceptional wines nearing prime.

**Aglianico dei Colli Lucani** r. dr. (s/sw.) (sp.) ★→ ★★  81 82 85 86
Table wine from Aglianico grown in E Basilicata, notaby around towns of Irsina and Tricarico in Matera province. Similar to Aglianico del Vulture when young (also in *amabile* and *spumante*), but it fails to rival the sheer grandeur of the DOC wine, though it does well with 5–6 years, often more, of aging. Also made in Apulia.
Miali

**Aglianico del Vulture** DOC r. dr. (s/sw.) (sp.)  ★★→★★★★  73 75 77 78 79 81 82 85 86
From Aglianico grapes grown on the E slopes of Monte Vulture and hills to the SE past Venosa to Genzano. Though it may be sold after a year as a dry wine or a lightly *amabile spumante*, it's the aged Aglianico that stands in the front rank of Italian wines. Deep ruby to garnet, taking on orange reflections with age in barrel and bottle, its bouquet heightens as it becomes richly smooth with unusual depth of flavors. The better grapes come from volcanic soil high up around Rionero and Barile where microclimates are similar to those in alpine regions.

Average production now exceeds 1 million bottles. The ★★★★ rating applies to '73, '77, '79, '81 and '85 vintages from Fratelli D'Angelo, though others can approach that level. The DOC permits vinification in Apulia.
Ag. 1 yr; *vecchio* 3 yrs (2 in barrel); *riserva* 5 yrs.

| | | |
|---|---|---|
| Botte | Fratelli D'Angelo | Fratelli Napolitano |
| Consorzio Viticoltori | Armando Martino | Paternoster |
|   Associati del Vulture | Miali | Torre Sveva |

**Asprino** or **Asprinio** w. dr. fz. ★ DYA
Curiously acidic little white from Asprinio grapes grown around the town of Ruoti. Most is sent with haste to Naples. Malvasia della Lucania, notably from Val Bradano, is similar.

**Lucanello** w. dr. ★★→★★★ 85 86
Fine dry white from Malvasia grown at Vulture with Pinot Bianco. Smooth and mouth-filling, its ample aroma recalls certain alpine whites. Fratelli D'Angelo

**Malvasia del Vulture** w. or am. dr. sw. sp. ★ DYA
Virtually the same as Malvasia della Lucania but restricted to the Vulture zone, where it is usually sweet and sparkling.

| | |
|---|---|
| Fratelli D'Angelo | Paternoster |
| Armando Martino | Sasso |

**Metapontum** r. w. dr. ★ 83 85 86
Table wines from the Ionian coastal plain around Metaponto: the *rosso* from Sangiovese, Negroamaro, Malvasia Nera, the *bianco* from Malvasia Bianca and Trebbiano.
C.S. del Metapontino

**Montepulciano di Basilicata** r. dr. ★→★★ 83 85 86
Table wine from Montepulciano grapes grown near Metaponto. Robust, round, well-scented, it is good for 2–6 years.
C.S. del Metapontino

**Moscato del Vulture** w. sw. sp. ★→★★ DYA
Dessert wines, usually sparkling, from Moscato grapes of the Vulture zone. Golden yellow, sweet, aromatic, low in alcohol, and best young.

| | |
|---|---|
| Botte | Armando Martino |
| Consorzio Viticoltori | Paternoster |
|   Associati del Vulture | Sasso |
| Fratelli D'Angelo | |

## Wine & Food

The cooking of Basilicata may be as lean and spare as the landscape, but it has a warmth that comes directly from the summer sun. Appetites are satisfied with ample servings of beans, pasta, soups, potatoes, and bread. Vegetables play a starring role in stews cooked with olive oil and plenty of herbs and spices. Pimento (known as *diavolicchio*) goes into a sauce called *piccante*, fiery enough to live up to its name and more. In the old days, meat was used thriftily in, for example, preserved pork products: *soppressata*, *coppa*, or the piquant *luganighe* sausages.

**Cazmarr** Stew of lamb's innards, *prosciutto*, cheese, and wine.
  ★★→★★★ Aglianica del Vulture *vecchio*.

**Ciammotta** Peppers, potatoes, eggplant, tomato, and garlic – first fried, then stewed.
  ★ Malvasia della Lucania *secco*.

**Lasagne e fagioli** Lasagne and beans laced with pepper and garlic.
  ★ Metapontum *rosso*, young.

**Minuich** Hand-made pasta rolled into cylinders around a slim metal stick, sometimes served with cabbage greens.
  ★ Malvasia del Vulture *secco*.

**Pignata** Lamb marinated with vegetables, hot peppers, cheese, and wine in a sealed earthenware pot (*la pignata*) and left to simmer on the hearth for hours.
  ★★ Aglianico dei Colli Lucani.

### Restaurants
Recommended near Monte Vulture: *La Pergola* at Rionero; *Delle Colline* at Muro Lucano.

# Calabria

Calabria

Once a garden of the Greeks, who favored its wines over others of Enotria, Calabria is striving gamely to recapture its antique vinicultural luster. They say Calabrian athletes returning in triumph from an early Olympiad were hailed with Krimisa, which, if not the "world's oldest wine," as some contend, was probably among the earliest in Europe. Krimisa was made where Cirò is made today, on the Ionian coast between the sites of the Greek cities of Sybaris and Kroton.

Cirò remains the paragon of Calabrian wines, the only well-known name among the 8 DOCs. Cirò *rosso* and *rosato* derive from Gaglioppo, as do most Calabrian reds, though the others, if sound and flavorful, rarely show the breed of the aged Cirò. White Cirò comes from Greco Bianco, a lively relic capable of both bright, modern dry wines and luxuriant, old-style dessert wines, the sweetest and best being Greco di Bianco.

The toe of the Italian boot is so mountainous that most vineyards are confined to rugged, relatively cool hillsides – probably a blessing because big yields are out of the question and the alternative is the pursuit of quality. Most Calabrian wines, Cirò excepted, can be found only on their home grounds. Several are well worth seeking out.

Calabria's tourist attractions are mostly natural: the Sila Massif (Italy's "Little Switzerland") in the north around Cosenza and Catanzaro (the region's capital); and the Aspromonte range in the south, overlooking Reggio di Calabria and, across the straits, Sicily's Mount Etna. Remnants of the Greeks are evident along the coasts, the most scenic of which is the Calabrian Riviera between Reggio and Gioia Tauro.

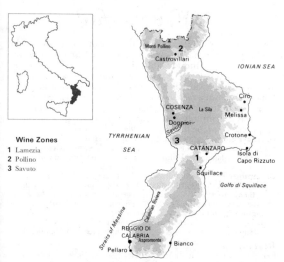

**Wine Zones**

1 Lamezia
2 Pollino
3 Savuto

## Recent vintages

The chart applies to Cirò, though it serves as a guideline to other Calabrian wines, such as Donnici, Pollino, Savuto, and Melissa.

1986   Fine crop of balanced wines, well suited to aging.
1985   Excellent year for long-lived reds.
1984   Late harvest of medium to good wines.
1983   Despite drought, Cirò was up in quality and quantity.
1982   Drought reduced crop of middling to good wines.
1981   Small harvest of generally good wines, notably Cirò.
1980   Some acceptable wines from select grapes.
1979   Fine, abundant crop of durable reds.
1978   Generally very good, long-lived wines.
1977   Mixed results, some good wines.

**Cerasuolo di Scilla** p. dr. or s/sw.  ★ DYA
Cherry-pink local wine of Scilla (the legendary Scylla at the top of the Straits of Messina) made from a mix that includes Alicante.

**Cirò** DOC r. p. w. dr.  ★→ ★★★  73 74 77 78 79 81 83 85 86
A name of ancient renown applied to three colors of wine from the Ionian coastal hills around Cirò and Cirò Marina. The *rosso*, from Gaglioppo with 10% of light Greco or Trebbiano permitted, is ample and strong (13.5%), with deep bouquet and velvety texture. With 5–8 years of age, sometimes more, it develops a distinct ruby-amber color. The *rosato*, from the same grapes as the red, can be a good all-purpose wine. The *bianco*, from the worthy Greco Bianco grape, was often lackluster, but cold fermentation and other techniques have immensely improved the white from certain producers. Wines from the heart of the zone may be labeled *classico*.
Ag. *riserva* (*rosso*) 3 yrs.

| | |
|---|---|
| Cantina Enotria | Vincenzo Ippolito |
| C.S. Caparra & Siciliani | Antonio Librandi |
| C.S. Torre Melissa | Antonio Scala |
| Fratelli Caruso | Tenute Pirainetto (Nicodemo) |

**Donnici** DOC r. dr.  ★→ ★★  83 85 86
Medium ruby to light red from Gaglioppo and Greco Nero grapes grown in hills adjacent to Cosenza. Fruity, fragrant, and unimposing, it is good fairly young and fresh.
Pasquale Bozzo                    Opera Sila C.S. di Donnici

**Greco di Bianco** DOC w. sw.  ★★→ ★★★★  77 78 79 81 83 85 86
Made from Greco grapes grown around the SE Calabrian seaside town of Bianco, this can be one of Italy's outstanding dessert wines. Golden, velvety, and luscious but not cloying, it has an entrancing orange blossom aroma and about 17% alcohol. With great age it tends to become drier and more richly scented, though its balance seems best in 4–8 years. Rare, expensive, and consistently excellent from Umberto Ceratti, who used to call the wine Greco di Gerace. New plantings promise more of this fine DOC wine.
Ag. 1 yr.
Cacib                              Francesco Saporito
Umberto Ceratti

**Lacrima di Castrovillari** r. dr. sw.  ★★  85 86
Full-flavored table wine from Lacrima Nera and Gaglioppo. *Secco* or *amabile*, it has deep ruby-violet color, fresh, richly fruity flavor and strength (14%). Drink in 1–3 years.
Alia                               C.S. Vini del Pollino

**Lametino** w. dr. (sw.)  ★ DYA
The white version of Lamezia, which is DOC only in *rosso*. Made from Greco and Malvasia, when dry it is soft and easy, when *amabile* mouth-fillingly rich.
C.S. di Sambiase

**Lamezia** DOC r. dr.  ⭐ DYA
Dry red from Nerello Mascalese, Nerello Cappuccio, Gaglioppo, and Greco Nero grown around Lamezia Terme, Sant' Eufemia, Sambiase,

and Filadelfia, W of Catanzaro. Cherry red, sometimes almost rosé, refreshingly uncomplex, it is best young.
C.S. di Sambiase

**Mantonico di Bianco** am. dr. or s/sw. **\*\*→\*\*\***   77 78 79 81 83 85 86
Made from semidried light Mantonico grapes grown around Bianco, it becomes a strong (15–16%) amber wine that needs barrel age to develop a Sherry-like style. Whether dry or slightly sweet, it retains a tannic, lightly bitter almond undertone and a curiously citrus-like aroma.
Cacib                                             Francesco Saporito
Umberto Ceratti

**Melissa** DOC r. w. dr. **\*→\*\***   78 79 81 83 85 86
Recent DOC from the Ionian coast around Melissa, Strongoli, and Crotone–adjacent (and similar) to Cirò. The *rosso*, based on Gaglioppo, is dry, rather full, capable of becoming interesting in 5–6 years. The *bianco*, based on Greco Bianco, can be dry and crisp, good with fish.
Ag. *superiore* (*rosso*) 2 yrs.
C.S. Torre Melissa                      Giuseppe Ippolito

**Moscato** w. s/sw. sw. (sp.) **\*→\*\*** DYA
Dessert wines made in many places from Moscato grapes, often semidried. Golden, aromatic, sometimes lightly sweet and sparkling but more often rich, strong and smooth.
Alia

**Nicastro** r. w. dr. (sw.) **\*** DYA
Recognized table wines from the town of Nicastro. The *rosso*, from Nerello and Gaglioppo, is a fruity wine, similar to the neighboring Lamezia. The *bianco*, usually dry, is based on Malvasia Bianca.

**Pellaro** r. p. dr. **\*→\*\***   83 85 86
Red and rosé table wines from Alicante and other varieties grown on the Pellaro promontory S of Reggio di Calabria. Light in color (cherry red to pink), it is robust, strong (up to 16%), and can improve over 3–5 years.
Vincenzo Oliva                          Pasquale Scaramozzino
Cristoforo Pastorino

**Pollino** DOC r. dr. **\*→\*\***   81 83 85 86
Sturdy red from Gaglioppo and Greco Nero grown in the Monti Pollino around Castrovillari and Frascineto. Light, almost rosé in color, it has fruity fragrance, good body, and can show class with 2–5 years.
Ag. *superiore* 2 yrs.
C.S. Vini del Pollino                    Basilio Miraglia

**Sant'Anna di Isola Capo Rizzuto** DOC r. dr. **\*** DYA
Inconsequential but tasty red from Gaglioppo and a host of other varieties grown on the Ionian coastal hills SW of Crotone near the town of Isola di Capo Rizzuto. Roseate red, it is best young and cool.
C.S. Sant'Anna

**Savuto** DOC r. p. dr. **\*\***   81 83 85 86
One of Calabria's better reds, from Gaglioppo and Greco Nero principally, grown on steep hills along the Savuto River S of Cosenza. Light ruby and fragrant, it can develop charm with 3–5 years of age.
Ag. *superiore* 2 yrs.
C.S. Vini di Savuto (G. Longo)        F. Todaro
Istituto Professionale di Stato

**Squillace** w. dr. **\*→\*\*\*** DYA
Fragile but convincing white from Greco Bianco, Malvasia, and others grown at Squillace SW of Catanzaro. Young (and on the spot) it is pale gold with a hint of sweetness, though it qualifies as dry.

**Villa Santelia** w. dr. **\*\*** DYA
Good white table wine based on Greco grown in the Cirò area.
Fratelli Caruso

*Wine & Food*

Calabria, behind its mountain barriers, has always lived in splendid isolation. Its cooking, although drawing on standard southern Italian ingredients, expresses this independence. Pork is so important that the pig has been called Calabria's "sacred cow." The great peasant tradition (which survives in home kitchens if rarely in restaurants) relies on soups, pastas, and vast arrays of vegetables. When not in season, peppers, zucchini (courgettes), artichokes, eggplant, and mushrooms are preserved in olive oil, of which the region is a major producer. Besides the usual range of shellfish, Tyrrhenian waters provide swordfish and tuna. Calabrians adore sweets, often based on citrus and other fruit, either candied or dried, such as figs filled with chocolate.

**Alalonga in agrodolce** Tender small tuna caught in Calabrian waters cooked sweet-sour.
   ★ Cerasuolo di Scilla.

**Cicirata** Christmas pastries flavored with either honey or cooked grape must and lemon.
   ★★★→★★★★ Greco di Bianco.

**Melanzane a polpetta** Eggplant stewed with eggs, garlic, pepper, and breadcrumbs.
   ★ Sant'Anna di Isola Capo Rizzuto.

**Mursiellu alla catanzarese** Rich stew of various pieces of pork, tomatoes, and peppers.
   ★★ Savuto or ★★ Cirò *rosso*.

**Mùstica** Newborn anchovies with oil and lemon.
   ★★ Squillace.

**Pesce spada** Swordfish, a speciality of Bagnara on the Calabrian Riviera, with peppers, lemon, garlic, capers, and herbs.
   ★★ Cirò *bianco*.

**Pitta chicculiata** Calabrian pizza – a sort of pie filled with tuna, tomato, anchovies, black olives, and capers.
   ★ Cirò *rosato*.

**Sagne chine** Festive lasagne baked with as many ingredients between the layers as possible, usually pork, peas, artichokes, and mushrooms.
   ★★ Savuto or ★★ Donnici.

### Restaurants

Recommended in or near wine zones: **Cirò-Melissa** *Il Gabbiano* at Cirò Marina; *Bella Romagna* and *Il Girrarosto* at Crotone; *Concordia* at Torre Melissa; **Donnici** *La Calavrisella* at Cosenza; **Lamezia** *Pesce Fresco* at Gizzeria Lido; **Pollino** *Alia* at Castrovillari.

# Campania

Campania

Both Greeks and Romans knew that vines thrived as nowhere else in the volcanic soil of Campania. The Greeks introduced vines now known as Aglianico and Greco and the Romans celebrated the wines of Avellino, Vesuvius, and Falernum. Sadly, Campanian viticulture has never fully recovered from a decline that began with the fall of the Roman Empire. Today, the region of Naples produces much less wine than conditions would permit. But what really lacks is a sense of quality; 99.6% of production is outside DOC. Though some table wines are admirable, many reinforce the notion that Campanian wines are lightweights masquerading under melodramatic names.

Still, what little serious wine there is confirms the wisdom of the ancients. Campania's best wines today come from Aglianico, Greco, and Fiano (a Roman favorite) in the hills of Avellino. One winery there stands out, Mastroberardino, which is also striving to restore the ancient luster of Vesuvius, which finally won its DOC in 1983, though the volcano's wines are burdened with the legendary but overworked name of Lacryma Christi (Christ's Tear).

Falernum or Falernian is not what it used to be, and just as well as modern palates wouldn't tolerate resin, salt water, and honey. However, a red called Falerno (from Aglianico) proves that the Romans understood the privileged nature of the place.

Though most wines of maritime Campania, from the Gulf of Naples to Sorrento and Salerno, are laughable at best, exceptions include certain wines of the island of Ischia and the resort town of Ravello on the Amalfi coast.

Campania's fabled tourist sites – Capri, Pompeii, Herculaneum, Sorrento, Amalfi, Ischia, Paestum, and Naples – need no further promotion. Wine lovers, who should find Ischia rewarding in the off-season, might be even more excited by the wines around Avellino and Benevento. The *Enoteca Partenopea* in Naples provides a discriminating selection from Campania and other regions.

1  Falerno
2  Greco di Tufo
3  Lacryma Christi
4  Taurasi

## Recent vintages

The chart applies to wines of Avellino. Recommended years for
others are shown with each entry.

1986 Fine harvest for reds and whites.
1985 Exceptional, possibly the best vintage since '68 for Taurasi.
1984 Generally mediocre due to damp and cold.
1983 Excellent harvest of durable wines.
1982 Sharply reduced due to drought, but wines were very good.
1981 Excellent harvest, though below normal in quantity.
1980 Latest harvest in memory resulted in excellent Fiano and Greco,
but earthquakes crippled Taurasi's production.
1979 Great but limited harvest for Fiano and Greco; rain spoiled
Taurasi's promising start, though a little fine wine was salvaged.
1978 Fine, abundant harvest; Taurasi drinking well now.
1977 Very good year for the whites, exceptional for Taurasi to drink
in the late 1980s.
Earlier fine vintages: '75, '73, '71, '68, '61, '58.

**Aglianico del Taburno** or **Taburno** r. dr.
A DOC has been proposed for red and rosé from Aglianico grown in the
Taburno hills of Benevento province not far from Taurasi.

**Amber Drops** am. sw. ★★ 77 78 79 81 83 85 86
Sherry-like sweet wine from raisined Biancolella grapes of Ischia.
Amber yellow with rich, woody aroma after aging in *barriques*, it
becomes soft and smooth over 7–10 years.
D'Ambra.

**Asprino** w. dr. ★ DYA
Fragile, acidic, lemon-yellow wine served over the counter in Naples as
a thirst quencher. Most of this light (8–9%) wine comes from Asprinio
grapes grown in Caserta province.

**Barbera** r. dr. ★→★★ 83 85 86
The Piedmont grape is used for table wines in several areas, notably the
Sannio and Irpinia hills around Benevento and Avellino, where it is also
blended with others. Dark and robust, the wines are best in 1–3 years.
La Vinicola Ocone

**Biancolella** w. dr. ★★ DYA
Table wine from Biancolella grapes of Ischia. Light golden yellow and
nicely scented, it is sharply dry but well textured. Good young.
D'Ambra

**Capri** DOC r. w. dr. ★ DYA
Simple wines designed to appeal to visitors of the lovely but touristy isle,
though grapes for their extremely limited production may also come
from certain spots on the mainland as well as Capri. The *rosso*, from
Piedirosso and others, is medium-ruby, dry, and drinkable if you're
lucky. The *bianco*, from Falanghina and Greco, can be drunk with fish.
De Rosa

**Chardonnay** w. dr.
Among plantings of this variety in the south is D'Ambra's vineyard at
400 to 500 meters on Ischia's Mount Epomeo, from which wines will be
made in the late 1980s.
D'Ambra

**Cilento** r. (p.) (s/sw.) (sp.) ★→★★ 83 85 86
Red, occasionally rosé, wines in various styles, even *amabile* and *spumante*.
The red from Primitivo, Guarnaccia, and others is often used for
blending, but it can also be a fine table wine with 3–5 years of aging.
C.S. di Cilento

**Falerno** r. w. dr. ★→★★★ 81 82 83 85 86
Italianized name for Falernum, the Roman favorite. The *rosso* from
Aglianico grown around the NW Campania coastal town of
Mondragone, is a fine, full-bodied table wine that improves with 4–6
years or more. The *bianco*, from Falanghina, is of little note.
Michele Moio                          Villa Matilde

**Fiano di Avellino** DOC w. dr. ★★→★★★★ 79 80 81 82 83 85 86
Exceptional dry white wine from Fiano – a derivation of Apianum, the
Roman name that acknowledged the bees' (*Apis*) attraction to the grape
– grown in hills surrounding Avellino. Light straw, smoothly textured,
with a scent of pears and hazelnuts, it has a dry, elegant, lingering flavor.
Wine from the community of Lapio, considered the most privileged part
of the DOC zone, may use Fiano di Lapio as a subdenomination.
Mastroberardino                              Struzziero

**Forastera** w. dr. ★ DYA
Pale straw table wine from Forastera grapes of Ischia – dry and fresh.
D'Ambra

**Gragnano** r. dr. (s/sw.) fz. sp. ★→★★ 85 86
Refreshing purplish table wine, often *frizzante* or *spumante*, sometimes off-
sweet. Made from various combinations of grapes, which may include
Aglianico, Olivella, and Per'e Palummo, grown near the town of
Gragnano in the hills of the Sorrentine peninsula.
Saviano

**Greco di Tufo** DOC w. dr. (sp.) ★★★ 83 85 86
Fine dry white from Greco grapes of antiquity grown around the village
of Tufo in the hills of Irpinia N of Avellino. Pale straw to medium yellow,
both its bouquet and flavor suggest almond. Mastroberardino's
Vignadangelo, from a special vineyard, has the character to evolve
favorably over 3–4 years. The *spumante* is rarely seen.
Mastroberardino                              Struzziero

**Ischia** DOC r. w. dr. ★→★★ 83 85 86
Light reds and whites from the resort island on the Gulf of Naples. Most
are common, but those from a couple of producers have deservedly wide
followings. The *rosso*, from Guarnaccia and Per'e Palummo, is a good all-
purpose wine, young and fresh. The *bianco*, from Forastera and
Biancolella, is a light refresher. Ischia *bianco superiore*, a very good fish
wine, comes from the same grapes grown in select parts of the island. It
may be fermented briefly with the skins and refermented with musts of
semidried grapes to give it character.
D'Ambra                                      Perrazzo

**Kalimera** w. dr. sp. ★★ DYA
Apparently the first *méthode champenoise* of Campania comes from
Biancolella, Forastera and Chardonnay grapes grown on Ischia's
Mount Epomeo and aged in cellars carved out of the isle's soft stone.
D'Ambra

**Lacrimarosa d'Irpinia** p. dr. ★★ DYA
Delicate rosé from Aglianico grapes of Irpinia processed under the
*lacrima* or teardrop system, which gives it a topaz-pink color and dry,
crisp, clean flavor.
Mastroberardino

**Lacryma Christi del Vesuvio**
See Vesuvio.

**Lettere** r. dr. ★★ DYA
Round, refreshing table wine of special drinkability, made from a
labyrinthian mélange of grapes, including Aglianico, Olivella, and Per'e
Palummo, grown at Lettere near Sorrento. Dry and supple, served cool
it goes with many dishes. Growers have requested DOC.
Antonio Pentangelo

**Per'e Palummo** r. dr. ★★ 82 83 85 86
Good table wine of Ischia made from Per'e Palummo with some
Guarnaccia. Well-structured, medium-ruby, it develops bouquet and
smooth flavor with 3–5 years.
D'Ambra

**Ravello** r. p. w. dr. ★★→★★★ 82 83 85 86
Fine table wines, the best of the Amalfi coast, from the lovely town of
Ravello. The *rosso*, from Per'e Palummo, Aglianico, Merlot, and others,
is dry, balanced, elegant, and capable of 5–10 years of aging (Episcopio
*rosso* is a superior example). The *rosato*, from the same grapes as the red, is
burnished pink, clean, and easy. The *bianco*, from Coda di Volpe, San

Nicola, Greco, and others, is a fish wine of more than usual character.
Episcopio (Vuilleumier)                Gran Caruso

**Solopaca** DOC r. w. dr. ★→ ★★ 83 85 86
Unsung DOC zone named after a town in the Sannio hills W of
Benevento. The *rosso*, from Sangiovese with some Aglianico and
Piedirosso, is ruby red and pleasantly soft, good in 2–4 years. The *bianco*,
from Trebbiano Toscano and Malvasia, is common.
C.S. La Guardiense                La Vinicola Ocone

**Taurasi** DOC r. dr. ★★→★★★★ 68 71 73 75 77 78 79 80 81 82 83 85 86
One of Italy's great aged red wines made from the late-maturing
Aglianico grape grown in the cool Irpinia hills NE of Avellino around
the village of Taurasi. Deep ruby when young, it takes on an onion-skin
color with age as its bouquet enhances and its youthful robustness tones
down to a velvety austerity. Rich, complete and highly personal, it
excels with roasts.
Ag. 3 yrs (1 in barrel); *riserva* 4 yrs.
Mastroberardino                Struzziero

**Vesuvio** DOC r. p. w. (sw.) (sp.) ★→★★★ 83 85 86
Finally approved as DOC in 1983, Vesuvio takes in *rosso*, *rosato* and *bianco*
of rather common stature and Lacryma Christi del Vesuvio in superior
versions. The red wine comes from Piedirosso and Olivella grapes, the
white from Coda di Volpe primarily grown on the lower slopes of Mt
Vesuvius or nearby. Lacryma Christi can become a notable, generous
garnet red, capable of 3–6 years of aging or more. The white can be dry,
semisweet, or sweet (also *liquoroso*) and may be sparkling.
Mastroberardino                Saviano

*Wine & Food*

It is hard to imagine that Naples was once a gastronomic capital
– under the Romans and again under various monarchs between
the late Middle Ages and Italy's unification. The sumptuous
dining of the past has since been replaced by the culinary
improvisations that perfume the alleyways of Naples: onions,
garlic, and herbs stewing with tomatoes for a *pommarola* sauce;
pastries frying in hot grease; steaming *espresso*; and fresh fish.
That many of Campania's specialities can be eaten standing up
should not detract from their inherent worth.

**Capretto in agrodolce** Sweet-
sour kid, a speciality of Irpinia.
Lamb is also done that way.
★★→★★★★ Taurasi.
**Cianfotta** Peppers, onions,
tomatoes, eggplant, and zucchini
stewed in oil and eaten cold.
★★ Ravello *rosato* or *bianco*.
**Mozzarella in carozza**
*Mozzarella* sandwiches coated with
batter and deep-fried in olive oil.
★★★★ Fiano di Avellino
or ★★★ Greco di Tufo.
**'Mpepata di cozze** Fresh mussels
served in their cooking water with
lemon, pepper, and parsley.
★★ Ischia *bianco*

**Parmigiana di melanzane** or
**melanzane alla parmigiana**
Campanian classic: eggplant
baked with tomato sauce,
*mozzarella*, and Parmesan.
★★ Lacrimarosa d'Irpinia.
**Pizza napoletana** The original,
with tomatoes, oregano, and fresh
basil – or, with *mozzarella* and
Parmesan added as a Margherita.
★ Asprino or ★ Vesuvio *bianco
secco*.
**Spaghetti alla puttanesca**
"Strumpet's spaghetti" dressed
with tomato, pepper, capers,
olives, and anchovies, a speciality
of Ischia.
★★ Biancolella.

### Restaurants
Recommended in or near wine zones: **Amalfi-Sorrento** *Cappuccini
Convento* near Amalfi; *Maria Grazia* at Nerano; *Buca di Bacco* and *La
Cambusa* at Positano; *Caruso al Belvedere* and *Da Palumbo al Confalone* at
Ravello; *La Spagnola al Porto* at Salerno; *Don Alfonso 1890* at Sant 'Agata;
*O'Parrucchiano* at Sorrento; **Avellino** *Barone* and *La Caveja* at Avellino;
**Capri** *Aurora* and *La Capannina*.

# Emilia-Romagna

Emilia-Romagna

Bologna "the fat" dotes over a region of plenty, comprising Lambrusco and other wines of the broad Po valley which have contributed to Emilia-Romagna's record as the most productive northern region with nearly a billion liters a year.

Lambrusco's conquests in America, where it once accounted for about half of Italian imports, has dwindled recently, though this bubbly red still steals the show from worthier wines of the Apennine foothills which stretch along the region's southern flank from Piacenza to the Adriatic. Emilia, the western sector, makes Lambrusco, as well as Gutturnio and a number of good varietals in the hills near Bologna and Piacenza. Romagna, between Bologna and the Adriatic, has three improving DOCs that bear its name – Sangiovese, Trebbiano and Albana, candidate for the first DOCG white – and a host of little known table wines that can be every bit as worthy.

Emilians prefer their wines bubbly, Romagnans tend to like theirs still, but both drink them young because they've learned

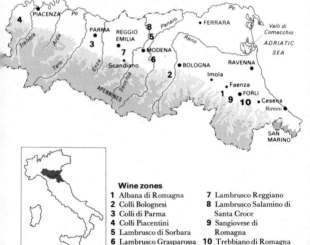

**Wine zones**

1 Albana di Romagna
2 Colli Bolognesi
3 Colli di Parma
4 Colli Piacentini
5 Lambrusco di Sorbara
6 Lambrusco Grasparossa di Castelvetro
7 Lambrusco Reggiano
8 Lambrusco Salamino di Santa Croce
9 Sangiovese di Romagna
10 Trebbiano di Romagna

that the richest, most glorified cooking of Italy is complemented by youthful freshness. Wines for aging are exceptions here.

Wine tourism is being developed in the region, notably in Romagna, through the *Ente Tutela Vini Romagnoli* (its symbol is the bearded *Passatore* in tilted hat, whose image graces bottles of approved wines). The wine house, a Romagnan institution, has been revived at Bertinoro (*Ca' de Bé*), Predappio Alto (*Ca' de Sanzves*), Ravenna (*Ca' de Vèn*), and Rimini (*Chésa de Vein*). Wine routes lead to vineyards of Sangiovese, Albana, and Trebbiano. In Emilia, the scenic Colli Bolognesi and Colli Piacentini offer many little-known good wines: the *enoteca* at

Castell'Arquato displays the Piacentini wines. Lambrusco's admirers can slake their thirst in the lush plains around Modena and Reggio, specifically at the *enoteca* in the castle at Levizzano Rangone near Castelvetro. The Enoteca Regionale Emilia-Romagna is housed in the Rocca Sforzesca, a medieval castle at Dozza in Romagna's hills.

## Recent vintages

ᴗThough Lambrusco and most other wines are to drink young, certain reds age well. Recent good years in Emilia (for Gutturnio, Barbera, Cabernet and Merlot) were '86, '85, '83, '82, '79, '78. Notable vintages in Romagna (for Sangiovese, Barbarossa and other reds) were '86, '85, '83, '82, '80, '79, '78, '77.

**Albana di Romagna** DOCG w. dr. or s/sw. (sp.) `*→***` 83 85 86
Romagna's preferred white from the time-honored Albana grape grown in a vast hilly zone between Bologna and Rimini. Either dry or *amabile*, it may also be *spumante*, which is increasingly popular. The *secco*, straw to golden yellow, delicately scented, at best cleanly dry, fruity, and smoothly textured with a bitter-almond background, is to drink in a year or two. The *amabile*, with golden highlights, has fruity fragrance and grapy sweetness from better producers; it holds up for 3–5 years from good vintages. Though DOCG has been approved, Albana has been a controversial choice, for quality among some four million bottles a year is uneven. New techniques, however, should help others to achieve the consistently superior class of Fratelli Vallunga, Fattoria Paradiso, and Ferrucci.

| | | |
|---|---|---|
| Luigi Baldrati | Ferrucci | Ruffo-Bacci |
| C.S. Forlì | Guarini | Spalletti |
| Cesari | C. Guidi & Figli | Tenuta Zerbina |
| Colombina | Marabini (Camerone) | Trerè |
| Comune di Faenza | Pambianco | Fratelli Vallunga |
| Fratelli Conti | Pasolini Dall'Onda | (Moronico) |
| Corovin | Fratelli Ravaioli | Vino dell'Olimpo |
| Costa-Archi | Ronchi | (Saporetti) |
| Fattoria Paradiso | Ronco | |

**Barbarossa di Bertinoro** r. dr. `***` 77 79 81 82 83 85 86
Unique red from vines discovered by Mario Pezzi and propagated within a plot called *Vigna del Dosso* near Bertinoro. Deep garnet and robust, with rich bouquet, it is already good after 2 years, and excellent from 5 to 10 as it becomes velvety and austere.
Fattoria Paradiso

**Barbera**
The dry, tasty, sometimes frothy table wines are made in Emilia's hills. DOC in Colli Bolognesi and Colli Piacentini.

**Bianco della Pusterla** w. s/sw. `**` 85 86
Lightly sweet, aromatic white from Malvasia, Moscato, Greco and Ortrugo grown at Vigolo Marchese in the Colli Piacentini. Suave and seductive, it is best in 1–3 years.
Pusterla

**Bianco di Scandiano** DOC w. dr. s/sw. fz. sp `*→**` DYA
Light white based on Sauvignon, grown around Scandiano SW of Reggio Emilia. Either *frizzante*, or *spumante*, the *secco* is soft and round, the *semisecco* aromatic.

| | |
|---|---|
| Cantina Cooperative | Elle (Conte Re) |
| Colli di Scandiano | Riunite |
| Casali | |

**Bonarda**
Varietal Bonarda (a strain of Croatina) is DOC in Colli Piacentini.

**Bosco Eliceo** or **Rosso del Bosco** r. dr. `*→**` DYA
Curious violet-garnet table wine from Uva d'Oro (known elsewhere as Fortana) grown in sandy plains around the Comacchio lagoon between Ferrara and the Adriatic. Warm, full-bodied, with acidic bite and grapy fragrance, it can be good young and cool.
C.S. Bosco Eliceo

**Cabernet** r. dr.  ★★ 78 79 82 83 85 86
Cabernet was prominent a century ago in Emilia, especially in the Colli
Piacentini. Some vines survived and more are being planted through
the Apennine foothills, signaling the advent of both varietal Cabernet
Sauvignon and Cabernet Franc, and Bordeaux-style wines with Merlot.
Cabernet Sauvignon is DOC in the Colli Bolognesi.
Marchese Malaspina

**Cagnina** r. s/sw.  ★★ DYA
Dessert wine of striking violet-pomegranate color that survives as a
vinicultural curio in the hills around Forlì. Made from the rare Cagnina
grape, it has a fruity aroma and mellow, ripe grape flavor – best young
and cool. A similar wine called Canena is made by Trerè.

| | | |
|---|---|---|
| C.S. Forlì | Fattoria Paradiso | Ronco |
| Colombina | Fratelli Ravaioli | |

**Calbanesco** r. dr.  ★★→★★★ 82 83 85 86
A unique table wine from the Calbanesco vine of undetermined origin
grown at Meldola south of Forlì. Of deep garnet color, it has an ample,
berry-like bouquet, dry, warm flavor with a hint of bitter underneath.
Best in 3–6 years.
Cesare Raggi

**Chardonnay** w. dr.  ★★★ 83 85 86
Chardonnay is not approved for Emilia-Romagna and therefore under
EEC policy cannot be planted. Nonetheless, one of Italy's pioneering
examples is the Chardonay of the Terre Rosse estate, SW of Bologna,
whose personality distinguishes it subtly from other wines of the variety.
Terre Rosse (Vallania)

**Colli Bolognesi-Monte San Pietro-Castelli Medioevali** DOC
Promising zone in the Apennine foothills SW of Bologna, split into two
subdivisions (Monte San Pietro and Castelli Medioevali), either of
which may appear on labels. Long a source of everyday wines to
Bologna, the zone's potential for quality has only begun to be realized
DOC covers eight types.

– **Barbera** r. dr.  ★→★★ 82 83 85 86
Most popular of the Colli Bolognesi wines, Barbera (which may contain
15% Sangiovese) has rich ruby-violet color and brisk flavor, mellowing
with 2–5 years.
Ag. *riserva* 3 yrs.

– **Bianco** w. dr. or s/sw.  ★ DYA
A rather plain, light golden wine from Albana and Trebbiano.

– **Cabernet Sauvignon** r. dr.  ★★→★★★ 82 83 85 86
Recently added to the DOC list, this is clearly the best red wine of
Bologna's hills. Deep in color with typical bouquet and flavor, its
natural gentility comes across even when styled to drink young (1–5
years). Terre Rosse's Cabernet exemplifies the style.
Ag. *riserva* 3 yrs.

– **Merlot** r. dr.  ★→★★ 83 85 86
Tasty red from at least 85% Merlot: dark ruby, softly dry, fruity and
good for 2–4 years.

– **Pignoletto** w. dr. (s/sw.) (fz.)  ★★ DYA
Newly approved as a distinct local clone somewhat resembling Riesling
Italico, this makes a lightly aromatic white, pleasantly fruity, usually
dry, though *amabile* and *frizzante* versions are permitted.

– **Pinot Bianco** w. dr. (s/sw.) (fz.)  ★→★★★ 85 86
Light greenish straw, usually dry (though *abboccato* is permitted), this
wine can reach admirable levels from certain producers in good years.

– **Riesling Italico** w. dr. (s/sw.) (fz.)  ★→★★ DYA
A light straw, delicately scented white of impressively fruity off-dry
flavor that comes across best young and chilled.

– **Sauvignon** w. dr.  ★★→★★★ 83 85 86
Best of the Colli Bolognesi DOC whites, it is pale greenish straw, crisply
dry, flinty, and amply scented. With a year of age, the Sauvignon of
Terre Rosse and Bruno Negroni can equal a good Loire white.

| | |
|---|---|
| Al Pazz (Fattoria Montebudello) | Aldo Conti |
| Cantina Consorziale | Bruno Negroni |
| Comprensorio Monte San Pietro | Terre Rosse (Vallania) |

**Colli di Parma** DOC
New zone in hills S and W of Parma around Salsomaggiore Terme and
the Taro River valley. DOC takes in three types, all still to be proven.
– **Malvasia** w. dr. s/sw. fz. (sp.) ★→★★★ DYA
From Malvasia di Candia with Moscato permitted at 15%, whether dry
or *amabile*, the typical aroma of Malvasia is heightened by a bit of fizz.
Oppici's *méthode champenoise* stands out.
– **Rosso** r. dr. (fz.) ★ 83 85 86
From Barbera with some Bonarda and Croatina, this is similar in style
to Lombardy's Oltrepò Pavese Rosso – dark ruby-violet, dry, bitter
underneath, often with a prickle.
– **Sauvignon** w. dr. (fz.) ★ DYA
Dry, delicately flinty, this noble variety could make a white of
significance here. Sometimes *pétillant*.
Cantine Dall'Asta                    Palazzo (Oppici)
Enopolio di Parma

**Colli Piacentini**
This large zone in the Apennine foothills south of Piacenza comprises
three former DOCs – Gutturnio dei Colli Piacentini, Monterosso Val
d'Arda, Trebbianino Val Trebbia – plus eight others, mainly varietal
wines. Though the appellation is yet to be fully developed, the zone
shows promise similar to the adjacent Oltrepò Pavese in Lombardy.
– **Barbera** r. dr. (fz.) ★→★★ 85 86
Sturdy red wines, sometimes fizzy, usually to drink inside 3 years.
Barbera from Ziano is of special note.
– **Bonarda** r. dr. s/sw. fz. ★→★★ 85 86
Dark ruby, often lightly sweet and fizzy, to drink in 2–3 years. Ziano's
Bonarda is prized by some.
– **Gutturnio** r. dr. (s/sw.) (fz.) ★→★★★ 82 83 85 86
Once *amabile* and *frizzante*, modern Gutturnio is usually dry and still.
From Barbera (60%) and Bonarda, it is deep garnet to violet in color,
generous and smooth with fine bouquet. Though some good young, some
bottles show style after 3–4 years.
– **Malvasia** w. dr. s/sw. fz. (sp.) ★→★★ DYA
The established pop wine of these hills: aromatic, fizzy, off-dry.
– **Monterosso Val d'Arda** w. dr. (s/sw.) fz. (sp.) ★★ DYA
Pleasant white, often *frizzante*, sometimes lightly *amabile*. Made from
Malvasia, Moscato, Trebbiano and Ortrugo in the Arda valley, it is
pleasantly fragrant, pale and delicate.
– **Ortrugo** w. dr. s/sw. (sp.) ★★ DYA
This fine local grape variety makes zesty whites of good class.
– **Pinot Grigio** w. dr. (sp.) ★→★★ DYA
Growingly popular, the variety is used for still wines and *spumante*.
– **Pinot Nero** r. (w.) (p.) dr. (sp.) ★→★★ 85 86
As in the Oltrepò Pavese, Pinot Nero will be used for both still red and
white and rosé sparkling wines.
– **Sauvignon** w. dr. (fz.) ★→★★ DYA
Good white wines made in the area indicate a bright future for this
distinctive varietal.
– **Trebbianino Val Trebbia** w. dr. (s/sw.) fz. (sp.) ★→★★ DYA
Fragile, spritzy white from Ortrugo, Malvasia, Trebbiano, Moscato and
Sauvignon grown in the Trebbia valley. Delicately dry and fragrant as a
rule, it may also be *amabile*.
– **Val Nure** w. dr. (s/sw.) fz. (sp.) ★ DYA
This fleeting white is similar to Trebbianino Val Trebbia.

| | |
|---|---|
| Fratelli Bonelli | Giancarlo Molinelli |
| Cascina di Fornello (Kustermann) | Montepascolo (Cardinali) |
| Castello di Luzzano (Fugazza) | Mossi |
| Castello di Prato Ottesola | Podere "Il Cristo" |
| Armando Clementoni | Pusterla |
| Colombo | Fratelli Rizzi |
| Remo Crosignani | Rocchetta |
| Gino Innocenti | Romagnoli |
| La Solitaria | Italo Testa & Figli |
| La Stoppa | Vitivinicola Colombi |

**Gutturnio dei Colli Piacentini**
See Colli Piacentini.

**Labrusca** p. dr. sp. ★★ DYA
Rapturous cherry-pink *spumante* from Lambrusco grapes processed by the *charmat* method at Correggio, near Reggio Emilia.
Oreste Lini & Figli

**Lambrusco** r. p. dr. s/sw. fz. ★→★★ DYA
Unclassified Lambrusco grown in Emilia's Po flatlands around Reggio and Modena. The dry is often consumed locally. Much of the *amabile*, sometimes pink, is exported to the United States. Some could qualify as DOC, but when it is sealed with plastic or metal caps (and not the corks required for DOC) it may not be so labeled. Invariably *frizzante*, its pressure is held under U.S. limits of sparkling wine to avoid excess taxes. (Producers do not include all bottler and shipper brands, which could also be dependable.)
Giacobazzi                          Riunite

**Lambrusco Bianco** w. dr. sp. ★★ DYA
The must from dark Lambrusco grapes separated from skins, vinified white and made sparkling by *charmat*. Clean and lively, its fine fruit-acid balance gives it unexpected tone.
Cavicchioli                          Oreste Lini & Figli

**Lambrusco di Sorbara** DOC r. dr. (s/sw.) fz. ★→ ★★★ DYA
Considered the most qualified DOC Lambrusco, it is made from Lambrusco di Sorbara grapes at 60% or more in a zone N of Modena that includes the village of Sorbara. Ruby to garnet with bright pink froth and well-scented, the *secco* goes with typical rich Emilian cooking, especially sausages, and the *amabile* (not often seen) with dessert. Like all DOC Lambrusco, it must be naturally *frizzante*, usually by *charmat*, sometimes by bottle fermentation.

| | |
|---|---|
| Mario Angiolini | Contessa Matilde |
| Francesco Bellei | Fini |
| Cancarini-Ghisetti | Giacobazzi |
| Cavicchioli | Italo Pedrotti |
| Chiarli | |

**Lambrusco Grasparossa di Castelvetro** DOC r. dr. (s/sw.) fz. ★→★★ DYA
Made from Lambrusco Grasparossa grapes in a zone S of Modena that includes Castelfranco Emilia, Spilamberto, and Sassuolo. Usually dry, sometimes *amabile*, but always *frizzante*, it has a ruby-violet color and a notable fragrance.

| | | |
|---|---|---|
| Cavicchioli | Contessa Matilde | Villa Barbieri |
| Chiarli | Giacobazzi | |

**Lambrusco Reggiano** DOC r. p. dr. s/sw. fz. ★→★★ DYA
Made from a blend of Lambrusco subvarieties grown around Reggio Emilia, this is the most heavily produced DOC Lambrusco (about 17 million liters a year) and the most exported. Considered the lightest in body and the most refreshing, whether dry or *amabile* its color varies from bright ruby to purple to pink.

| | |
|---|---|
| G. Alberini & Figli | Remigio Medici & Fratelli |
| Adolfo Donelli & Figlio | Moro |
| Oreste Lini & Figli | Riunite |

**Lambrusco Salamino di Santa Croce** DOC. r. dr. (s/sw.) fz. ★→★★ DYA
Made from Lambrusco Salamino grapes in a zone surrounding Modena that includes the village of Santa Croce. Ruby to purple, usually dry (as Modena's typical table wine), it can also be *amabile*.

| | |
|---|---|
| C.S. di Santa Croce | Contessa Matilde |
| Cavicchioli | Nedo Masetti |
| Chiarli | Severi Vini |

**Malvasia**
Wines from light Malvasia grapes are made in many parts of Emilia's hills. Usually spritzy and either off-dry or off-sweet, they can also be still and quite sweet, as is the fine Terre Rosse Malvasia from Bologna. Malvasia is DOC in Colli di Parma and Colli Piacentini.

**Merlot**
The popular vine is found in several parts of the region, most notably in Colli Bolognesi, where it is DOC, also in the Colli Piacentini and the Po Delta E of Ferrara.

**Monterosso Val d'Arda**
See Colli Piacentini.

**Müller Thurgau** w. dr.  ★★  DYA
Crisp whites from the Riesling-Sylvaner cross have been successful at Ziano in the Colli Piacentini as table wines.
Giancarlo Molinelli

**Pagadebit** or **Pagadebito** w. dr. (s/sw.)  ★★→★★★  DYA
Delicate white from the nearly extinct Pagadebit Gentile vine being revived on a limited scale around Bertinoro. Though sometimes *amabile*, the Pagadebit of Fattoria Paradiso is now usually dry with graceful texture and fruitiness, due to low-temperature fermentation.

| | | |
|---|---|---|
| Fattoria Paradiso | C. Guidi & Figli | Fratelli Ravaioli |
| Guarini Matteucci | Mossi | Ronco |

**Picòl Ross** r. dr. fz.  ★★★  DYA
One of the best of the Lambrusco family, Picòl Ross is grown at Sant'Ilario d'Enza, SE of Reggio.
Moro

**Pinot Bianco**
Grown in various parts of the region; DOC only in Colli Bolognesi.

**Pinot Grigio** w. dr.  ★→★★  DYA
Increasingly planted, Pinot Grigio is DOC in Colli Piacentini. The table wine of Terre Rosse near Bologna can match Pinot Grigio from more northerly places.
Terre Rosse (Vallania)

**Pinot Nero**
New interest in this vine both for red wines and sparkling whites is being shown in the hills. Pinot Nero is DOC in Colli Piacentini.

**Pinot Spumante** w. dr. sp.  ★★  DYA
Good sparkling wines are made from Pinot and Chardonnay grapes in several places, both by the *charmat* and Champagne methods.
Bruno Negroni                    Italo Testa & Figli

**Rèfolo** w. dr. fz.  ★★  DYA
Exhilarating bubbly from Trebbiano, Prosecco and Pinot made in Romagna. Bright straw, cleanly dry, it has a nice mix of bitter and soft.
Cesari

**Riesling**
Riesling Italico is DOC in Colli Bolognesi.

**Ronco Casone, Ronco dei Ciliegi, Ronco delle Ginestre** r. dr.  ★★★
80 81 82 83 85 86
Three "crus" from Sangiovese Grosso grown at Casale near Modigliana in Romagna's hills. Aged in small barrels of new French oak, they develop elegant tone in deep ruby color, flowery bouquet in dry but rich and complex flavor. With age, potential for  ★★★★  seems within reach.
Gian Matteo Baldi (Castelluccio)

**Ronco del Re** w. dr.  ★★★→★★★★  81 82 83 84 85 86
Sauvignon Blanc from a tiny plot on the Castelluccio estate, fermented and aged in a single barrel of French oak by winemaker Vittorio Fiore into 725 bottles of a singular white of luxuriant tone with extraordinary nuance, depth and staying power.
Gian Matteo Baldi (Castelluccio)

**Rosso Armentano** r. dr.  ★★★  78 79 82 83 85 86
Fine combination of Sangiovese di Romagna with Cabernet Franc and Pinot Nero orchestrated by Tommaso Vallunga in a red that needs 6–8 years to show elegance in bouquet and flavor.
Fratelli Vallunga

**Rosso della Bissera** r. dr. ** 82 83 85 86
Robust table wine from Montepulciano grown at Tenuta Bissera SW of
Bologna. Dark ruby, rounded, and perfumed, it is good in 3–5 years.
Bruno Negroni

**Sangiovese di Romagna** DOC r. dr. *→ ★★★ 79 80 82 83 85 86
Varietal red from the Romagnan (as distinguished from the Tuscan)
strain of Sangiovese grown in a vast zone of Romagna from the outskirts
of Bologna to the Adriatic coast S of Rimini. Though produced in
quantity (10 to 20 million liters a year), Sangiovese is not well known
outside Italy. Habitually consumed fairly young, some *riserva superiore*
(exemplified by Spalletti Rocca di Ribano and Fattoria Paradiso's
Vigneti delle Lepri) after 4–5 years shows breed well above its price
level. Bright ruby tending to garnet, with rich, flowery bouquet, smooth
balance and long finish. The *superiore* comes from specified places long
noted for quality.
Ag. 5 months; *riserva* 2 yrs.

| | |
|---|---|
| Luigi Baldrati | Marabini (Camerone) |
| Otello Burioli & Figli | Pasolini Dall'Onda |
| Cantina Baldini | Fratelli Picchi |
| Cantina di Villa I Raggi | Plauto (Premiovini) |
| Cantina Produttori Predappio | Cesare Raggi (Le Calbane) |
| C.S. Riminese | Fratelli Ravaioli |
| Cesari | Ronchi |
| Colombina | Ronco |
| Fratelli Conti | Spalletti (Rocca di Ribano) |
| Corovin | Tenuta Amalia |
| Fattoria Paradiso (Vigneti delle Lepri) | Tenuta del Monsignore |
| | Tenuta Zerbina |
| Ferrucci (Domus Caia) | Arturo Tesini |
| Carla Foschi Calisese | Fratelli Vallunga (Moronico) |
| Guarini | |

**Sauvignon**
Sauvignon white wines are increasing in the Apennine foothills. The
style has been bright and light (sometimes bubbly), yet there is evidence
of wines of real class (Terre Rosse, Ronco del Re). DOC in Colli
Bolognesi, Colli di Parma and Colli Piacentini.

**Scorza Amara** or **Scorzamara** r. dr. fz. ★★ DYA
Full-bodied, dark red *frizzante* from Scorza Amara grapes, a relative of
Lambrusco, grown at San Polo d'Enza, SW of Reggio.
Remigio Medici & Fratelli          Ina Maria Pellerano

**Trabense** w. dr. sp. ★★ DYA
Refreshingly delicate bottle-fermented *spumante* from Trebbiano and
Ortrugo grown at Travo in the Colli Piacentini.
Valentino Migliorini

**Trebbianino Val Trebbia**
See Colli Piacentini.

**Trebbiano di Romagna** DOC w. dr. (s/sw.) (sw.) (sp.) *→ ★★ DYA
White, usually dry and still, from the Trebbiano di Romagna vine,
considered distinct from other Trebbiano clones, but, like most, it yields
profusely of rather neutral wines. The zone covers much the same
territory as Albana and Sangiovese di Romagna but extends farther N
to the flat terrain around Lugo. Pale straw yellow, bone dry, with a faint
odor of the grape, it has always been a wine to drink young, though new
vinification methods have improved its fruit-acid balance and even
given it some character. Production approaches 10 million liters
annually. The *spumante* (dry, semisweet, or sweet) is not often seen.

| | | |
|---|---|---|
| Antica Fattoria Brocchi | Fratelli Conti | Ravaglia |
| Luigi Baldrati | Corovin | Fratelli Ravaioli |
| Cantina di Villa i Raggi | Fattoria Paradiso | Ronco |
| | Ferrucci | Ronchi |
| Cantina Produttori Predappio | Guarini | Tenuta Amalia |
| | C.Guidi & Figli | Tenuta del Monsignore |
| C.S. Forlì | Le Calbane (Raggi) | |
| C.S. Riminese | Marabina (Camerone) | Tenuta Zerbina |
| Cesari | Pasolini Dall'Onda | Trerè |
| Colombina | Fratelli Picchi | Fratelli Vallunga |
| | Plauto (Premiovini) | |

# Wine & Food

Pasta alone elevates Emilia-Romagna's cooking to the divine. The making of *tagliatelle*, *tortellini*, *tortelli*, *anolini*, *cappelletti*, *passatelli*, *lasagne*, *gnocchi*, and *gnocchetti*, to name a few, is a daily routine performed by the *sfogliatrice*, living testimony to the regional conviction that pasta must be fresh and made by hand. But pasta is just the entrée of a culinary heritage as religiously adhered to as any of France (whose chefs drew more inspiration than they would care to admit from the cooks of Bologna's region). Bologna, with its *mortadella* and *lasagne verdi* and a dozen other delights of its own, is the capital of Italian gastronomy, but some provincial centers – Parma, Modena, and Reggio – can rival its battery of good things to eat. Foremost are Parmigiano-Reggiano cheese (Parmesan) and *prosciutto* di Parma, but Modena weighs in heftily with its pig's feet sausage (*zampone*) and *aceto balsamico*, which is almost too glorious to be considered vinegar. There is so much more to Emilia-Romagna's cornucopia that this list could only whet your appetite.

**Anatra alla romagnola** Duck cooked with bacon, wine, and seasonings in Romagna.
  *** Sangiovese *riserva superiore* or *** Barbarossa.
**Burlenghi** Hot fried pastry flavored with lard, pork crackling, rosemary, garlic, and grated cheese, famous at Vignola near Modena.
  ** Lambrusco Grasparossa di Castelvetro.
**Cappelletti in brodo** The hat-shaped pasta with meat filling served in broth.
  *** Albana *secco*
**Culatello** Prized tenderest part of the *prosciutto*, from the Po flatlands.
  ** Monterosso Val d'Arda *secco*.
**Grana** Parmigiano-Reggiano, the greatest of grating cheeses, is also eaten in chunks.
  ** Gutturnio.
**Lasagne verdi al forno** Green lasagne cooked with layers of meat

*ragù* and béchamel.
  ** Lambrusco di Sorbara.
**Pasticcio di tortellini** Small ear-shaped pasta cooked with *ragù* then baked in a pie crust Bologna style.
  *** Cabernet Sauvignon
**Piadina** Romagnan flat bread eaten with *pecorino* cheese, *prosciutto*, or salame, like a sandwich.
  ** Sangiovese di Romagna.
**Prosciutto di Parma con melone** Parma ham with cantaloupe (or fresh figs).
  ** Malvasia dei Colli Piacentini.
**Tortelli all'erbetta** Large pasta squares filled with *ricotta* and *erbetta*, a chard-like green, served with melted butter and Parmesan.
  ** Monterosso Val d'Arda *secco* or ** Sauvignon.
**Zampone** Pig's feet sausage made in Modena, served with lentils or mashed potatoes.
  ** Lambrusco Salamino di Santa Croce.

## Restaurants

Emilia-Romagna has fine restaurants nearly everywhere. Recommended in or near wine zones: **Colli Bolognesi** *Rocca* at Bazzano. **Colli di Parma** *Aquila Romana* at Noceto; *Trattoria Da Eletta* at Sala Braganza. **Colli Piacentini** *La Coccinella* at Albarola; *Antica Trattoria della Paolina* at Bobbio; *Da Faccini* and *La Rocca* at Castell'Arquato; *Roma* at Pianello Val Tidone. **Lambrusco zones** *La Noce* at Borzano; *Fini* and *Oreste* at Modena; *Arnaldo Aquila d'Oro* at Rubiera; *Al Portone* at Scandiano. **Romagna** *Gigiolè* and *La Grotta* at Brisighella; *La Frasca* at Castrocaro Terme; *Amici Miei* at Faenza; *Al Maneggio* at Forlimpopoli; *San Domenico* at Imola; *La Meridiana* at Lugo; *Locanda della Colonna* at Tossignano.

# ~Friuli-Venezia Giulia~

Friuli-Venezia Giulia

Friuli is the realm of the new Italian white wine. The climate of this northeastern corner of Italy, which borders on Austria and Yugoslavia, is determined by the propitious intermingling of alpine and Adriatic air. The DOC zones of Collio Goriziano, Colli Orientali del Friuli and parts of Grave del Friuli boast remarkably even growing seasons for the venerable local Tocai, Verduzzo, Ribolla, Malvasia, and Picolit and an honor roll of outsiders that comprises Sauvignon, Riesling Renano, Traminer, Müller Thurgau, Pinot Grigio and, just lately, Chardonnay.

Tocai, the local favorite, has the makings of an international celebrity, though its name gets confused with the dissimilar Tokays of Hungary and Alsace. The region's most heavily planted white, Tocai can match the class of Sauvignon, Pinot Bianco, Chardonnay, and coppery Pinot Grigio, which reach peaks of splendor in the hills between Gorizia and Udine.

Picolit is Italy's most fabled dessert wine. Some insist on comparing it with Château d'Yquem, though about all the two have in common is that they are white, sweet, and uncommon. Unproductive, due to a congenital weakness known as floral

**Wine Zones**
1 Collio Goriziano
2 Colli Orientali del Friuli
3 Grave del Fruili
4 Carso

abortion, and prohibitively expensive, Picolit has nonetheless managed a rapid comeback which has raised suspicions that most of what is being sold derives from blends or else from grapes of a cross between Picolit and Verduzzo.

Surprisingly, Friuli produces more red than white. Merlot dominates, though Cabernet (more often Franc than Sauvignon), the native Refosco, and some exciting oddities also thrive. Merlot and Cabernet, which are usually light, soft, fruity wines to drink young, are heavily produced in the flats that take in the DOC zones of Aquileia, Isonzo, Latisana, and parts of Grave.

The smallest of the Tre Venezie – the territory of the Venetian Republic which includes the Veneto and Trentino-Alto Adige – Friuli also has the smallest wine production (130 million liters a year), but a third of that is DOC and much of the rest is still very drinkable.

The land of the ancient Friulian people, and an outpost of the Roman Empire, the region is a crossroads of Germanic, Slavic, and Italianate cultures. There is a prominent Slovenian minority in the southeast around Gorizia and the capital of Trieste.

A short drive from Venice along the *Autostrada la Serenissima*, Friuli has become a prime attraction to wine buffs. Collio's hills are traversed by wine roads. The *Strada del Merlot* follows the Isonzo River southwest of Gorizia. The well-stocked *Enoteca La Serenissima* at Gradisca di Isonzo was one of Italy's first public wine libraries. Wineries large and small offer exceptional hospitality, as do the cozy country taverns and inns.

## Recent vintages

As a rule, Friulian dry whites are at their flowery best when young, though increasingly Tocai, Sauvignon and Pinot Bianco defy the rule. Even reds are usually styled for early drinking, but some Cabernet, Merlot and Refosco improve notably with age.

1986    Early harvest of unexpectedly fine, structured reds and nicely balanced whites with aging potential.

1985    Hail in Collio and drought took a toll, but some outstanding reds and full-blown whites were realized.

1984    Generally weak due to cool and damp, though some better than adequate whites were made.

1983    A fine year for reds and whites, though heat caused problems with wines not processed at low temperature.

1982    Abundant crush, though whites often lacked acidity and may be short lived. Excellent for reds.

**Aquileia** DOC
Flat zone stretching from the Adriatic north past the ancient Roman city of Aquileia to Palmanova and Trivignano. Vines for red wine prevail in the sandy clay soil, though good white wines are also made. Production is centered in the large Cantina Sociale Cooperativa del Friuli Orientale at Cervignano, which sells under its own Molin di Ponte label and supplies Valdo. The DOC list has expanded to include 10 varietals and a rosé.

– **Cabernet** or **Cabernet Franc** or **Cabernet Sauvignon**
r. dr. ★→★★   82 83 85 86
The wines may be labeled in three ways. All tend to be bright ruby, rather light, round, fresh and fragrant, best in 2–4 years.

– **Merlot** r. dr. ★→★★   85 86
Light, tasty, fruity, medium-ruby color, to drink in 1–3 years. The most heavily produced of Aquileia's varietals.

– **Pinot Bianco** w. dr. ★→★★   DYA
Straw yellow, soft, perfumed, and smooth with good varietal character.

– **Pinot Grigio** w. dr. ★★→★★★   DYA
Though production is limited, this is often the best Aquileia white: smooth, fruity, dry but flowery with light golden-copper color.

– **Refosco** r. dr. ★★→★★★ 82 83 85 86
From Refosco del Peduncolo Rosso grapes, this has a deep garnet-violet
color, a fairly full body and a pleasant fruity flavor with typically bitter
undertone. To drink in 2–5 years, sometimes more.
– **Riesling Renano** w. dr. ★→★★ DYA
Very small production of this light golden, dry wine that does somewhat
better in cooler places.
– **Rosato** p. dr. ★ DYA
Based on Merlot with other varieties permitted, this is light cherry hued,
soft, subtly grapy.
– **Sauvignon** w. dr. ★→★★★ DYA
Bright, flinty whites with personality in Aquileia's coastal climate.
– **Tocai Friulano** w. dr. ★→★★ DYA
More delicate and drier than Tocai from the hills, but a good fish wine.
– **Traminer** w. dr. ★ DYA
New and unproven.
– **Verduzzo Friulano** w. dr. ★ DYA
This should make a light, lemony white.

| | | |
|---|---|---|
| Ca'Bolani | Molin di Ponte | Villa Chiozza |
| Giacomelli | Valle | |

**Cabernet**
Qualified as DOC in six of Friuli's seven zones. The traditional
Cabernet Franc is being supplemented by Cabernet Sauvignon, often in
medium weight wines, but increasingly in bigger, barrel-aged reds often
blended with Merlot.

**Carso** DOC
Recent appellation applies to two reds based on the Terrano grape (a
strain of Refosco) and a white Malvasia grown in the Carso hills, the
narrow strip of land that extends into Yugoslavia between Trieste and
Gorizia.
– **Carso** r. dr. ★→★★ DYA
This must contain at least 70% Terrano grapes in a dark ruby, grapy,
fleshy, rather simplistic wine.
– **Carso Malvasia** w. dr. ★→★★ DYA
Based on Malvasia Istriana, this straw-colored wine is dry, fruitily
aromatic, fairly soft.
– **Terrano del Carso** r. dr. ★→★★★ 83 85 86
At least 85% of Terrano grapes, perfumed (of raspberries), dry but round
and fruity, as epitomized by the Terrano di Sagrado of Castelvecchio.

**Chardonnay**
Previously considered a Pinot, Chardonnay has been singled out and
boosted rapidly to star status as the most frequently planted new vine of
Friuli. Pioneered by EnoFriulia and Plozner as a *vino da tavola*,
Chardonnay has become DOC in Grave del Friuli and seems sure to
gain recognition elsewhere as major producers such as Abbazia di
Rosazzo, Collavini, Gravner, Jermann, Puiatti and Ronco Blanchis
polish up their styles.

**Colli Orientali del Friuli** DOC
An elite zone that extends N along the Yugoslav border from Corno di
Rosazzo to Tarcento at the foot of the Julian Alps, Colli Orientali has
conditions similar to neighboring Collio (p. 46) and more space in
which to develop. Its axis is Cividale del Friuli on the site of the Roman
city of Forum Julii. The zone has most of the varietals of Collio, plus
Verduzzo, Refosco, Cabernet Sauvignon, and Riesling Renano to
enhance its possibilities. Picolit is DOC only here.
– **Cabernet** r. dr. ★★→★★★ 79 81 82 83 85 86
Either Cabernet Sauvignon or Cabernet Franc or both may be used in
this red, which at best shows more elegance in body and bouquet than
other Friulian Cabernets. Deep ruby with herb-like, tarry flavors typical
of the family, the *riserva* shines with 3–7 years.
Ag. *riserva* 2 yrs.
– **Merlot** r. dr. ★★→★★★ 82 83 85 86
Supple, smooth, and versatile, it is tastiest in 1–3 years, or, if *riserva*, 3–5.
In either case, it can rank with Italy's best.
Ag. *riserva* 2 yrs.

**– Picolit** w. s/sw. or sw. ★★→★★★ 79 82 83 85 86

In Colli Orientali, uniquely, Picolit's authenticity is controlled. Yet, among some 40,000 bottles issued annually from an estimated 50–60 producers, quality is rarely up to price. Permitted yields are 4000 kilograms of grapes per hectare (about 1500 standard bottles from an acre), the lowest for any DOC wine anywhere. Most growers say they get less. Up to 10% of other varieties may be included under DOC, which prescribes wine of at least 15% alcohol of deep straw color, with lightly perfumed aroma and warm, harmonious, delicate flavor, whether *amabile* or *dolce*. The best examples surpass that description.

Ag. *riserva* 2 yrs.

**– Pinot Bianco** w. dr. ★★→★★★★ 82 83 84 85 86

Some of Italy's finest Pinot Bianco originates here: fragrant, fruity, with remarkable harmony and structure to improve over 2–5 years.

**– Pinot Grigio** w. dr. ★★→★★★ DYA

The best of Colli Orientali can equal any Pinot Grigio in both the light and *ramàto* (coppery) styles.

**– Pinot Nero** r. dr. ★→★★ 82 83 85 86

Red Burgundy's grape rarely achieves grandeur here, though it tends to show more stuff than in Collio and can take a little more aging.

Ag. *riserva* 2 yrs.

**– Refosco** r. dr. ★★→★★★ 79 80 81 82 83 85 86

Wine from this native can rival the imported varieties in class and age somewhat longer. Deep violet tending to garnet with age, its warm, full, lightly tannic flavor comes into its own in 4–7 years.

Ag. *riserva* 2 yrs.

**– Ribolla** w. dr. ★★→★★★ 84 85 86

Coming back into vogue, this white is zesty when young, becoming broader and dignified with 2–3 years.

**– Riesling Renano** w. dr. ★★ DYA

Not enough has been done with this true Riesling, which is clearly superior to Riesling Italico. Pale golden yellow with blossomy bouquet and fruity freshness in a basically dry, smooth flavor.

**– Sauvignon** w. dr. ★★→★★★ 85 86

This can stand with Sauvignon from Collio, Alto Adige and all but the best of France.

**– Tocai Friulano** w. dr. ★★→★★★★ 85 86

From certain producers – Abbazia di Rosazzo, for instance – this can rival the best of Collio, holding impressively for 2–3 years.

**– Verduzzo (Ramandolo)** w. dr. or s/sw. ★★→★★★ 78 79 80 81

Wine from this antique, indigenous vine may be either dry or sweet or, better yet, in between. The dry version is bright greenish gold, nicely fruity with flowery bouquet, and of light body – good when young with summer dishes. The *amabile*, from slightly dried grapes, has more of everything – color, aroma, and smoothness – its ripe fruit sweetness offset by a sensational dry finish (Abbazia di Rosazzo and Ronchi di Fornaz make outstanding Verduzzo *amabile*). The Verduzzo *amabile* from a sector of the community of Nimis may be called Ramandolo (G.B. Comelli and Giovanni Dri excel).

| | |
|---|---|
| Abbazia di Rosazzo | I Moros (Tavagnacco) |
| Angoris | La Viarte |
| Bandut | Livon |
| Bosco Romagno (Arzenton) | Francesco Lui |
| Bosco Romagno (Zambotto) | Giovanni Monai |
| Mario Budini | V. Nascig |
| Livio Olivo Buiatti | G. Franco Pascolini |
| Valentino Butussi | Giuseppe Picogna |
| Campeglio | Pitotti |
| Cantarutti Alfieri | Poggiobello |
| Casa di Legno (Lesizza) | Fratelli Pozzo |
| Collavini | Rocca Bernarda |
| Colli di Spessa | Paolo Rodaro |
| G.B. Comelli | Ronchi di Cialla |
| Marina Danieli | Ronchi di Fornaz |
| Gianfranco d'Attimis Maniago | Ronco del Gnemiz |
| Girolamo Dorigo | Rubini |
| Giovanni Dri | Dante Sara |
| Marino Ermarcora | Cisiro Snidero & Figli |
| Livio Felluga | Isidoro Tilatti |

Valle                                Vinicola Udinese
Vigne dal Leon                       Volpe Pasini
Villa Belvedere

## Collio Goriziano or Collio DOC

A strip of hills against the Yugoslav border running from near Gorizia
W and N past Cormons, reputed to have one of Europe's most
privileged microclimates for white wines. The wines of numerous small-
scale growers have improved steadily as expert assistance has become
available. Besides 12 DOC types, Chardonnay, Cabernet Sauvignon,
Müller Thurgau and Riesling Renano make impressive table wines.
Though whites dominate, reds are notable for supple, youthful style.
– **Cabernet Franc** r. dr.  **→***  82 83 85 86
Light and bright, with understated varietal character, pleasant to drink
in 1–4 years, rarely more.
– **Collio** w. dr.  *→**  DYA
The only non-varietal among the region's DOCs, Collio comes from
Ribolla, Malvasia, and Tocai, a delicate dry white wine, sometimes a
touch *pétillant*, to drink very young.
– **Malvasia Istriana** w. dr.  *→**  DYA
Zippy white with subtle Malvasia aroma, very dry, good with fish.
– **Merlot** r. dr.  **→****  79 81 82 83 85 86
Usually light in body and color, soft, nicely scented with herb-like traits
of the grape, but Merlot can be full and even aristocratic gaining stature
with age.
– **Pinot Bianco** w. dr.  **→****  83 84 85 86
Sometimes light and fruity, occasionally luxuriant, enhanced by the
unannounced presence of Chardonnay and, from a few producers, a
little barrel seasoning. Younger Pinot Bianco tends to have a light straw
color, crisp acidity, and flowery fragrance. With a year or more of age,
the better examples tend to golden with ample bouquet suggesting of
vanilla and almonds, and the buttery texture of white Burgundy.
– **Pinot Grigio** w. dr.  **→****  85 86
Some vinify for light yellow wine, fruity and crisp when young. Others
leave the fermenting wine in contact with the skins to achieve a pale
smoky gold *ramato* (coppery) style, fuller in body, flavor, and aroma – a
fine aperitif with a year or more of bottle age.
– **Pinot Nero** r. dr.  *→**  83 85 86
Pleasant red from the temperamental variety that even in better years
shows only a vague resemblance to red Burgundy. Ruby and rotund, it
can be fragrant, fleshy, and smooth in 1–4 years, but never dramatic.
– **Ribolla** w. dr.  **→***  85 86
Recently added to the Collio collection, this white from the ancient,
indigenous Ribolla Gialla vine has a lemon-yellow color, delicate grapy
aroma and a fairly full, distinctive flavor mellowing with age.
– **Riesling Italico** w. dr.  *→**  DYA
Good, lively, dry to off-dry white with fruity flavor and aroma and pale
gold color; however, the non-DOC Riesling Renano does better.
– **Sauvignon** w. dr.  **→***  85 86
Not enough of this noble Bordelaise is planted, but some of what is yields
results to compare with fine Sauvignons of France and California. Pale
straw with golden-green highlights, elegant fruit-acid balance and
flowery, flinty nose, it is smooth and long, full of Sauvignon personality.
– **Tocai Friulano** w. dr.  **→****  85 86
Even workaday Tocai is good in Collio, where it is drunk as a versatile
meal wine. In the hands of a few, it reaches heights unequalled
elsewhere. Pale straw with lemon-yellow reflections, its scent is of wild
flowers and its flavor, dry but ample, is full of nuances, most markedly
ripe fruit and almond, with velvety texture and length.
– **Traminer** w. dr.  *→**  DYA
Produced in miniscule quantity, this native of Alto Adige has probably
not realized its full potential, though Mario Schiopetto, for one, has
raised it to significant levels from some vintages. Medium golden yellow,
its usually spicy aroma is somewhat subdued here, but the inherent
richness comes through in the otherwise dry flavor.

Attems                               Borgo del Tiglio
F. Berin                             Fratelli Buzzinelli
Collavini                            Paolo Caccese
Borgo Conventi                       Campagnis (Zampar)            ▶

Cantina Produttori Vini Cormons
Ca' Ronesca
Carlo Drufovka
Conti Formentini
EnoFriulia
Livio Felluga
Marco Felluga
Giulio Furlani
Gradimir Gradnik
Francesco Gravner
Marcello & Marino Humar
Jermann
Alessio Komjanc
La Ginesta
Pighin
Silvestro Primosic

Doro Princic
Radikon
Roncada
Ronco Blanchis
Ronco della Chiesa
Russiz Superiore
Mario Schiopetto
Subida di Monte
Riccardo Terpin
Redento Vazzolar
Venica
Villa Russiz
Villa San Giovanni
Vinicola Udinese
P. Zorutti (Comis)
Luigi Zorzon

**Dragarska** r. dr. ★★★ 82 83 85 86
Merlot and Cabernet grown at Oslavia in Collio and mixed with more
aplomb than most Friulian varietals of either type.
Carlo Drufovka

**Engelwhite**
See Pinot Nero.

**Franconia** or **Blaufränkisch** r. dr. ★★→★★★ 81 82 83 85 86
An oddball that can be excellent. Made from a grape known variously
as Franconia, Limberger, Blaufränkisch, and Bleufrancs, believed to
have come from Croatia. Bright ruby red, it has a generous bouquet,
good body and a clean, dry flavor against a background of raspberry-
like sweetness. Reaches prime in 3–6 years.
Cantina Produttori Vini Cormons     Giuseppe Toti
V. Nascig                           Valle
Roncada

**Grave del Friuli** DOC
This zone, which dwarfs all others, accounts for about half the region's
DOC wine. Grave covers low hills and plains from the border of Veneto
eastwards past Udine. More than half of Grave's output is in Merlot,
which thrives in gravelly lowlands similar to parts of Bordeaux. Grave is
also a major producer of Tocai and Cabernet and has no shortage either
of Refosco or of the white Pinots. Several of Friuli's largest wineries, both
cooperative and private, are here. Recently expanded, the appellation
takes in 13 types, including three styles of Cabernet and the first DOC
Chardonnay in Italy. Though much of the wine is of sound, everyday
quality, some is superb, for Grave has microclimates similar to those of
Collio and Colli Orientali. Within its confines is the world's largest vine
nursery, the *Vivai Cooperativi Rauscedo*, which prepares 30 million shoots a
year for Italy and other nations.

– **Cabernet** or **Cabernet Franc** or **Cabernet Sauvignon**
r. dr. ★→★★★ 81 82 83 85 86
Cabernet Sauvignon exists, but Cabernet Franc is favored for its quicker
maturation and *gout de terroir*, the earthy, herby taste that inspires its
admirers. Most is to drink young, but some holds up for 5 years or more.

– **Chardonnay** w. dr. ★→★★★ 85 86
Italy's first DOC Chardonnay, this can show good balance and varietal
character here, as exemplified for years by Plozner.

– **Merlot** r. dr. ★→★★★ 82 83 85 86
Grave is Italy's capital of Merlot, with some 10 million liters a year,
some of it solid enough to improve over 3–5 years. Even the everyday
stuff is good – supple, fruity and fragrant.

– **Pinot Bianco** w. dr. ★→★★★ 85 86
Quality ranges from pedestrian to very good in wine of solid class and
character.

– **Pinot Grigio** w. dr. ★→★★★ DYA
Whether light or coppery, Pinot Grigio at its best concedes nothing to its
neighbors in Collio and Colli Orientali.
– **Pinot Nero** r. dr. ★→★★ 83 85 86
Just approved, this should in some cases compare with Pinot Nero of
Colli Orientali.

– **Refosco** r. dr. ★→★★★ 79 81 82 83 85 86
This seductive red, popular locally, from better producers ranks with
the region's finest. Ages 4–7 years or more.
– **Riesling Renano** w. dr. ★ DYA
Though new and unproven, this could be admirable from the cool
heights of Grave.
– **Rosato** p. dr. ★ DYA
Just introduced, this will make light use of dark varieties.
– **Sauvignon** w. dr. ★→★★★ DYA
Another newcomer, this could be the most promising white in this
gravelly zone.
– **Tocai Friulano** w. dr. ★→★★★ 85 86
Grave makes more Tocai than Collio and Colli Orientali combined;
choice bottles stand with the region's elite.
– **Traminer Aromatico** w. dr. ★ DYA
A new and still questionable entry.
– **Verduzzo** w. dr. ★→★★ DYA
The dry is preferred here in a golden-yellow wine with greenish tints,
best young when its fruity freshness is offset by an almost salty dryness.

| | |
|---|---|
| Antonutti | Lis Gravis |
| Duca Badoglio | Molino delle Streghe |
| Cantina del Friuli Centrale-Bertiolo | Morassutti |
| Cantine Bidoli | Morelli De Rossi |
| Cantoni | Pighin |
| Castello di Porcia | A. Pittau |
| Collavini | Plozner |
| Marina Danieli | Pradio |
| Fantinel | Santa Margherita |
| Germano Filiputti | Vigneti Le Monde |
| Friulvini | Vigneti Pittaro |
| Antonio Furchir | Villa Ronche |
| Giacomelli | Vinicola Udinese |
| La Delizia (C.S. Casarsa) | |

## Isonzo DOC

Small zone along the Isonzo River reaching from the coastal plain near
Monfalcone to gentle rises around Gradisca d'Isonzo, Cormons, and
Gorizia. Isonzo's terrain and microclimate favor Cabernet and Merlot,
which, among its ten types, most consistently rate with Friuli's finest.
– **Cabernet** r. dr. ★★→★★★ 82 83 85 86
From either Cabernet Sauvignon or Cabernet Franc, a soft, smooth,
buoyantly fragrant wine, light but remarkably drinkable in 2–6 years.
– **Malvasia Istriana** w. dr. ★ DYA
From the native Istrian strain of Malvasia, a light, fragile, pale fish
wine.
– **Merlot** r. dr. ★★→★★★ 82 83 85 86
The most heavily produced Isonzo wine, Merlot tends to show more
consistent class here than in any other zone. Light in color and body,
brilliantly fresh in bouquet and flavor, it hits peaks in 1–4 years.
– **Pinot Bianco** w. dr. ★→★★ DYA
Pleasantly brisk when young, Pinot Bianco does better in high places.
– **Pinot Grigio** w. dr. ★→★★ DYA
Usually made in the light, pale style here.
– **Riesling Renano** w. dr. ★★ DYA
The small amount made shows more class than might be expected. Pale,
greenish yellow, and fragrant, it is best very young.
– **Sauvignon** w. dr. ★★ DYA
Isonzo's climate favors consistent if unspectacular quality in this variety.
– **Tocai** w. dr. ★★ DYA
The favorite white is solid and good, if never up to Collio's top echelon.
– **Traminer Aromatico** w. dr. ★ DYA
Very little of this cold-climate vine is planted. Maybe just as well.
– **Verduzzo Friulano** w. dr. ★ DYA
Simple, tasty, of limited production; Verduzzo's heights are reached
elsewhere.

| | |
|---|---|
| Angoris | Fratelli Brotto |
| Bader | Antonio Burdin |
| Bortoluzzi | Cantina Produttori Vini Cormons ▶ |

| | |
|---|---|
| Cappelletti | Stelio Gallo |
| Luisa Eddi | S. Elena |
| Conti Prandi d'Ulmhort | Tenuta Villanova |

**Latisana** DOC
This zone in the coastal plains follows the Tagliamento River N from the Adriatic past the town of Latisana. Similar in geography to Aquileia and Isonzo, Latisana's seven types are dominated by Merlot, Cabernet, and Tocai.

– **Cabernet** r. dr. ★→★★ 85 86
Cabernet Sauvignon and/or Franc make soft, light, scented wine to drink in 2–4 years.

– **Merlot** r. dr. ★→★★ 85 86
Popular everyday wine, its easygoing nature is appreciable in 1–3 years.

– **Pinot Bianco** w. dr. ★★ DYA
Made in limited quantity, finely scented, smooth, with varietal tone.

– **Pinot Grigio** w. dr. ★→★★ DYA
The light style prevails here in very limited quantities.

– **Refosco** r. dr. ★★ 82 83 85 86
Though overwhelmed in numbers by the other reds, Refosco is more robust and durable and can show distinctive style.

– **Tocai** w. dr. ★→★★ DYA
The favored white can rival some good Tocai of the hills.

– **Verduzzo** w. dr. ★ DYA
Common here.

| | |
|---|---|
| Isola Augusta | Volderie (Dal Ferro Galvan) |
| Sergio Pevere | |

**Lison-Pramaggiore**
The DOC zone centered in the Veneto extends into Friuli.

**Malbec** or **Malbeck** r. dr. ★★ 79 82 83
The Bordeaux vine, usually secondary in composites with Cabernet and Merlot, makes a good varietal in W Friuli around Pordenone.
Castello di Porcia

**Malvasia** or **Malvasia Istriana** w. dr. ★ DYA
DOC in Carso, Collio and Isonzo.

**Merlot**
Table wines, usually red, occasionally rosé, from Friuli's most popular grape variety may carry the varietal name and a place when not qualified for DOC. Merlot is DOC in six of the seven zones.

**Montsclapade** r. dr. ★★★ 82 83 85 86
A classic Bordeaux blend of Cabernets, Merlot and Malbec aged in small, new oak barrels, this promises to evolve into a red of notable class with 5–6 years of aging.
Girolamo Dorigo

**Müller Thurgau** w. dr. ★★→★★★ 85 86
The Riesling-Sylvaner cross has been gaining favor in Friuli, especially in Collio, where it can make impressive wine. Pale in color, subtly but distinctively perfumed, it tends to be bone dry and crisply fruity when young, becoming smooth, almost voluptuous, with bottle age.

| | |
|---|---|
| Fratelli Buzzinelli | Ronco Blanchis |
| Cantoni | Ronco del Gnemiz |
| Maria Danieli | Mario Schiopetto |
| EnoFriulia | Redento Vazzolar |

**Picolit**
DOC in Colli Orientali, Picolit is also made in other parts of Friuli though its authenticity isn't controlled.

**Pignolo** r. dr. ★★★ 84 85 86
Ancient indigenous vine of Colli Orientali revived in a *vino da tavola* of resilient individuality. Of a luminous ruby-cherry color, Pignolo has enticingly fresh aromas and vibrant flavors of ripe fruit and berries which should be enhanced by 3–5 years aging, possibly more.
Abbazia di Rosazzo

**Pinot Bianco**
DOC in six of the seven zones, it also makes good *vino da tavola*.

**Pinot Grigio**
DOC in six of the seven zones. Much wine from this overtaxed vine is
loosely identified as Pinot Grigio delle Venezie and the like. Excessively
popular, much more "Pinot Grigio" is sold than grapes could provide.

**Pinot Nero**
DOC in Collio, Colli Orientali and Grave, Pinot Nero also makes table
wines, usually red or rosé. Grapes are used increasingly for *brut spumante*,
but it can make a fine, still white: Puiatti's Pinot Nero in Bianco and
Jermann's Engelwhite.

**Ramandolo**
DOC as a subdenomination under Colli Orientali del Friuli Verduzzo.

**Refosco**
Friuli's preferred native red is DOC in all zones but Collio and Isonzo.
The best known clone is Refosco del Peduncolo Rosso, though there is
also Refosco Nostrano and the related Terrano del Carso.

**Ribolla** or **Ribolla Gialla**
An impressive native approved as DOC in Colli Orientali and Collio.

**Riesling Italico**
DOC only in Collio; occasionally used for table wine elsewhere.

**Riesling Renano**
DOC in Aquileia, Colli Orientali, Grave and Isonzo, this noble
Rhinelander makes a fine wine from Mario Schioppetto in Collio.

**Ronco del Gnemiz** r. dr.  **\*\*\***  82 83 85 86
The Cabernets combine with Merlot grown in Colli Orientali in a red of
sturdy backbone and soft flavors that need 5–6 years to gain the desired
poise.
Ronco del Gnemiz

**Ronco delle Acacie** w. dr.  **\*\*\*→\*\*\*\***  84 85 86
Evidence that Italy's new wave whites stand in a class apart is
eloquently expressed in this blend of Tocai, Pinot Bianco, Ribolla and
Malvasia grown in a special vineyard at Rosazzo in the Colli Orientali.
Youthful redolence of flowers and fruit is soothed by a kiss of oak in a
wine of remarkable finesse.
Abbazia di Rosazzo

**Ronco dei Roseti** r. dr.  **\*\*\*→\*\*\*\***  82 83 84 85 86
Bizarre blend of local curiosities – Franconia, Tazzelenghe, Refosco –
with Cabernet and Merlot seasoned in new oak by Walter Filiputti.
Though rather wild at first, with bottle age the elements come together
in a red of singular personality.
Abbazia di Rosazzo

**Runk** w. dr.  **\*\*\***  85 86
Pinot Bianco with a flattering 20% of Tocai in a convincing table wine
made at Oslavia in Collio.
Carlo Drufovka

**Sauvignon**
This promising variety is DOC in Collio, Colli Orientali, Grave and
Isonzo.

**Schioppettino** r. dr.  **\*\*→\*\*\*\***  82 83 85 86
A cult has grown around this esoteric red from the indigenous Ribolla
Nera or Schioppettino vine, which makes its home at Albana di
Prepotto in the heart of the Colli Orientali. Schioppettino rates
superlatives for its singular rustic breed, marked by bright ruby color,
fragrance of ripe berries, and marked acidity that only seems to enhance
its depth and length of flavors over 5–6 years.
Rieppi                          Giuseppe Toti
Ronchi di Cialla                Vigne dal Leon
Ronco del Gnemiz

**Spumante** w. (p.) dr. (s/sw.) sp.  **\*\*→\*\*\*\***
Production of sparkling wines has exploded in Friuli recently,
capitalizing on Pinots, Chardonnay and other varieties. Much
production is by the long charmat method, but *méthode champenoise*
(marked m.c.) is also used, notably in the Collavini Applause Nature

and Puiatti Extra Brut, both *pas dosé*.
– **Conte Bolani (m.c.)**
Ca' Bolani
– **Cormons Pinot Brut, Riesling Brut, Sauvignon Brut**
Cantina Producttori Vini Cormons
– **La Delizia Brut (m.c., also charmat)**
C.S. Casarsa (La Delizia)
– **Applause Nature (m.c.), Il Grigio**
Collavini
– **Brut Mus**
Marina Danieli
– **Il Blanc-Blanc, Il Flut**
Duca Badoglio
– **Livio Felluga Brut**
Livio Felluga
– **Fornaci di Manzano Brut**
Fornaci di Manzano
– **Giacomelli Brut (m.c.)**
Giacomelli
– **Brut Pinot**
Pighin
– **Puiatti Extra Brut (m.c.)**
Puiatti
– **Rubini Brut**
Rubini
– **Brut Valle**
Valle
– **Vigneti Pittaro (m.c.)**
Vigneti Pittaro
– **La Plume Brut**
Vinicola Udinese

**Tazzelenghe** or **Tacelenghe** r. dr. ★★→★★★ 82 83 85 86
The name, dialect for *tazzalingua*, alludes to its tannic sharpness on the
tongue, though this dark ruby-violet table wine has a way of being
gratifyingly smooth with 3–6 years of age.

| | |
|---|---|
| Brava | Girolamo Dorigo (Ronc di Juri) |
| Marina Danieli | Vigne dal Leon |

**Terrano del Carso**
See Carso.

**Terre Alte** w. dr. ★★★ 84 85 86
From Tocai, Pinot Bianco and Sauvignon grown in the Oleis vineyards
in Colli Orientali, this is a soft, flowery white whose youthful tone might
belie its keeping capacities.
Livio Felluga

**Tocai Friulano**
Friuli's favorite white is DOC in six of seven zones.

**Traminer** or **Gewürztraminer** or **Traminer Aromatico**
Though marked differences between Traminer and the superior
Gewürztraminer exist, they are often ignored in Italy where wines are
usually labeled Traminer or Traminer Aromatico. DOC in Collio,
Grave and Isonzo, it makes table wine elsewhere.

**Verduzzo**
DOC in Colli Orientali, Grave, Isonzo, and Latisana, Verduzzo is used
for both dry and sweet whites.

**Vigne dal Leon** r. dr. ★★★→★★★★ 82 83 85 86
Merlot combines with Cabernet and rare local varieties grown in Colli
Orientali in a red of authoritative size but seductive tones and textures.
Seasoned in small barrels of French oak, it should mellow nicely for 5–8
years or longer.
Vigne dal Leon

**Vintage Tunina** w. dr. ★★★→★★★★ 82 83 84 85 86
Singular white from Pinot Bianco, Chardonnay, Sauvignon and a hint
of Picolit selected by Sylvio Jermann in his Tunina vineyard in Collio.
Among Italy's whites of greatest stature, it can resemble a fine

Burgundy in texture, bouquet, nuance of flavors and breed, yet its
personality is inimitably its own.
Jermann

**Zuc di Volpe** r. dr. ★★★ 82 83 85 86
An unlikely mix of Pinot Nero at 70% with Cabernet Sauvignon and
Merlot grown in the Colli Orientali. Though young, the '81 and '82 had
fine bouquet and fascinating flavor that should reach harmony in 4–6
years after the harvest.
Volpe Pasini

In Friuli, East meets West around the *fogolar*, the cozy open
hearth with a conical chimney that expresses the region's warm
hospitality in nearly every dining room. A melting pot of
European cookery, Friuli-Venezia Giulia gives its own touch to
*gulasch*, *knödel*, Viennese pastries, cabbage soups, and strudel. But
the tangs of Slovenia, Croatia, Bohemia, Austria, and Hungary
are merely a bonus added to Friuli's own tasty peasant heritage
of pork, beans, mutton, sausages, soups, blood puddings,
polenta, turnips, game, and cheese. Venezia Giulia, the coastal
strip, contributes fish to the menu with soups, chowders, and
refined risottos with prawns, squid, or scallops that reflect the
influence of Venice. From the hill town of San Daniele comes a
*prosciutto* which some consider to be the most exquisite made.

**Boreto alla gradese** Fish (turbot
is ideal) cooked in oil, vinegar,
garlic, and water, a speciality of
the isle of Grado.
   ★ Malvasia Istriana
or ★ Verduzzo *secco*.
**Brovada** Turnips marinated in
fresh wine pressings, then cut into
strips and cooked with *muset*, a pork
sausage.
   ★★ Merlot or ★★ Cabernet.
**Capriolo in salmi** Venison in a
rich wine sauce.
   ★★★ Refosco
or ★★★ Schioppettino.
**Frico** Cheese, both fresh and aged,
fried with onions in butter until
crunchy.
   ★★★ Sauvignon.
**Granzevola alla triestina**
Tender spider crab meat baked

with breadcrumbs, garlic, and
seasonings.
   ★★★→★★★★ Tocai
or ★★★→★★★★ Pinot Bianco.
**Gulasch** or **gulyas** Beef cooked
with tomato, onions, paprika.
   ★ Terrano del Carso or beer.
**Jota** Nourishing and tasty soup of
pork, beans, cabbage, cornmeal.
   ★★ Cabernet Franc.
**Paparot** Cream soup that includes
spinach and corn flour.
   ★★→★★★ Pinot Grigio.
**Prosciutto di San Daniele** Paper
thin slices of air-cured ham.
   ★★★ Tocai.
**Strucolo** Friuli's answer to
strudel, made with *ricotta* or apples
or other fruit.
   ★★★→★★★★ Verduzzo
Ramandolo.

### Restaurants

Recommended in or near wine zones: **Carso** *Suban* at Trieste. **Collio** *Al
Cacciatore della Subida*, *Felcaro* and *Il Giardinetto* at Cormons; *Venica* at
Dolenga; *Trattoria Blanch* at Mossa; *Parco Formentini* at San Floriano.
**Collio Orientali** *Locanda alle Officine* at Buttrio; *Locanda al Castello* and
*Zorutti* at Cividale del Friuli. **Grave** *Da Toso* at Leonacco di Tricesimo;
*Del Doge* in the Villa Marin at Passariano del Codroipo; *Da Gildo* at
Porcia; *Trattoria La Primula* at San Quirino; *Al Grop* at Tavagnacco;
*Boschetti* at Tricesimo; *Astoria Italia* and *Là di Morèt* at Udine. **Isonzo** *Al
Ponte* at Gradisca d'Isonzo; *Da Bruno* and *Hannibal* at Monfalcone.
**Latisana** *Da Toni* at Gradiscutta; *Bella Venezia* at Latisana; *Bidin* at
Lignano Sabbiadoro.

# Latium
Lazio

Rome calls to mind wines of golden hue, which is not to suggest that their memories are always golden. Frascati and Est! Est!! Est!!!, the legends on Latium's wine list, are white, as are more than 90% of the region's DOCs and most of the table wines, too. Frascati is prima donna of the Castelli Romani, the green-clad clump of spent volcanoes southeast of Rome that harbors six of Latium's 16 DOC zones and lies within view of seven others. Est! Est!! Est!!!, whose vineyards surround the yawning crater of Lake Bolsena north of Rome, is primogenitor of that species of wine (like Liebfraumilch and California Burgundy) that lurks behind a trumped-up name.

Every established white of Latium is based on Malvasia or Trebbiano or, most often, combinations of the two. Both make wines prone to oxidation, which explains why they were habitually drunk up quickly and close to home. Hot bottling and more recently, cold processing, have stopped premature browning and enabled them to be sold worldwide, but their most sincere admirers still prefer them close to home.

Latium's finest wines are red, though the evidence is not easy to find. Some consist of the native Cesanese, or else Montepulciano and Sangiovese or, most remarkably, Cabernet and Merlot. Three alone – Torre Ercolana, Fiorano *rosso*, and Colle Picchioni – could advance Latium's case for eminence, if only a few bottles remained after local fans take their quotas.

Latium is central Italy's most prolific wine region, with more than half-a-billion liters a year. Not all the good wines appear in the A–Z listing, for the simple reason that they are rarely available in labeled bottles. Some carry recognized names, such as Baccanale, Bolsena *rosso*, Colli Cimini, Colli Etruschi, Colli Rufeno, Colli Sabini, Feronia, Greghetto di Gradoli, Maccarese, Quintaluna, Ronciglione and Torre in Pietra, though that doesn't mean they'll be easy to find.

An enchanting wine trip from Rome is a circuit of the Castelli Romani, taking in Frascati, Marino, Colli Albani, Colli Lanuvini, Montecompatri Colonna, and Velletri. An extended trip includes Zagarolo, Cori, Aprilia and the three Cesanese DOC zones in the ruggedly pretty Ciociaria hills.

Among several shops with good choices of regional and national wines are the *Enotica Trimani, Enoteca Cavour, Enoteca Costantini* and *Enoteca Palombi* in Rome.

## Recent vintages

For red wines and the few whites that may be kept more than a couple of years, recommended vintages appear with each entry.

**Aleatico di Gradoli** DOC r. sw.  ★★  78 79 80 81 82 83 85 86
Little of this fragrant dessert wine from the antique Aleatico grape is made in the hills W of Lake Bolsena. The basic version is violet-red, lightly alcoholic, and aromatic, best in early years with fruit, especially cantaloupe. The *liquoroso* of 17.5% is for after dinner, like Port. It can last 5–10 years or more.
C.S. di Gradoli

**Aprilia** DOC
Three outside varieties grown in the plains around Aprilia S of Rome are prolific, the wines usually pedestrian though experiments underway in vineyards and cellars are aimed at notable improvements.
– **Merlot** r. dr.  ★→★★  83 85 86
Soft, balanced, tasty with 1–3 years of age, this tends to be the best of the Aprilia trio. Casale del Giglio's barrel-aged '83 showed new dimensions.
– **Sangiovese** r. or p. dr.  ★  DYA
Whether pale red or dark pink, this rates little interest.
– **Trebbiano** w. dr.  ★→★★  DYA
This neutral white is plentiful and widely distributed. Casale del Giglio's Satrico exemplifies the type.

| | |
|---|---|
| Bolla | Enotria (C.S. di Aprilia) |
| Casale del Giglio (Santarelli) | Villa dei Priori |
| Colli del Cavaliere | |

**Bianco Capena** DOC w. dr. or s/sw.  ★→★★  DYA
From Malvasia and Trebbiano grown around Capena and Morlupo, N of Rome, the *superiore* (of 12%) can rival the best Castelli Romani whites. The DOC will soon become Capena and include a red wine.
C.S. Feronia

**Castelli Romani** r. p. w. (s/sw.)  ★  DYA
Recognized table wines from various grape varieties grown in the Castelli Romani SE of Rome. The *bianco*, usually dry, occasionally *abboccato*, is similar to the several DOC whites (Frascati, Marino, etc.) of the hills. Unclassified red and rosé wines also often carry the Castelli Romani name. They are based on Sangiovese, Montepulciano, and Cesanese, and are good young.

| | |
|---|---|
| Gotto d'Oro (C.S. Marino) | Fontana di Papa (C.S. Colli Albani) |

**Cecubo** r. dr.  ★★  79 80 81 82 83 85 86
Contemporary red from Abbuoto, Negroamaro, and other grapes grown where the ancient Roman Caecubum originated along the S Latium coast near Gaeta. Deep ruby, perfumed, dry, and robust, it ages well for 3–8 years, sometimes more.
Cantine Cenatiempo

**Cerveteri** DOC r. w. dr. s/sw. ★→★★ 83 85 86
Large zone along the coast NW of Rome around Cerveteri and
Civitavecchia. The *rosso*, from Sangiovese and Montepulcano, is
balanced ruby red wine of good body that holds up well for 1–4 years.
The *bianco*, from Trebbiano and Malvasia, dry or *abboccato*, is mellow
with a light bitter undertone. Drink young.
Cantina Cooperativa di Cerveteri

**Cesanese del Piglio** DOC r. dr. (s/sw.) (sw.) (fz.) (sp.) ★★ 81 82 83
85 86
Good basic red from Cesanese grapes grown in the Ciociaria hills SE of
Rome around villages of Piglio, Anagni, and Paliano. Though made in a
confusing range of types – *secco, asciutto, amabile, dolce, frizzante*, and
*spumante* – the dry versions are the most convincing. Garnet red, well-
scented, tannic, and warm, dry Cesanese is good in 2–6 years. The
semisweet and sweet wines have local admirers.
C.S. Cesanese del Piglio

**Cesanese di Affile** DOC r. dr. (s/sw.) (sw.) (fz.) (sp.) ★★ 81 82 83
85 86
Virtually the same as neighboring Cesanese del Piglio, the zone
surrounds the town of Affile. Some consider this rarity the best.

**Cesanese di Olevano Romano** DOC r. dr. (s/sw.) (sw.) (fz.) (sp.)
★★ 81 82 83 85 86
Grown around Olevano Romano, this is nearly identical to its
neighbors.
C.S. Vini Tipici Cesanese

**Colle Picchioni** r. dr. ★★★ 81 82 83 85 86
Though unclassified, this might be the best wine from the Castelli
Romani in commerce, proof that the volcanic soil of the hills suits reds at
least as well as whites. From Merlot and Cesanese with some Sangiovese
and Montepulciano, this robust, dark ruby wine develops warmth, poise,
and winning bouquet with 4–6 years, sometimes more. Wine from tiny
Vigna del Vassallo and Vigna Due Santi are the estate's special "crus".
Paola Di Mauro

**Colli Albani** DOC w. dr. (s/sw.) (sw.) ★ DYA
White from various Malvasia and Trebbiano subvarieties grown in the
Castelli Romani around Lago Albano and Castelgandolfo. Soft, straw
yellow to golden, it is usually dry but may be *abboccato, amabile* or *dolce*.
Colli Albani *superiore* must have 12% alcohol.
Fontana di Papa (C.S. Colli Albani)

**Colli Lanuvini** DOC w. dr. (s/sw.) ★→★★ DYA
Scarcely known, this can be among the better Castelli Romani whites.
Grown between Lago di Nemi and Aprilia around the town of Lanuvio,
it is soft, usually dry, convincingly fresh, and fragrant.

| | |
|---|---|
| Colle Rubro | Mone Giove |
| Colle San Gennaro | Fratelli Silvestri |
| La Selva | Valle Vermiglia |

**Cori** DOC r. w. (s/sw.) (sw.) ★ 85 86
Obscure zone adjacent to the Castelli Romani around the town of Cori.
The *rosso*, from Montepulciano, Nero Buono di Cori, and Cesanese, can
be interesting. The *bianco*, from the usual mélange of Castelli grapes, has
little to say, whether dry, *amabile*, or *dolce*.

**Est! Est!! Est!!! di Montefiascone** DOC w. dr. (s/sw.) ★→★★ DYA
The wine was once as ludicrous as the name, a hangover from a 12th-
century legend about a tippling bishop's servant whose antics suggest he
was a victim of *delirium tremens*. Legends aside, this white from Trebbiano
and Malvasia grown beside Lake Bolsena is getting better from certain
producers. Usually dry, lightly fruity, almondy, and, lately, crisper than
most other Latium whites. Annual production is about 1 million liters.

| | |
|---|---|
| Bigi | Marchesi Antinori |
| C.S. di Montefiascone | Italo Mazziotii |

**Falerno** or **Falernum** r. w. dr. ★→★★ 81 82 83 85 86
Table wines from S. Latium where Falernum, the Roman favorite, once
thrived. The *rosso*, from Aglianico and Barbera grown around Formia,
Gaeta, and Fondi, is rich and full, improving with 4–6 years, sometimes
more. The white, from Falanghina, has golden tones and goes well with

fish when young. With age it turns amber and flat.
Cantine Cenatiempo

**Fiorano** r. w. dr. s/sw. ★★→★★★★  75 77 78 79 80 81 82 83 85 86
Fine table wines made along the ancient Appian Way just outside
Rome. The *rosso*, from Merlot and Cabernet Sauvignon, is a leading
Italian example of a Bordeaux composite, with the breed to improve
over a decade or more. Deep ruby tending to garnet-amber, it is austere,
rich in extract, taking on bouquet and nuance of flavor with age. The
golden Fiorano *bianco* comes from Malvasia di Candia, worthiest of local
light grapes. Barrel age gives it more elegance and depth than any of the
Roman DOCs. It can take several years of age. Fiorano Sémillon, from
the Sauternes *cépage*, is a refined rarity, delicately off-dry with pale
crystalline color and light, flowery aroma.
Boncompagni Ludovisi, Principe di Venosa

**Frascati** DOC w. dr. s/sw. (sw.) (sp.) ★→★★★  DYA
Latium's most famous wine. Historically often *cannellino* (rather sweet as
a result of raisining grapes), it was sold from the vat in Frascati or in
cooled containers in Rome's *trattorie*. Today it is usually dry and bottled.
Made from a blend of Malvasia, Trebbiano, and other light grapes grown
around the towns of Frascati, Grottaferrata, and Monteporzio Catone,
the wine is soft, smooth, and dry or off-dry, with plenty of Malvasia aroma
and a straw-golden color. Romans drink it with everything from *fettuccine*
to fish to fruit. Crisper, cleaner, and paler than before, the wine's fragility
is often combated with hot or cold stabilization. Of nearly 20 million
liters a year, much is exported. *Cannellino* and *amabile* are sometimes
seen, *spumante* rarely. *Superiore*, of which Villa Simone and Fontana
Candida's Vigneti Santa Teresa stand out, must have 12% alcohol.

| | |
|---|---|
| C.S. di Monteporzio Catone | Grigione |
| Cantine San Marco | Fratelli Mennuni |
| Casa Vinicola Pavan | San Matteo |
| Castel De' Paolis (Lepanto) | Principe Pallavicini |
| Colli di Catone | Tusculum |
| Colli di Tuscolo (C.S. di Frascati) | Valle Vermiglia |
| Conte Zandotti | Villa Beatrice |
| De Sanctis | Villa di Catone |
| Fontana Candida | Villa Simone |
| Gotto d'Oro (C.S. di Marino) | Villaporziana |

**Marino** DOC w. dr. (s/sw.) (sw.) (sp.) ★→★★★  DYA
Marino is second to Frascati in volume and prestige among Castelli
Romani whites, though some Romans prefer it, for it tends to be a shade
stronger, deeper in color and aroma, with a marked almondy finish in
its soft, grapy flavor. Best young in the simple *osterie* of Marino, much is
now shipped by the huge cooperative. Made from a similar combination
of grapes in a zone adjacent to Frascati NW of Lake Albano. Marino is
sometimes fermented briefly with the skins and aged in barrels to give it
old-fashioned character. It may also be *abboccato, amabile* or *dolce*.
*Spumante* is rare. *Superiore* must have 12%. Paola Di Mauro's special
bottling called "Oro" can be as precious as the name.

| | |
|---|---|
| Paola Di Mauro | Gotto d'Oro (C.S. di Marino) |
| Due Santi (Lepanto) | Principe Pallavicini |

**Montecompatri Colonna** DOC w. dr. s/sw. ★  DYA
White from the NE corner of the Castelli Romani, made from the usual
mélange of grapes. Labels may carry the full denomination or the name
of either town.

**Orvieto**
Part of the DOC zone centered in Umbria extends S into Latium.

**Torre Ercolana** r. dr. ★★→★★★★  75 77 78 79 80 81 83
Table wine from nearly equal parts of Cesanese, Cabernet, and Merlot,
grown at Anagni in SE Latium. Only 1,000 to 1,500 bottles are made
from good vintages, enough to have convinced a fortunate few in Italy
of its class while remaining a secret from the rest of the world. Different
each year, because of the way each variety responds to the season, from
outstanding vintages ('78, '83) it is singular, opulently perfumed with
an authoritative concentration of flavors that explode on the palate and
linger there. Suited to roast beef and game, it's also worth
contemplating all alone – if you can find a bottle.
Cantina Colacicchi

**Velletri** DOC r. w. dr. (s/sw.) ★→★★ 82 83 85 86

The lone DOC red of the Castelli Romani and a stereotypical but better-than-average white originate around the town of Velletri S towards Cisterna. The *rosso*, from Cesanese, Montepulciano, and Sangiovese, is fresh and fruity, best on the young side. The *bianco*, whether *secco* or *amabile*, is more delicate and fragrant than most Castelli whites.

| | |
|---|---|
| Cantina Viticoltori Velletri | Consorzio Produttori Vini Velletri |
| Casa Vinicola Pavan | Villa Ginnetti |
| Colle Piombo (Gabrielli) | |

**Zagarolo** DOC w. dr. s/sw. ★ DYA

Only a few thousand liters of this white are made annually in a zone E of the Castelli Romani from the same sort of grapes. Mellow and grapy, whether dry or *amabile*, it is best on the spot. *Superiore* must have 12.5%. Nati Panfilio

## *Wine & Food*

Contemporary Roman cooking is a monument to hodge podge, the foundations of which – the recipes of the ancient Romans and the bourgeoisie of ensuing epochs – have all but crumbled away. What remains has been patched together by the poor and propped up by what could be borrowed or stolen from other places. Yet, for all the salt cod and salt pork, tripe, brains, entrails, feet, tails, dried beans, mussels, anchovies, chickpeas, and salty *pecorino romano*, Rome lays one of the most pungently tasty and vividly colored tables of Italy. A rare extravagance is *abbacchio*, sucking lamb so tender that even poor people can't resist it. But what really enriches the Roman diet are the vegetables that arrive fresh daily from the region's truck gardens. Many dishes of Rome (and Latium) don't seem to go with wine. The Roman answer is to quaff carafe whites from the beloved Castelli Romani – sometimes mercifully diluted with effervescent mineral water.

**Abbacchio alla cacciatora** Baby lamb cooked with rosemary, garlic, anchovies, and vinegar.
  ★★★→★★★★ Torre Ercolana
  or ★★★→★★★★ Fiorano *rosso*.

**Bucatini alla matriciana** Long, narrow pasta tubes with a sauce of *guanciale* (salt pork from the pig's jowl), red peppers (sometimes tomatoes), and grated *pecorino*.
  ★ Castelli Romani *rosato*
  or ★ Colli Albani.

**Carciofi alla giudia** Tender artichokes flattened flower-like and deep-fried, a speciality of Rome's Jewish quarter. *Carciofi alla romana* are artichokes sautéed in oil, garlic, and mint.
  Water

**Coda alla vaccinara** Oxtail stewed with onion, tomatoes, lots of celery, and wine.

  ★★ Cesanese *secco*.
**Cozze alla marinara** Mussels cooked in their juice with parsley, garlic, and sometimes tomato.
  ★★ Marino *superiore secco*.
**Fettuccine al burro** Feather-light egg noodles with lashings of butter, cream, and Parmesan.
  ★★ Frascati *superiore secco*.
**Penne all'arrabbiata** Pasta tubes with raging hot pepper sauce.
  ★ Any carafe white.
**Saltimbocca alla romana** Veal filets with *prosciutto* and sage sautéed in butter.
  ★★★ Colle Picchioni.
**Spaghetti alla carbonara** The hot pasta is plunged into a mix of *guanciale*, grated Parmesan, *pecorino*, hot peppers, and raw eggs, which curdle and adhere to the strands.
  ★★ Colli Lanuvini.

### Restaurants

Recommended in or near wine zones: **Castelli Romani** *Cacciani* at Frascati; *Il Castagnone* at Genzano; *Le Quattro Stagioni* at Grottaferrata; *La Perla* at Marino; *D'Artagnan* at Montecompatri; *Da Micara* at Monteporzio Catone; *Benito* at Velletri; *Giardino* at Zagarolo. **Cerveteri** *Da Nazareno* at Cerveteri. **Cesanese zones** *Del Gallo* at Anagni; *La Vecchia Osteria* at Labico; *Sora Maria e Arcangelo* at Olevano Romano. **Montefiascone** *Dante* at Montefiascone.

# Liguria

Wine is an almost irrelevant item in the economy of the Italian Riviera which flanks Italy's busiest seaport of Genoa. Still, on the verdant hillsides of this slender crescent arching along the Ligurian Sea from France to Tuscany grow more than 100 types of vines. This remarkable testimony to self-reliance in the region with the next to the lowest volume of production (Valle d'Aosta trails) is also a factor behind the obscurity of Liguria's myriad local wines.

A conspicuous exception is Cinqueterre, whose reputation was built more on past achievements than present. Other wines merit greater esteem, especially Rossese di Dolceacqua and also the white Pigato and Vermentino, which are the stars of the new Riviera Ligure di Ponente DOC.

There's a definite fascination in tracking down local wines. Most are white and go well with fish or even *pesto* (basil and garlic sauce) and can seem divine when sipped on a terrace at Rapallo or Portovenere (what they'd taste like back home probably doesn't matter). Local wines to look for are Coronata and Polcevera on the outskirts of Genoa; the whites and reds of Piematone (near Bordighera); and the red Granaccia of Quiliano near Savona. Most others are called simply *nostrano* (ours) – but proudly.

Visitors may find the rusticity of the Dolceacqua zone against the French border a relaxing counterpoint to the crowded playgrounds of nearby San Remo and Monte Carlo. The vineyards of Cinqueterre northwest of La Spezia are also out-of-the-way and posed dramatically on cliffs above the sea. The *Enoteca Sola* in Genoa provides an intelligent selection of Ligurian wines with the best from other places. Also recommended are the *Enoteca Mantelli* in Genoa and the *Enoteca Baroni* at Lerici.

## Recent vintages

Recommended vintages appear with each entry for the few Ligurian wines for aging.

**Buzzetto di Quiliano** w. dr. *→** DYA
Local wine from the Buzzetto grape grown at Quiliano above Savona. Bright straw yellow, fragile (10% or so), zestfully acidic, its underripe freshness makes it right for *pesto*. Growers issue bottles with a uniform label.

**Cinqueterre** DOC w. dr. * DYA
Praised and poeticized through the ages, Cinqueterre's romantic history alone is worthy of respect, but, sadly, the modern wine rarely lives up to past notices. From Bosco grapes with some Albarola and Vermentino grown on steep seaside slopes of the "Five Lands" – the villages of Monterosso, Vernazza, Corniglia, Manarola, and Riomaggiore – the wine is (ideally) straw green, dry, fresh, and delicately scented.
– **Sciacchetrà** am. s/sw. sw. ** 82 83 84 85 86
The dessert version of Cinqueterre from the same grapes semidried. Of at least 17% alcohol, it is golden amber, smooth, sometimes dry enough for aperitif, and it keeps for years. Very rare.
Ag. 1 yr.

Cooperativa Agricoltura di
 Cinqueterre

Silvano Cozzani
Liana Rolandi

**Lumassina** w. dr. ★ DYA
Lumassina, probably the same as the Buzzetto grape of Quiliano, makes
this simple white, noted near Pietra Ligure as the perfect match for *pesto.*
Giuseppe Maffei                          Zanobbio

**Riviera Ligure di Ponente** DOC
Recently approved, this DOC groups four wines grown along the
western Riviera between Savona and Imperia, centered in the towns of
Albenga, Finale and Pornassio.
– **Ormeasco** r. dr. ★★→★★★ 85 86
From Pornassio in the Apennines, this ruby-cherry hued wine employs
Dolcetto as convincingly as most any Piedmontese of the variety and
can surpass most in longevity, becoming velvety in texture with a rich
bouquet of berries and spices.
– **Pigato** w. dr. ★★→★★★ DYA
An outstanding variety for rich, mouth-filling whites that reach peaks
from vineyards around Albenga. Strong (13–14%) and amply
structured, its smooth flavors are best within a year or two after harvest.
– **Rossese** r. dr. ★★→★★★ 85 86
From Liguria's excellent dark variety, Rossese is usually light ruby-
violet in color, flowery and fluently tasty when young, though some
vintages produce wine of deeper tone that are good for 2–5 years.
– **Vermentino** w. dr. ★→★★★ DYA
Liguria's preponderant light variety makes pale straw green to
yellowish wines, finely scented and whether light and crisp or smooth
and rich are usually best young.

| | |
|---|---|
| Anfossi | Fratelli Pozzo |
| Cantine Calleri (Salea) | Romano Ramoino |
| Cascina Fèipu dei Massaretti | Lino N. Spotorno |
| Bruna Donato Francesco | Vairo |
| Eno Val d'Arroscia (Lupi) | Vio |
| Vincenzo Mariano | |

**Rosa di Albenga** p. dr. ★★ DYA
The best-known of several rosés from the native Barbarossa grape
prominent around Albenga. Cherry pink, dry, convincing.
Cantine Calleri

**Rossese di Dolceacqua** or **Dolceacqua** DOC r. dr. ★★→★★★ 82 83
85 86
The inherent beauty of this red was appreciated by Napoleon, but its
glamor still isn't fully expressed. Yet, even when rustic, it's seductive.
From Rossese grown on hills behind Ventimiglia, Bordighera, and San
Remo, centered in the town of Dolceacqua, it is bright ruby to deep
violet, as flowery on the nose as it is fruity on the palate, with warmth
and plushness after 2–5 years, sometimes more. The trend is toward
youthfully soft wines similar in style to some Beaujolais *crus.*

| | |
|---|---|
| Silvio Anfosso (Roquin) | Rubino Balestra & Tornatore |
| Crespi | Solamito & Garoscio |
| Enzo Guglielmi | Tenuta Giuncheo (Diamonti) |
| Michele Guglielmi | Pippo Viale |
| Nano | Vigneti d'Arcagna |
| Antonio Orrigo | Vigneto Curli (Croesi) |

**Terizzo** r. dr. ★★→★★★ 83 85 86
Stylish ruby-garnet wine from Sangiovese and Cabernet grown at
Castelnuovo Magra. Aged in chestnut casks, it is full-bodied with a
lovely bouquet and an opulence that lasts at least 3–4 years.
La Colombiera (Ferro)

**Vermentino** w. dr. ★★ DYA
DOC in Riviera di Ponente, Vermentino also makes good whites in
eastern Liguria, in the Colli di Luni above La Spezia.
Il Becco (Poggianti)                     La Colombiera (Ferro)

# Wine & Food

As seafaring people, Ligurians rely on fish prepared in artistic and savory ways. There are tiny white *bianchetti* (whitebait), *datteri* (sea dates), *tartufi del mare* (oyster-like sea truffles), shrimp, squid, octopus, mullet, seabass, and dozens of others, many of which appear in the fish soups known as *buridda* or *ciuppin*. But fish isn't all. Cramped for space between the sea and the precipitous Apennines, Ligurians resourcefully work magic with nearly anything edible their terraced gardens, orchards and herb-scented hillsides provide. Basil is revered, the base of the glorious *pesto* among many uses. Nuts, herbs, mushrooms, and spices are features of the exotic sauces and dressings for pasta and other dishes, so deftly delicious that they're called *tocchi* (touches). Meat is secondary, though rabbit braised with olives is adored along the western Riviera. Another exquisite speciality of that region is dried tomatoes under oil. Though day-to-day dining is simple enough, Ligurians like the elaborate on special occasions, expressed in *cima alla genovese*, *torta pasqualina*, and, the epitome of indulgence, *cappon magro*.

**Branzino in tegame** Sumptuous Mediterranean seabass cooked with white wine, tomato, and seasonings.
  \*\*\* Vermentino.

**Cappon magro** At least a dozen types of fish are piled pyramid-style on a base of sea biscuits and topped with oysters and lobsters.
*Capponada* is a simpler version that contains preserved fish.
  \*\*\* Pigato

**Castagnaccio** Crunchy chestnut cake with raisins and pine nuts.
  \*\* Cinqueterre Sciacchetrà.

**Cima alla genovese** Veal breast rolled with vegetables, nuts, herbs, spices, eggs, and cheese.
  \*\* Riviera di Ponente Rossese

**Coniglio al Rossese** Rabbit braised in Rossese with tomato, garlic, rosemary, and olives.
  \*\*→\*\*\* Rossese di Dolceacqua.

**Farinata** Irresistible snack of chickpea paste cooked in oil and served in crisp slabs like pizza; known as *panissa* when onions are included.
  \*\* Rosa di Albenga.

**Pansôti** Type of ravioli filled with *ricotta* and chard and topped with a walnut cream sauce.
  \*\*\* Pigato.

**Torta pasqualina** Monumental Easter tart, its multitude of ingredients spread through 33 layers.
  \*\*\* Vermentino

**Trenette al pesto** Slender ribbon noodles (sometimes with boiled potatoes included) topped with Genoa's sauce of basil, cheese, nuts, oil, and garlic.
  \* Lumassina.

**Troffie al pesto** Slender pasta and potato spikes with the famous sauce.
  \*→\*\* Buzzetto di Quiliano.

## Restaurants

Recommended in or near wine zones: **Cinqueterre** *Aristide* at Manarola; *Da Claudio* at Monterosso; *Gambero Rosso* at Vernazza; **Colli di Luni** *Paracucchi-Locanda dell'Angelo* at Ameglia; *La Lucerna* at Bocca di Magra; *La Luna* at Campiglia; *Le Due Corone* at Lerici; **Dolceacqua-Riviera di Ponente** *Palma* at Alassio; *La Capanna* at Apricale; *L'Uliveto* at Castellaro; *Nannina* at Imperia; *Gino* at Piani di Camporosso; *Balzi Rossi* at Ponte San Ludovico.

# Lombardy
Lombardia

Lombardians, perhaps uniquely among Italians, prefer other wines to their own. The nation's most populous and prosperous region has three outstanding wine areas: the Valtellina in the north, the Oltrepò Pavese in the southwest and the province of Brescia (with seven DOC zones) in the east. And yet, in Milan, the commercial capital of Italian wine, it's harder to find a bottle from the home region than a white from Friuli or Trentino, a red from Piedmont, or one of the omnipresent triumvirate from Verona. Though Lombardy grows more Pinot for *spumante* than does any other region, well-heeled Milanese habitually celebrate with Champagne at double the cost.

This cosmopolitanism may be admirable in some ways, but when it comes to wine, Lombardians don't seem to know what they're missing. True, the Oltrepò Pavese, which shares neighboring Piedmont's aptitude for quality, hasn't lived up to its

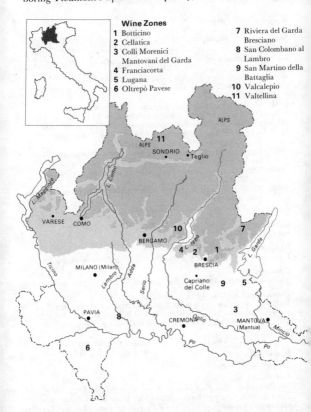

**Wine Zones**
1 Botticino
2 Cellatica
3 Colli Morenici Mantovani del Garda
4 Franciacorta
5 Lugana
6 Oltrepò Pavese
7 Riviera del Garda Bresciano
8 San Colombano al Lambro
9 San Martino della Battaglia
10 Valcalepio
11 Valtellina

promise – yet. Growers still sell their best Pinot grapes to outsiders, who rarely mention the origins on labels.

The Valtellina produces more DOC wine from Nebbiolo grapes than any other (Barolo follows), but its reputation is better abroad than at home. Brescia's wines have only recently begun to rise from obscurity. Franciacorta Pinot *spumante* leads the way, but the reds of Franciacorta, Botticino, and Cellatica, the white Lugana and Tocai di San Martino della Battaglia, and the *rosso* and *chiaretto* of Riviera del Garda Bresciano have winning personalities, too.

Visitors to the Lombardian lake country can take in Lugana and the Riviera del Garda on the shores of Lake Garda, and Franciacorta, which touches on pretty Lake Iseo. The Valtellina is a gorgeous valley in the Alps. The Oltrepò Pavese lies in rustically scenic hills south of Pavia. Oltrepò wines are screened for display and tasting at the *enoteca* in Certosa di Pavia.

Milan has some of the nation's best supplied wine shops – *Enoteca Solci, Enoteca Cotti, Enoteca Ronchi, N'Ombra de Vin* and *Provera* among many – as well as restaurants with impressive cellars. Also in the provinces are outstanding collections, such as *Enoteca Italo Castelletti* at Ponte San Pietro near Bergamo, *Enoteca Rocco Lettieri* at Cantù near Como, *Enoteca Merigalli* at Monza and *Enoteca Malinverno* at Isola Dovarese near Cremona.

## Recent vintages

Lombardy's longest-lived wines are the reds of Valtellina, which may improve for a decade or more. In Oltrepò Pavese, Brescia and other zones, most reds are drunk inside 6–7 years.

1986　Generally very good for reds and whites in all zones.
1985　Fine crop of reds in Valtellina and Oltrepò Pavese; medium to good for whites.
1984　Generally poor, though some decent whites were made.
1983　Fine year in Oltrepò; good to very good in the northeast.
1982　Outstanding harvest everywhere, one of the best in Oltrepò.
1981　Sharply reduced, especially in Oltrepò; quality was generally acceptable, but subpar in Valtellina.
1980　Late harvest with whites better than reds in Oltrepò and Brescia; fine, durable wines in Valtellina.
1979　Very good, abundant crop in Oltrepò; good to excellent in Valtellina and Brescia.
1978　Though reduced in volume, quality was good to excellent in long-lived reds.

Earlier good vintages in Valtellina include '71, '70, '69 and '64.

**Barbacarlo**
See Oltrepò Pavese.

**Barbera**
Lombardy's most heavily planted vine. DOC in Oltrepò Pavese.

**Bonarda**
Strain of Croatina popular in SW Lombardy. DOC in Oltrepò Pavese.

**Botticino** DOC r. dr. ★★ 82 83 85 86
Bright garnet-red wine from Barbera, Marzemino, Schiava, and Sangiovese grown in limited quantity E of Brescia. Warm, fairly robust, and lightly tannic, it develops bouquet and touches of grace in 3–4 years.
Al Romanino (Giossi)　　　　　Tenuta Bettina (Bracchi)

**Buttafuoco**
See Oltrepò Pavese.

**Cabernet**
Grown here for decades, Cabernet Franc figures in the DOC red of Franciacorta, Cabernet Sauvignon in Valcalepío DOC. Numerous table wines are also made: see Colle del Calvario and Maurizio Zanella.

**Capriano del Colle** DOC r. w. dr. ★ 85 86
Little-known DOC from the town of Capriano del Colle S of Brescia.
The *rosso*, from Sangiovese and Marzemino, is supposedly bright and
lively when young. The Trebbiano is pale straw green and tart.

**Cellatica** DOC r. dr. ★★ 83 85 86
From Schiava Gentile, Barbera, and Marzemino grapes grown at
Cellatica, N of Brescia, this tasty, scented, ruby-red is good in 2–4 years.
Barbi
Cooperativa Vitivinicola Cellatica-Gussago

**Chardonnay**
Already established in sparkling wines, Chardonnay is coming on strong
in still wines, most notably Ca' del Bosco's Chardonnay from
Franciacorta, whose '83 ranks with the finest new whites of Italy,
promising ★★★★.

**Clastidium** w. dr. ★★★ 78 82
Extraordinary white from Pinot Nero and Pinot Grigio grown at Broni
in Oltrepò Pavese and vinified at Casteggio (the Roman Clastidium)
under a secret method that involves several years' aging in oak casks.
Dry but mouth-filling and silky, it maintains light color, gorgeous fruity
flavor, and flowery bouquet for 8–10 years or more. Very rare.
Angelo Ballabio

**Colle del Calvario** r. w. dr. ★★ 81 82 83 85 86
Table wines from the town of Grumello between Bergamo and Lake
Iseo. The *rosso*, from Merlot, Cabernet Sauvignon, and Marzemino,
illustrates potential for Bordeaux-style reds in these alpine foothills. It
ages well with 6–8 years. The *bianco*, from Pinot Bianco and Grigio, is
fruity and fresh, good young.
Tenuta Castello

**Colli Morenici Mantovani del Garda** DOC r. p. w. ★→★★ DYA
Localized DOC between Mantua and Lake Garda. The *rosso*, from
Rondinella, Merlot, and Rossanella, is lightweight and dry; it may be
called *rubino*. The *rosato*, from the same grapes, pale cherry in color and
delicate, may be called *chiaretto*. The *bianco*, from Garganega and
Trebbiano, bears a vague family resemblance to Soave.
C.S. Colli Morenici Alto Mantovano

**Cortese**
See Oltrepò Pavese.

**Franciacorta** DOC
Zone NW of Brescia centered in the town of Cortefranca and fronting
on Lake Iseo, noted for two distinctive categories of wine.
**– Pinot** w. (p.) dr. sp. ★★→★★★★
Both still white (Pinot Bianco di Franciacorta, based on Pinot Bianco
grapes) and sparkling white and rosé (Pinot di Franciacorta *spumante*,
which may include Pinot Nero and Grigio, as well as Chardonnay) are
covered by this category. The still wine is pale yellow with hints of
green, smooth, fruity and balanced – best within 2–3 years. The *spumanti*
may be either non-vintage *charmat* or vintage *méthode champenoise brut*,
which includes the *pas dosé* or *nature*. The model estate of Ca' del Bosco
makes *spumante* to rival in class fine Champagne with its vintage Brut,
Crémant and elegant Dosage Zero. Among others of special note are
Bellavista, Monte Rossa and Guido Berlucchi, though Italy's largest
producer of *champenoise* is outside DOC (see under Spumante).
**– Rosso** r. dr. ★★→★★★ 82 83 85 86
Bright ruby red from a unique combination of Cabernet Franc,
Barbera, Nebbiolo, and Merlot. Fragrant, smooth, and dry, with a
round, mellow flavor, it is versatile and impressive in 2–5 years.

| | | |
|---|---|---|
| Bellavista | Cornaleto | Nobili Barboglio de' |
| Fratelli Berlucchi | Lorenzo Faccoli | Gaioncelli |
| Bersi Serlini | Il Mosnel | G. Ragnoli |
| Ca' del Bosco | Longhi-De Carli | Ricci Curbastro |
| Cattarich-Ducco | Monte Rossa | Uberti |
| Cavalleri | Monti della Corte | |

**Gaggiarone**
See Oltrepò Pavese Bonarda.

**Groppello** r. dr.  ★★→★★★  83 85 86
Fine table wine from the Valtenesi on SW shore of Lake Garda. Based
on Groppello, it has a lively ruby color, medium body, and a dry, fresh,
fruity flavor with an almondy finish. Good in 2–4 years, sometimes
more.
Redaelli de Zinis

**Grumello**
See Valtellina Superiore.

**Inferno**
See Valtellina Superiore.

**Lambrusco Mantovano** r. dr. fz.  ★  DYA
Lambrusco from the province of Mantova, similar to Emilian types.
Alberini                              C.S. Cooperativa di Revere

**Lugana** DOC w. dr. (sp.)  ★★→★★★  DYA
Fine white from Trebbiano di Lugana grown S of Lake Garda in a zone
reaching into the Veneto at Peschiera. Straw green to sunny yellow,
delicately flowery, its considerable grace and personality make it one of
the most consistently good whites of the Garda-Verona area (including
Soave). Good young, some Lugana develops depth with a year or more
in bottle. A passable *spumante* is made, usually by *charmat*.

| | | |
|---|---|---|
| Ambrosi | Pellizzari di San | Tenuta Sansonina |
| Ca' Furia | Girolamo | Vigneti Venturelli |
| Pietro Dal Cero | Podere Co' de Fer | Villa Flora |
| Fratelli Fraccaroli | Prandell | Visconti |
| Lamberti | Provenza | Zenato |
| Andrea Pasini & | San Grato | Zenegaglia |
| Figli | (Premiovini) | |

**Merlot**
Varietal table wines of good quality are made in Oltrepò Pavese, San
Colombano al Lambro, Bergamo, and Brescia, among other places.

**Moscato**
See Oltrepò Pavese.

**Moscato di Scanzo** r.–am. sw.  ★★★
From the Merera clone of dark Moscato grown at Scanzo in the
province of Bergamo, this ruby-amber dessert wine with exquisite
Muscat fragrance and refined sweetness. Extremely rare, the few bottles
produced are considered priceless.

**Müller Thurgau** w. dr.  ★★  85 86
Table wines from the Riesling-Sylvaner cross, grown in the Oltrepò
Pavese, can do as well as DOC whites in class. Fine, fragrant and
smooth, they are often good young but can take on persuasive nuances
with 2–3 years in bottle.

| | |
|---|---|
| Italo Contardi | Membretti-Balestreri |
| Fratelli Faravelli | Montelio (Mazza Sesia) |
| Giovanni Ferrari & Fratelli | Fratelli Padroggi |
| Isimbarda | |

**Narbusto** r. dr.  ★★★  74 78
Though made from the usual Oltrepò red grapes, this is kept apart as an
unusually long-lived table wine aged at least 8 years in casks, 2 in bottle,
and capable of lasting another decade beyond. Rich bouquet of berries
and tar, deep ruby color, the flavor is austere with lingering warmth.
Angelo Ballabio

**Oltrepò Pavese** DOC
A large zone in hills S across the Po from the city of Pavia in SW
Lombardy. Despite outstanding capacity (100 million liters a year, 17%
DOC) and a tradition of millennia, Oltrepò Pavese remains a potential
giant of Italian wine groping for an identity. Italy's leading source of
Pinot for *spumante* (usually made in Piedmont), the zone also produces
fine Barbera, Bonarda, Riesling, Moscato, and Müller Thurgau grapes.
Still, the few wines with widespread reputations (Frecciarossa, Ballabio,
and Monsupello, for example) rely on individual identities. The DOC
covers 15 general types: eight varietal names (though Moscato and
Pinot Nero apply to two different versions); a *rosso* (of Barbera,
Croatina, Uva Rara, and Ughetta) and *rosato*; plus three special
denominations (Barbacarlo, Buttafuoco, and Sangue di Giuda, all

based on grapes for the red). To confuse things, some wine that could qualify as DOC isn't sold as such. Still, an active consortium is making progress in this major zone.

**– Barbacarlo** r. dr. s/sw. fz. ★★→★★★ 81 82 83 85 86
Restricted zone near Broni named after Barbacarlo estate of Maga Lino, which continues to make the best wine among several producers. Deep ruby, robust, and dry (though an *amabile* is permitted), it has the almondy bitter background typical of Oltrepò reds. Among the longest-lived, most expensive and best of Italy's *frizzante* reds. Ag. 1½ yrs.

**– Barbera** r. dr. ★→★★★ 79 81 82 83 85 86
Whether drunk young, when its tannic robustness is inviting, or after 5–10 years, when it develops bouquet and composed character, this can rank with the finest wines of the name.

**– Bonarda** r. dr. ★→★★★ 83 85 86
Dark, thick, grapy, bitter, Bonarda epitomizes the rustic goodness of Oltrepò reds. Usually good in 3–4 years, it can age to garnet red and austere, as epitomized by the Gaggiarone of Giacomo Agnes.

**– Buttafuoco** r. dr. (fz.) ★★→★★★ 82 83 85 86
Colorfully named (sparks like fire), this inky, generous, dry, often bubbly wine has distinctive personality from Bianchina Alberici. Good after 3–4 years, from special vintages it can last longer.

**– Cortese** w. dr. (fz.) (sp.) ★→★★ DYA
The tiny amount of wine from Piedmont's prime white grape is light and crisp, sometimes bubbly.

**– Moscato** w. s/sw. sw. fz. sp. ★★ DYA
Dessert wines, nearly always bubbly, can match all but the best Moscatos of Piedmont.

**– Moscato Liquoroso** w.–am. s/sw. sw.
New category for fortified Moscato in both *secco* (semisweet) and *dolce naturale* (very sweet) versions with up to 22% alcohol.

**– Pinot Grigio** w. dr. (fz.) ★★ DYA
Usually still, sometimes *frizzante*, this can rival much Pinot Grigio from the Venezie. Color ranges from light straw to coppery.

**– Pinot Nero** r. p. w. dr. (fz.) ★→★★★ 82 83 85 86
Applies to red, still wines which can occasionally match a minor Burgundy, as well as pink and white. The latter can be fairly full and deep, fresh when young, smooth with 2–3 yrs. of age.

**– Pinot Nero Spumante** w. (p.) dr. sp.
Though some DOC is produced, much sparkling wine from Pinot Nero and other varieties is unclassified, (see Oltrepò Pavese Spumante).

**– Riesling Italico** w. dr. (fz.) ★→★★ DYA
When right, this variety can make whites of fresh tone and lively character.

**– Riesling Renano** w. dr. (fz.) ★→★★ DYA
Not up to Rieslings of Alto Adige, but wines of light distinction can be realized at times.

**– Rosato** p. dr. (fz.) ★→★★ DYA
From the basic grapes for *rosso*, this can be a zesty, cherry-hued rosé.

**– Rosso** r. dr. ★→★★★ 79 81 82 83 85 86
Made by many in somewhat different styles and under many different names. Some are common, but quite a few are good to excellent. Dark ruby turning to garnet, the best versions are ample in body, nicely tannic and lightly bitter, with smoothness and bouquet after 3–4 years. Ag. *riserva* 2 yrs.

**– Sangue di Giuda** r. dr. fz. (s/sw.) ★→★★ 85 86
Usually the fizziest of the Oltrepò reds, "Judas's Blood" is let in limited quantities from a restricted zone near Broni. Lively, soft, sometimes with a hint of sweetness, it is dominated by Croatina. Best inside 3 years.

| | |
|---|---|
| Pietro Achilli | C.S. Intercomunale di Broni |
| Giacomo Agnes | C.S. Retorbido |
| Bianchina Alberici | C.S. Santa Maria della Versa |
| Fratelli Bagnasco | Casa Rè |
| Marco Bellani | Castello di Luzzano |
| Bersano | Cella di Montalto |
| Broglio | Cinzano |
| Ca' Longa (Brega) | Clastidio (Ballabio) |
| Ca' Montebello (Scarani) | Italo Contardi |
| C.S. Casteggio | Fratelli Faravelli |

Frecciarossa (Odero)
Fratelli Gancia
Fratelli Giorgi
Il Frater (Bellani)
Isimbarda
La Marzuola
Le Fracce (Mairano)
Madonna Isabella (Venco)
Maga Lino
Maggi
Malpaga
Mangiarotti
Martini & Rossi
Membretti-Balestreri
Mombrione (Cavazzana)
Monsupello (Boatti)
Montelio (Mazza Sesia)

Nazzano
Enrico Orlandi & Figli
Fratelli Padroggi
Pezzolo
Piccolo Bacco dei
  Quaroni
Poggiopelato (Agnes)
Quattro Castagni
Tenuta Mazzolino
Tenuta Pegazzera
Dino Torti
Travaglino
Edmondo Tronconi
Luigi Valenti
Vigna al Castello (Dezza)
Vilide (Fontanarossa)

**Oltrepò Pavese Spumante** (Pinot-based) DOC/non-DOC w. p. dr.
sp. ★★→★★★
Many Italian sparkling wines are based on *cuvées* from Oltrepò (mainly
Pinot Nero, also Pinot Grigio and Bianco and Chardonnay) though
the source is not always clear on labels. Many are processed outside
the zone, often in Piedmont. The following, produced in the area, offer
good quality and value, especially when made by the *méthode
champenoise*, marked (m.c.), whose producers may use the trademark
Classese.
– **Ballabio Brut (m.c.), Ballabio Rosé (m.c.)**
Angelo Ballabio
– **Cristal Pinot Brut (m.c.), Fontanachiara Brut (m.c.),
  Fontanachiara Pinot (m.c.)**
Maggi
– **Giorgi Gran Spumante (m.c.)**
Fratelli Giorgi
– **Gran Spumante La Versa Brut (m.c.)**
C.S. Santa Maria La Versa
– **Malpaga Brut (m.c.)**
Malpaga
– **Il Doppio Tappo, Monsupello Brut (m.c.)**
Monsupello (Boatti)
– **Pegazzera Brut (m.c.)**
Tenuta Pegazzera
– **Santa Maria Brut**
Pietro Achilli
– **Scarani Brut (m.c.)**
Ca' Montebello
– **Vilide Brut Gran Riserva (m.c.)**
Vilide

**Pinot**
Lombardy is Italy's leading producer of Pinot, both light and dark
varieties, for use in still wines and, most notably, sparkling. See
Franciacorta Pinot, Oltrepò Pavese Pinot Nero and Oltrepò Pavese
Spumante.

**Riesling**
Both Riesling Renano and Riesling Italico are grown in Lombardy,
notably in Oltrepò Pavese as DOC wines.

**Riviera del Garda Bresciano** DOC r. p. dr. ★→★★★ 83 85 86
A large zone W and SW of Lake Garda in Brescia province. Both the
*rosso* and *chiaretto* are from Groppello, Sangiovese, Barbera, and
Marzemino – bright, clean, tasty, dry wines that can match the more
famous reds from across the lake (Valpolicella and Bardolino) The *rosso*
gets a little barrel age, but its light, fruity qualities make it best inside
3–4 years. The *chiaretto*, light and delicate, is refreshing very young.
Andrea Pasini's *rosso* and *chiaretto* stand out.
Ag. *superiore (rosso)* 1 yr.
Nevio Baruffolo                    Bertanzi                         ▶

Cascina La Torretta Spia d'Italia
Castello di Drugolo
Fabio Bottarelli & Figlo
Franco & Valerio Bottarelli
Domenico Chiappini & Figli
Colombaro (Pinna Berchet)
Fattoria Saleri
Giuseppe Fontanella
Girolamo Frassine
Giuseppe Giovanelli
Lamberti

Monte Cicogna
Andrea Pasini & Figli
Pellizzari di San Girolamo
Prandell
Redaelli di Zinis
Giovanni Robazzi
San Grato (Premiovini)
Vigneti Venturelli
Visconti
Zenato
Italo Zuliani

**Ronco di Mompiano** r. dr. ✶✶ 83 85 86
Bright red table wine from Marzemino and Merlot grown at Mompiano
on the edge of Brescia. Dry, smooth, and scented, it is good in 3–4 years.
M. Pasolini

**San Colombano al Lambro** or **San Colombano** DOC r. dr. ✶→✶✶
82 83 85 86
Hearty red from Croatina, Barbera and Uva Rara grown on the gentle
rises around San Colombano SE of Milan. Best drinking is usually in
2–4 years.
Banino (Panigada)
Nettare dei Santi (Riccardi)

Podere Costa Regina
(Pietrasanta)

**Sangue di Giuda**
See Oltrepò Pavese.

**Sassella**
See Valtellina Superiore.

**Sfursat** (or **Sfurzat, Sforzato**)
See Valtellina.

**Spumante** (Pinot or Chardonnay based) w. (p.) dr. (s/sw.)
sp. ✶✶→✶✶✶
Lombardy produces a growing quantity of unclassified *spumanti* by both
the *champenoise* and *charmat* methods. Guido Berlucchi in Franciacorta
makes some four million bottles a year of *champenoise*, about a third of
Italy's total, but since the *cuvées* consist of Pinot and Chardonnay from
Franciacorta, Trentino-Alto Adige and Oltrepò Pavese (along with
Cortese from Gavi), they cannot be DOC. Other producers listed are
outside recognized zones. (See also Franciacorta and Oltrepò Pavese
Spumante.) *Méthode champenoise* is marked (m.c.)
– **Carlozadra Brut (m.c.)**
Perlage
– **Cuvée Antica Fratta Brut (m.c.), Brut Millesimato (m.c.), Pas
Dosé (m.c.), Rosé (m.c.)**
Antica Cantina Fratta (Berlucchi)
– **Cuvée Imperiale Berlucchi Brut (m.c.), Brut Millesimato (m.c.),
Grand Cremant (m.c.), Max Rosé (m.c.), Pas Dosé (m.c.)**
Guido Berlucchi
– **Prandell Brut (m.c.), Prandell Rosé (m.c.)**
Prandell
– **Villa Mazzucchelli Brut (m.c.)**
Vila Mazzucchelli

**Tocai di San Martino della Battaglia** DOC w. dr. ✶✶ DYA
Good white from Tocai Friulano grown S of Lake Garda around San
Martino della Battaglia. Bright lemon yellow, flowery, with dry, lightly
bitter almond flavor, it is best very young.
Cascina La Torretta Spia d'Italia
Pellizzari di San Girolamo
A. & G. Pergreffi
Prandell

Giovanni Robazzi
Ercole Romano
Vigneti Venturelli
Zenato

**Valcalepio** DOC r. w. dr. ✶→✶✶ 83 85 86
DOC zone between Bergamo and Lake Iseo. The *rosso*, from Merlot and
Cabernet Sauvignon, is dark ruby with dry, robust flavor and herb-like
bouquet after 2–4 years. *Bianco*, from Pinot Bianco and Grigio, is straw
yellow, delicate, dry, and light, good young.
Ag. (*rosso*) 2 yrs.

▶

C.S. Bergamasca
Fuzier a Negrone
Le Corne
Bortolo Locatelli & Figli

Tenuta Castello
Tenuta La Cornasella
Villa di Serio (Casselle Alte)

**Valgella**
See Valtellina Superiore.

**Valtellina** DOC
Zone along the Adda River around Sondrio near the Swiss border, with
terraced vineyards split into minuscule plots. Praised since Roman times,
the Valtellina is one of the few places outside Piedmont where Nebbiolo
(here called Chiavennasca) thrives. In fact, it is the most prolific of all
Nebbiolo zones with about 9.5 million bottles a year, of which less than
half is Valtellina Superiore (see below). Much of the production is controlled by foreign capital for consumption in Switzerland. Good white
table wines are made in the zone from Nebbiolo vinified off the skins
and exemplified by Enologica Valtellinese's Nebbia and Il Grappolo.
– **Sfursat** (or **Sfurzat, Sforzato**) r. dr. ★★→★★★  78 79 82 83 85 86
The names are dialect versions of the vinification process that depends
on semidried grapes (same as for basic Valtellina) to bring alcohol to the
required 14.5%. Ample in body, with rich ruby-orange color, it
becomes warm and perfumed after 4–5 years and can age for a decade
or more. Some consider this to be the Valtellina's best.
Ag. 1 yr.

– **Valtellina** r. dr. ★→ ★★ box  82 83 85 86
The basic Valtellina red can be made throughout the DOC zone from at
least 70% Nebbiolo with other dark varieties permitted. It has lively red
color, delicate scent, and somewhat tannic flavor. Good in 3–5 years.
Ag. 1 yr.
(See producers under Valtellina Superiore.)

**Valtellina Superiore** DOC r. dr. ★★→★★★  78 79 82 83 85 86
DOC applied to four subdenominations, each named for a delimited
area within the Valtellina zone. All wines must consist of at least 95%
Nebbiolo. Though subtle variations exist, basic traits are similar: ruby-
red color, tending to garnet with age as bouquet becomes ethereal and
the dry, lightly tannic flavor becomes smoother and more austere over
6–7 years (longer from outstanding vintages). Bottles often appear with
individualistic names – Antica Rhaetia, Castel Chiuro, Fracia,
Paradiso, Perla Villa, Sassorosso, Signorie, and Villa – in addition to the
formal appellation. Ultimately, winemaking skill is often more
important than a precise place of origin.
Ag. 2 yrs. (1 in barrel); *riserva* 4 yrs.
– **Grumello**
The vineyards take the name of a 13th-century castle between Sondrio
and Montagna in Valtellina.
– **Inferno**
The zone is adjacent to Grumello to the E around Poggiridenti. Best
plots are known as Inferno and Paradiso.
– **Sassella**
Most often considered the best of the four, the zone lies W of Sondrio
toward Castione Andevenno.
– **Valgella**
Between the towns of Chiuro and Teglio, this is the most heavily
produced of the four.

Franco Balgera
Fratelli Bettini
Cantina Cooperative Villa-
    Bianzone
Enologica Valtellinese
La Castellina (Fondazione
    Fojanini)
Nino Negri

Nera
A. Pelizzatti
Fratelli Polatti
Rainoldi
San Carlo
Tona (G. Bonisolo)
Fratelli Triacca

**Maurizio Zanella** r. dr. ★★★→★★★★  81 82 83 84 85 86
Cabernet Sauvignon and Franc with Merlot grown in Franciacorta
carries the name and signature of Lombardy's pace-setting producer in
a table wine that may be Italy's best Bordeaux blend to date –
exemplified by the '83. Warm, generous, complex and loaded with
personality and style, this should reach peaks in 5–8 years of harvest.
Ca' del Bosco

# Wine & Food

Natural opulence is reflected in Lombardy's multifarious diet. Milan, unavoidably, instigates food forms called "fast," "international," "nouvelle," but the city also has more fine "Italian" restaurants than any other. Milanese gourmets still relish their ossobuco, costoletta and risotto alla milanese. The outlying seven provinces have so clung to tradition that Lombardian cooking is more accurately described as provincial than regional. Still, everybody eats veal, beef, pork (though cuts and cooking differ), and cheese (besides blue-veined gorgonzola there are grana padano to rival Parmesan, stracchino, taleggio, robiola, and bitto). Risotto reigns in the flatlands, polenta and pasta in the hills, though there is plenty of crossover. In Pavia, they eat frogs and snails, in Bergamo small birds, in Mantua pasta with pumpkin, and in Cremona candied fruit laced with mustard (mostarda). Perhaps the leading preserve of provincial cooking is the Valtellina around Sondrio where, among other nutritious eccentricities, buckwheat is used for pasta and polenta.

**Bresaola** Beef cured much as prosciutto and served in paper-thin slices.
  ** Inferno.

**Busecca** Richly flavored Milanese tripe soup.
  ** Franciacorta rosso
  or ** Oltrepò Pavese rosso.

**Casonsei** Ravioli of Brescia filled with sausage, cheese, and bread.
  ** Riviera del Garda chiaretto.

**Cassoeula** Various cuts of pork cooked with cabbage, celery, and carrots and often served with polenta.
  *** Oltrepò Pavese Barbacarlo
  or ** San Colombano al Lambro rosso.

**Costoletta alla milanese** Breaded veal cutlet with mashed potatoes.
  *** Oltrepò Pavese Pinot Nero.

**Ossobuco e risotto alla milanese** Braised veal shank with saffron risotto, the pride of Milan.
  *** Oltrepò Pavese Barbera.

**Panettone** Milan's dome-shaped Christmas cake.
  ** Oltrepò Pavese Moscato spumante.

**Pizzoccheri** Rustic buckwheat noodles served with boiled potatoes, cabbage, and melted cheese in the Valtellina.
  ** Valtellina, fairly young.

**Polenta e osei alla bergamasca** Polenta with small game birds cooked with butter and sage, a speciality of Bergamo.
  *** Colle del Calvario rosso
  or ** Valcalepio rosso.

**Risotto alla certosina** Elaborate risotto with freshwater prawns, frogs, perch, and vegetables, cooked in white wine.
  *** Oltrepò Pavese Riesling
  or *** Müller Thurgau.

**Sciatt** Fritters of buckwheat and white flour, bitto cheese, and grappa.
  ** Sfursat.

**Tortelli di zucca** Pasta envelopes filled with pumpkin paste flavored with amaretto and nutmeg, served with butter and grated grana.
  *** Lugana.

**Vitello tonnato** Veal filet dressed with a tuna-flavored cream sauce.
  *** Pinot spumante méthode champenoise.

## Restaurants

Recommended in or near wine zones: **Franciacorta** Bertoli and XVII Miglio at Erbusco; Il Volto at Iseo; Tortuga at Rovato. **Garda** and **Colli Morenici** Miramonti at Caino; La Capra at Cavriana; Tre Corone at Desenzano; Tortuga at Gargnano del Garda; Il Bersagliere at Goito; Vecchia Lugana at Lugana di Sirmione; Trattoria alle Piante at Manerba del Garda. **Oltrepò Pavese** Locanda La Buta at Bosnasco; Castello di San Gaudenzio at Cervesina; Chalet della Certosa at Certosa di Pavia; Hostaria Il Casale at Sante Maria della Versa; Il Gallo at Stradella; **San Colombano** Albergo del Sole at Maleo. **Valtellina** Baita da Mario at Ciuk di Bormio; Sassella at Grosio; San Fedele at Poggiridenti; Della Posta at Sondrio; Cerere at Ponte in Valtellina.

If Verdicchio is the only wine of the Marches with an international reputation, much credit is due to its instantly recognizable green amphora bottle. Not to detract from the wine's basic worth: even the French concede that with fish it rivals Muscadet. But the exported Verdicchio is often a standardized, non-vintage product that does not express the maximum that this temperamental vine can give in the chalky-clay soil of the Marches.

Rosso Picenco is also produced in quantity, but, oddly enough, only a fraction of this attractive red leaves the Marches. Another ruby-colored gem is Rosso Cònero, based on Montepulciano grown on the Cònero massif near Ancona, the ancient Greek seaport that is now the region's capital. Most of the other wines are meant to go with regional food, fish in particular, which is always fresh and usually modestly priced at the many good restaurants.

Most people come to the Marches to bask on Adriatic beaches, but those who wander off into the interior in search of wine will also find eye-pleasing scenery in the hills – topped with castles, monasteries, and walled towns – that roll down in green waves from the Apennines to the Adriatic. Urbino is an art center, Loreto a religious shrine, and Ascoli Piceno is one of many well-preserved medieval towns.

A tasteful choice of wines can be found at the *Enoteca Internazionale Teodoro Bugari* at San Benedetto del Tronto.

**Wine Zones**
1 Bianchello del Metauro
2 Bianco dei Colli Maceratesi
3 Falerio dei Colli Ascolani
4 Rosso Cònero

5 Rosso Piceno
6 Sangiovese dei Colli Pesaresi
7 Verdicchio dei Castelli di Jesi
8 Verdicchio di Matelica

## *Recent vintages*

Most white wine is to drink young, so the chart applies mainly to
Rosso Piceno and Rosso Cònero, which only rarely benefit from
more than 4–8 years of aging.

1986  Fine crop of white and red wines.
1985  Hot, dry, better for reds than Verdicchio.
1984  Poor for reds, acceptable for Verdicchio.
1983  A good year for red wines.
1982  Generally fine year, though drought cut the size.
1981  Small, uneven harvest; some good wines, many mediocre.
1980  Normal crop of mostly average wines, good Rosso Cònero.
1979  Fine, abundant, exceptional for Rosso Cònero.

**Antico di Casa Fosca** w. dr. 83 85 86
Practically a Verdicchio di Matelica, but aged in new oak barrels as a
novel *vino da tavola*. Finely aromatic with hints of honey and walnuts in
its flavor, time will tell if this experiment is a success.
Enzo Macella

**Bianchello del Metauro** DOC w. dr. ★→★★ DYA
A snappily acidic little white noted for its affinity with seafood. From
Bianchello grapes grown along the Metauro River valley.
Anzilotti-Solazzi          COVIM                    Roncosambaccio
Basili/Crescentino         Giovanetti               Umani Ronchi
Bianchini                  Le Terrazze di

**Bianco dei Colli Maceratesi** DOC w. dr. ★→★★ DYA
The zone is large, stretching from the Adriatic inland past Macerata
toward the Apennines, but little of this light white from Trebbiano
Toscano and Maceratino is made. Delicate in odor, scent, and flavor.
Attilio Fabrini            Villamagna (Campagnucci-
La Torraccia (Costantini)  Compagnoni)

**Falerio dei Colli Ascolani** DOC w. dr. ★→★★ DYA
White based on Trebbiano Toscano grown in hills N of the Tronto
River between Ascoli Piceno and the Adriatic. Straw green and rather
neutral with an acidic vein, it should be drunk young with fish.
Boccabianca               Picenum
Cantina Sant' Angelo      Tattà
Fratelli Cocci Grifoni    Vallone
Costadoro                 Villa Pigna (Rozzi)

**Fontanelle** w. dr. ★★ 85 86
Good white from Verdicchio grown at Cossignano near Ascoli Piceno.
Bright golden, dry, perfumed, and smoothly textured with fine fruit-
acid balance, it rounds into form in 2 years.
Tattà

**Lacrima di Morro** DOC r. dr. (fz.)
Exotic purple to dark crimson wine apparently from vines outside the
vinifera family planted around the ancient town of Morro d'Alba S of
Senigallia. To my taste coarse and kinky with that foxy odor peculiar to
non-vinifera wines, but it beat the odds to win official classification by
having enough friends in high places to override opposition by the DOC
committee.

**Montepulciano delle Marche** r. dr. ★→★★★ 81 82 83 85 86
Though usually blended with Sangiovese (as in Rosso Cònero and
Rosso Piceno), Montepulciano also makes a varietal table wine. Villa
Pigna's aptly named Vellutato rivals the Abruzzi's best.
C.S. Val di Nevola          Villa Pigna (Rozzi)
Tattà

**Rosato di Montanello** p. dr. ★★ DYA
Fine rosé from Sangiovese and Montepulciano grown outside Macerata.
Pale roseate, flowery on the nose, it is light, dry, and fruity.
Villamagna (Compagnucci-Compagnoni)

**Rosso Cònero** DOC r. dr. ★★→★★★ 79 80 82 83 85 86
Distinguished red from the Monte Cònero massif overlooking the
Adriatic S of Ancona. From Montepulciano (though it may include
15% Sangiovese), it is deep ruby, robust, and rather austere, with fine

bouquet and plenty of depth in its warm, somewhat tannic flavor, which mellows over 3–6 years, sometimes more.

| | |
|---|---|
| Castelfiora | MecVini |
| Fazi-Battaglia | Moroder |
| Fattoria Le Terrazze | Cesare Serenelli |
| Federici & Gagliardini | Fratelli Torelli |
| Garofoli (Vigna Piancarda) | Umani Ronchi (Casal di Serra) |
| Marchetti | Vallerosa (Bonci) |

**Rosso di Corinaldo** r. dr. ★★→★★★ 82 83 85 86
Can be one of central Italy's better Merlots, from a special vineyard at Corinaldo in hills inland from Senigallia. Dark ruby red, rich, and silky smooth, with hints of tar and herbs, it peaks in 3–6 years.
C.S. Val di Nevola

**Rosso Piceno** DOC r. dr ★★→★★★ 79 81 82 83 85 86
Flexible red from Sangiovese at 60%, Montepulciano at 40%, made in quantity in a zone covering much of E Marches between Ascoli Piceno and Senigallia. Aging in oak casks (not required by DOC) and storage in bottle bring out the natural finesse that make it one of central Italy's most promising red wines. Ruby red tending to garnet, in 3–7 years it becomes smooth, composed, with bouquet and charm. *Superiore* covers a restricted area between Ascoli Piceno and San Benedetto del Tronto.
Ag. *superiore* 1 yr.

| | |
|---|---|
| Boccabianca | Picenum |
| C.S. di Cupramontana | Tattà |
| C.S. Val di Nevola | Umani Ronchi |
| Fratelli Cocci Grifoni | Vallone |
| Costadoro | Villamagna (Compagnucci- |
| Fazi-Battaglia | Compagnoni) |
| La Torraccia (Costantini) | Villa Pigna (Rozzi) |
| Giuseppe Pennesi | |

**Sangiovese dei Colli Pesaresi** DOC r. dr. ★→★★ 82 83 85 86
Made in the N around Pesaro and Urbino, this unassuming red can be as savory as most any Sangiovese from neighboring Romagna.

| | |
|---|---|
| Anzilotti-Solazzi | COVIM |
| Basili/Crescentino | Fattoria di San Cristoforo |
| Bianchini | Giovanetti |
| C.S. dei Colli Pesaresi | Le Terrazze di Roncosambaccio |
| Ciardiello/Evalli | |

**Tenuta di Pongelli** r. dr. ★★★ 83 85 86
An intuitive combination of three noble varieties – Sangiovese, Montepulciano and Cabernet – grown at Serra de' Conti near Jesi, this fine-tuned red *vino da tavola* aged in Slavonian oak casks shows the master touch of consulting enologist Giorgio Gray.
Villa Bucci

**Tristo di Montesecco** w. dr. ★★→★★★ 85 86
Table wine of singular personality from Trebbiano Toscano, Malvasia di Candia, Riesling Italico, and Pinot Grigio grown at Montesecco near Pergola in N Marches. Pale brassy yellow with fruity aroma, it is soft but complex with a pleasant bitter background after 2–3 years, including a spell in wood conducted by enologist-owner Massimo Schiavi.
Fattoria di Montesecco

**Verdicchio dei Castelli di Jesi** DOC w. dr. (fz.) (sp.) ★→★★★ DYA
The renowned Verdicchio comes from hills drained by the Esino, Misa and Musone rivers adjacent to the town of Jesi. *Classico* takes in all but the NW portion of this large zone west of Ancona. Popularized as a fish wine in green amphora bottles, Verdicchio was often blended down and pasteurized for the international market. But lately low-temperature processing and, more important, careful selection of grapes has resulted in superior wines from both large and small producers. Brunori's San Nicolò is the product of a skilled artisan; Villa Bucci reflects studied techniques. The new class is evident also from Fazi-Battaglia and other large producers with single vineyard bottlings: Garofoli's Macrina, Monte Schiavo's Il Pallio and Umani Ronchi's Casal di Serra. Verdicchio also makes fine bubbly wine, exemplified by C.S. di Cupramontana's Colonnara Brut and Garofoli's *metodo classico*.

| | |
|---|---|
| Bianchi | C.S. di Cupramontana (Colonnara) |
| Brunori (San Nicolò) | C.S. di Montecarotto |

►

C.S. Val di Nevola
Castelfiora
Castellucci
Fazi-Battaglia
Federici & Gagliardini
Garofoli (Fiorese, Macrina)

Monte Schiavo (Colle del Sole,
 Il Pallio)
Umani Ronchi (Casal di Serra)
Vallerosa (Bonci)
Villa Bucci
Zaccagnini

**Verdicchio di Matelica** DOC w. dr. (sp.) ✭✭→✭✭✭ DYA
Insiders contend that the best Verdicchio comes from this high zone in
the W Marches between Fabriano and Camerino. Though evidence is
scarce, the '82 from Fratelli Bisci was remarkable 3 years later, imbued
with the size, nuances and depth of what are considered nobler whites
and the only Verdicchio to which I'd unhesitatingly give ✭✭✭✭.
Spumante is rarely seen.
Fratelli Bisci
La Monacesca

Pagliano (MecVini)
Vinimar

**Verdicchio di Montanello** w. dr. ✭✭✭ DYA
Table wine made at Montanello near Macerata. With its fragrance and
smooth balance, it compares favorably with most DOC Verdicchio.
Villamagna (Compagnucci-Compagnoni)

**Verdicchio Pian delle Mura** w. dr. sp. ✭✭→✭✭✭ DYA
The still version is good, the *brut nature spumante* superior, with
Verdicchio's best traits enhanced by the persistent *perlage* and delicately
yeasty scent of a skillfully made *méthode champenoise*.
Attilio Fabrini

**Vernaccia di Serrapetrona** DOC r. dr. s/sw. sw. sp. ✭→✭✭✭ DYA
Curious sparkling red based on Vernaccia di Serrapetrona grapes
grown around Serrapetrona W of Macerata. Deep garnet-purple, grapy
and fragrant with mouth-cleansing bitterness on the finish, it can be
dry, *amabile*, or *dolce*. Most producers have replaced the traditional
special process of bottle fermentation with *charmat*, but Attilio Fabrini
insists on the *méthode champenoise*, which gives clearly superior results.
Attilio Fabrini

## Wine & Food

The food of the Marches, immediately likeable – like the wine or,
for that matter, the people – never lets you down. Cooks draw
from land and sea and, without too much fuss, put the best of
both on the table, often together. Roast pig (*porchetta*) is cooked
with wild fennel, rosemary, garlic, and pepper, as are duck,
rabbit, and even shellfish. Both fowl and fish may be cooked *in
potacchio*, with tomato, rosemary, garlic, onion, and white wine.

**Anatra in porchetta** Duck
cooked with wild fennel, garlic,
ham, and bacon. *Coniglio* (rabbit)
may be done the same way.
 ✭✭✭ Rosso Piceno.
**Brodetto** Among many fish soups
of the name, Ancona's version is
most famous, maybe because it
includes at least 13 types of fish.
 ✭✭ Verdicchio dei Castelli di Jesi.
**Faraona in potacchio** Guinea
fowl cooked with onion, garlic,
rosemary, and tomato in wine.
 ✭✭✭ Rosso Cònero.

**Olive all'ascolana** Hollowed
giant green olives of Ascoli with a
meat stuffing, fried in olive oil.
 ✭ Falerio dei Colli Ascolani.
**Piccione ripieno** Squab stuffed
with chestnut-butter purée and
baked.
 ✭✭✭ Vernaccia di Serrapetrona
*secco.*
**Vincisgrassi** An elaborate
lasagne which includes butter,
cream, *prosciutto*, and black truffles.
 ✭✭✭ Verdicchio *spumante méthode
champenoise.*

### Restaurants
Recommended in or near wine zones (which take in all but the
mountainous areas): *Il Passetto* at Ancona; *Posta Vecchia* at Calcinelli;
*Ilario* and *Villa Amalia* at Falconara Marittima; *La Quinta* at Fano;
*Boschetto* at Filetto di Senigallia; *Galeazzi* at Jesi; *Da Secondo* at Macerata;
*La Cantinetta del Cònero* at Osimo Scalo; *La Cantinella* at Ostra; *La Ginestra*
at Passo del Furlo; *Da Carlo al Mare* and *Lo Scudiero* at Pesaro; *Emilia* and
*Giacchetti* at Portonovo; *Albula* at San Benedetto del Tronto; *Albatros* at
Senigallia.

# Molise

After years of deprivation as the only region without a DOC, Molise has emerged with two new appellations. Neither Biferno nor Pentro has been widely tested, so they remain to be proven.

However, Molise already had some good wines. Examples are the Montepulciano del Molise and Ramitello *rosso* from Masseria Di Majo Norante near the Adriatic. The Biferno DOC wines of Serra Meccaglia or Rocca del Falco (both from a cooperative at Gambatesa) show promise. Conceivably, Molise's neglected hillsides may one day make wine of real class. The climate is right and those rocky inclines aren't suitable for much else.

Perhaps the most inviting thing about Molise is that few people go there, possibly because few people know where it is. It has a narrow strip of Adriatic coast (at Termoli) and extensive uplands to explore, while enjoying the rustically tasty wine and food at true bargain prices.

## Recent vintages

Data has not been recorded long in Molise. Recommended vintages are given with red wines, which rarely last more than 4 years.

**Bianco del Molise** w. dr. ★ DYA
From Trebbiano Toscano and/or Bombino Bianco grown in various parts of Molise, this is straw yellow, dry, neutral in scent and flavor.
Cantina Valbiferno                    Colle Sereno

**Biferno** DOC r. p. w. dr. ★→ ★★ 83 85 86
The zone along the Biferno River valley which traverses Molise from the Apennines to the Adriatic is beginning to show promise, as expressed by Di Majo Norante's Molì and the Serra Meccaglia and Rocca del Falco brands of the Vita Coop. The *bianco* from Trebbiano compares with the middle range of Abruzzi whites and the *rosato* from Montepulciano could stand with most Cerasuolo. The *rosso* needs some work to match the Abruzzi's best.
Ag. *superiore* (*rosso*) 3 yrs.
Cantina Valbiferno                    Rocca del Falco (Vita)
Molì (Di Majo Norante)               Serra Meccaglia (Vita)

**Montepulciano del Molise** r. dr. ★→ ★★★ 82 83 85 86
Table wine from Montepulciano grapes grown in several parts of the region. Ruby to brick red, it is robust and dry, acquiring smoothness and style with 3–4 years.
Masseria Di Majo Norante

**Moscato** w. s/sw. (fz.) (sp.) ★ DYA
Dessert wines, both still and bubbly, are made from light Moscato grapes in various places. Sometimes good, rarely memorable.

**Pentro** or **Pentro di Isernia** DOC r. p. w. dr. ★ 85 86
A new name in Isernia province for *rosso* and *rosato* from nearly equal parts of Montepulciano and Sangiovese and *bianco* from Trebbiano Toscano with some Bombino Bianco.

**Ramitello** r. w. (fz.) ★★→ ★★★ 82 83 85 86
Wines from the Ramitello vineyards near Campomarino. The *rosso*, from Sangiovese and Montepulciano, is deep ruby and smooth with a light bitter aftertaste, good in 3–4 years. The *bianco*, from Trebbiano and Malvasia, is aged a little to develop a golden color and some aroma. *Frizzante* wines are made too, a light red from Sangiovese and a white from Trebbiano, both to drink young and cool.
Masseria Di Majo Norante

**Rosato del Molise** p. dr. ★ DYA
Table wines from Montepulciano and Sangiovese vinified as rosé are
made in several places.
Masseria Di Majo Norante

**Rosso del Molise** r. dr. ★ 83 85 86
Montepulciano, Sangiovese and other both dark and light grapes go
into these ruby, rather soft table wines, best to drink in 1–4 years.

**Sangiovese** r. dr. ★ 85 86
Table wines from Sangiovese are made in various places. Light ruby
and dry, they become smooth over 2–3 years.

**Tifernum** r. p. dr.★ 83 85 86
Table wines from Montepulciano, Sangiovese, and Aglianico grown at
Petrella Tifernina. The *rosso* is deep red and scented, with good body
and balance over 3–4 years. The *rosato* is tasty when young.
Colle Sereno

**Vernaccia di Serra Meccaglia** w. dr. sp. ★★ DYA
Impressive white from Vernaccia di San Gimignano grapes grown at
Gambatesa. A *spumante* version is known as Monforte Brut.
Serra Meccaglia (Vita)

*Wine & Food*

Molise doesn't have a *cucina* all its own, but instead shares recipes
with the Abruzzi, while picking up an occasional idea from
neighboring Apulia, Campania, and Latium. The cooking is
rustic and authentically good. Lamb and kid are stalwarts in the
hill country, where *pecorino* cheese is eaten in chunks or grated
over pasta, and pork is preserved in *prosciutto* and salame.
Mountain streams provide trout and crayfish. Along the coast,
the usual range of Adriatic fish is consumed.

**Calcioni di ricotta** Circular
pasta shells folded over a paste of
*ricotta, provolone, prosciutto,* and eggs,
then deep-fried in oil.
  ★★ Biferno *bianco.*
**Fiadone** Easter tart filled with
beaten eggs, mild *pecorino,* sugar,
cinnamon, and lemon rind.
  ★ Moscato *amabile* or *dolce.*
**Gamberi d'acqua dolce ai ferri**
Freshwater crayfish grilled over
coals.
  ★★ Vernaccia di Serra
Meccaglia.
**Mazzarelle d'agnello** Lamb's

lung and intestines wrapped in
beet greens and cooked in oil and
white wine.
  ★★ Montepulciano del
Molise.
**Tacconi** Quadrangular pasta
often served with meat sauce.
  ★★ Tifernum.
**Trota alle brace** Fresh brook
trout grilled over coals.
  ★★ Ramitello *bianco.*
**Zuppa di ortiche** Soup of nettle
sprouts, tomato, bacon, and onion.
  ★★ Biferno *rosato.*

### Restaurants
Recommended near wine areas: *Da Emilio* at Ferrazzano; *Lo Squalo Blu*
and *Torre Saracena* at Termoli; *Vittoria* at Venafro.

# Piedmont

Piemonte

Techniques may be reforming at a faster clip elsewhere, but Piedmont provides lasting proof that Italy produces wines of the highest order. A visit to the Langhe hills around Alba where Barolo and Barbaresco are grown ought to convince any doubter. There is something reminiscent of Burgundy there: in the manicured vineyards fragmented into single-owner plots on every south-facing slope; in the trim villages, where the lusty odor of fermenting grapes perfumes the autumn air; in the self-assured way the *vignaiolo* hands you a glass of his best. In the Langhe, as in the Côte d'Or, wine is a way of life.

But, without doubt, Piedmont and its wines stand alone, so alone that they demand concentration to truly comprehend. Every important Piedmontese wine derives from a native vine. Most are from single varieties, though not all carry varietal names. The noblest vine is Nebbiolo, the source of Barolo and Barbaresco, as well as Gattinara, Ghemme, Carema, Lessona, Nebbiolo d'Alba, and other distinguished reds.

Piedmontese consume far more red wine than white. Nearly half the red is Barbera, much of which is for everyday, some of which is remarkable. Dolcetto is often more seductive, smooth and supple with an almondy finish and too good to escape international acclaim. Grignolino and Freisa, though declining because of meager yields, remain more than local curiosities.

Among whites, Asti Spumante, from the Moscato di Canelli grape, is the world's second most lauded sparkling wine after Champagne. Cortese, at its best from Gavi, is a rising star among dry whites.

Though Piedmont ranks only seventh among Italian regions in volume of production, its quality wines are the most thoroughly categorized; it has 37 DOC or DOCG zones, the most of any region. Viticulture is most intense in the Langhe and Monferrato hills around Alba, Asti and Alessandria, where thousands of growers work vineyards that are often little larger than a hectare. Many sell grapes to industrial wineries centered in Canelli, Asti, and Turin, firms which often base their economies on vermouth, Asti and other sparkling wines. The trend to make wine from individual vineyards, either directly by the grower or by small-scale winemakers, should preordain a *cru*-style classification of vineyards, starting with Barolo and Barbaresco, the zones best prepared for such distinction.

Piedmont's other outstanding wine district is in the alpine foothills between Valle d'Aosta and Lake Maggiore in the provinces of Vercelli and Novara. There Nebbiolo prevails in Gattinara, Ghemme, Lessona, and other fine wines.

Piedmont is by far the best organized Italian region for wine tourism. Focal points for travelers are the Langhe and Monferrato hills and the towns of Alba and Asti, reachable by car in just over two hours from Milan and in even less time from Turin and Genoa. Well-marked wine roads cover a score of production zones. Signs from Alba lead to vineyards and cellars of Barolo, Barbaresco, Dolcetto d'Alba, Barbera d'Alba, Nebbiolo d'Alba, and Moscato d'Asti. Public *enoteche* provide places to buy and drink the wines. Not to be missed are the castles

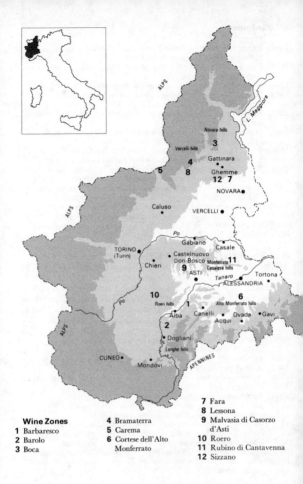

**Wine Zones**

1 Barbaresco
2 Barolo
3 Boca
4 Bramaterra
5 Carema
6 Cortese dell'Alto Monferrato
7 Fara
8 Lessona
9 Malvasia di Casorzo d'Asti
10 Roero
11 Rubino di Cantavenna
12 Sizzano

of Grinzane Cavour (Alba wines), Costigliole d'Asti (Asti and Monferrato wines), and Vignale Monferrato (Monferrato Casalese wines), all with good restaurants serving local specialities. The villages of Barolo and Barbaresco have *enoteche* to show off their production. Interesting wine museums include *Abbazia dell'Annunziata* near La Morra, *Bersano* at Nizza Monferrato, and *Martini & Rossi* at Pessione. Good wine shops include *Enoteca Bava* and *Enoteca Conca d'Oro* at Cannobio, *Enoteca Eporediese* at Ivrea and *Enoteca Vivian* at Novara.

### Recent vintages

#### Alba: Barolo and Barbaresco
As a rule, Barbaresco from an average-to-good harvest rounds into form at 4–6 years and Barolo at 5–8, after which they hold well for several more years. From the best vintages, a couple of years more are needed. In both cases, *riserva* should be designated for longer aging, often well over a decade.

| 1986 | Spring hail cut the crop in Barolo, but otherwise a fine year of balanced wines for medium long aging. |
|---|---|
| 1985 | Vies with '82 as the greatest recent vintage. Time will tell. Excellent for Barbera. |
| 1984 | Cool and damp made this largely a write-off. |
| 1983 | Fine fall weather made this a good to very good year for Nebbiolo wines and Barbera. |
| 1982 | Hailed as one of the greatest years this century; wines of unusual size and harmony. |
| 1981 | Disappointing after a promising start, but select wines were satisfactory or better. |
| 1980 | Record quantity despite curious weather that forced the latest harvest in memory. Middling-to-very-good wines. |
| 1979 | Nearly equal to '80 in size, easily superior in quality. Early maturing, charming wines to enjoy from now onwards. |
| 1978 | Near disaster from early damp and cold turned to an unexpected glorious vintage. Rare, luxuriant wines for long aging. |

Notes on earlier vintages: Only 1974 stood out between the great '78 and '71 vintages, the latter of which overshadowed the excellent '70 crop. Other fine harvests: '67, '65 (especially Barolo), '64 (especially Barbaresco), '62, '61, '58, '57, '52, '51 and '47.

## Novara-Vercelli hills and Carema

Though Nebbiolo is often mixed with Bonarda and Vespaiola in these alpine foothills, some wines can equal Barolo in longevity. Gattinara, Carema, Lessona, Ghemme, Caramino, and choice Spanna need 4–6 years to be drinkable and sometimes more than a decade to reach prime. Wines containing less Nebbiolo – Boca, Fara, Sizzano, and Bramaterra – usually mature sooner.

| 1986 | Fine crop of harmonious wines for medium aging. |
|---|---|
| 1985 | Drought did scattered damage in what was otherwise a fine year. |
| 1984 | Lightweight wines, generally below standard. |
| 1983 | A good year but it lacked consistency. |
| 1982 | A fine year almost everywhere; balanced wines should age well. |
| 1981 | Mediocre. Select wines may be good but short lived. |
| 1980 | Late harvest resulted in good wine from select grapes. |
| 1979 | Big year in both volume and quality in well-structured wines with better-than-average life expectancy. |
| 1978 | Miracle vintage, thanks to a warm, dry autumn after a miserable spring and early summer reduced size. Great in Carema, near great elsewhere in wines which are rounding into form. |

Notes on earlier vintages: '76 and '74 were good for Gattinara, which however had less than full satisfaction in '71, but a great year in '70. Other fine harvests: '69, '64, '61, '52.

**Arengo** r. dr. (fz.)  **★→★★**  DYA
Trendy little red, softly fruity and sometimes lively, conceived by 18 wineries to use up excess Barbera and other red grapes.

**Arneis dei Roeri** w. dr. **★★→★★★** DYA
An ancient vine of the Roeri hills N of Alba, Arneis is enjoying a revival, though production is still limited. Soft but richly textured, it can range from moderately interesting to elegant, complex and fascinating.

| | |
|---|---|
| G. Battista Arduino | Malvirá (Damonte) |
| Blangè (Ceretto) | Produttori Montaldesi Associati |
| Castello di Neive | Renato Rabezzana |
| Bruno Giacosa | Fratelli Rabino |
| La Brenta d'Oro | |

**Asti Spumante** or **Asti**
See Moscato d'Asti.

**Barbaresco** DOCG r. dr.  **★★→★★★★**  71 74 78 79 80 82 83 85 86
One of Italy's great red wines. Made from Nebbiolo grown around the villages of Barbaresco, Neive, and Treiso, adjacent to Alba, Barbaresco production is at most 3 million bottles a year. With its neighbor Barolo it shares the robust, austere, dramatic elegance of well-aged Nebbiolo. Though Barbaresco rarely equals the sheer power of the biggest Barolo and requires less maturing in barrel and bottle to develop bouquet (4–8

years), it is sometimes credited with more finesse and more consistent quality from year to year. Certain bottlings – notably Gaja's special vineyards – command prices near the top for Italian wines from recent vintages. Gaja and Bruno Giacosa are the producers who have won highest praise internationally, though Produttori del Barbaresco, Bricco Asili, Castello di Nieve and Marchesi di Gresy have also built fine reputations. Special vineyard bottlings of proven worth are cited after the producer's name. DOCG took effect with the '81 vintage and could be applied retroactively back to '79.

Ag. 2 yrs. (1 in wood); *riserva* 4 yrs.

Accademia Torregiorgi (Messoriano)
Fratelli Barale (Rabajà)
Bera
Luigi Bianco & Figlio
Carlo Boffa & Figlio
Franco Bordino
Bricco Asili-Ceretto (Bricco Asili, Faset)
Cantina del Glicine (Curà, Marcorino)
Cantina della Porta Rossa
Cantina Vignaioli Elvio Pertinace (Casotto, Marcorino)
Fratelli Casetta (Vigna Ausario)
Castello di Neive (Messoriano, Santo Stefano)
Ceretto (Asij)
Fratelli Cigliuti (Serraboella)
Confratelli di San Michele
Contratto (Cascina Alberta)
Giuseppe Cortese (Rabajà)
Anfosso De Forville
Paolo De Forville
Fontanafredda
Franco-Fiorina
Gaja (Costa Russi, Sori San Lorenzo, Sori Tildin)
Gemma (Gallina)
Bruno Giacosa (Gallina, Santo Stefano)
Fratelli Giacosa

Giovanni Giordano & Figli
Enrico Giovannini-Moresco (Pajorè)
Granduca-Duca d'Asti
La Spinona-Berutti
Le Colline
Marchesi di Gresy (Camp Gros, Gaiun, La Martinenga)
Giuseppe Mascarello & Figli (Bernardotti)
Fratelli Oddero
Parroco di Neive
Secondo Pasquero-Elia (Sori-d'Paytin)
Luigi Pelissero
Pio Cesare
Produttori del Barbaresco (Asili, Moccagatta, Ovello, Pora, Rabajà)
Alfredo Prunotto (Montestefano, Rabajà)
Renato Ratti
Francesco Rinaldi & Figli
Rizzi
Roagna-I Paglieri (Crichët Pajé, Opera Prima)
Dario Rocca & Figli
Roche
Gigi Rosso
Scarpa (I Tetti di Neive, Payoré Barberis)
Vietti (Masseria, Rabajà)

## Barbera or Barbera del Piemonte

About half of Piedmont's red derives from Barbera, often sold under the generic name. Some is rustic and inexpensive, but a bit is unexpectedly refined (see Bricco Uccellone). There are also white and rosé Barberas and even sparkling and sweet versions. DOC under Alba, Asti, Colli Tortonesi, Gabiano, Monferrato and Rubino di Cantavenna.

**Barbera d'Alba** DOC r. dr. ★★→★★★ 78 79 82 83 85 86

Rich in color and body, smooth in scent and flavor, lightly tannic, this is often the longest-lived Barbera. Some producers vinify for drinking within a year, others in 2–3 years, others for longer aging. Quality has improved steadily. Worthy special vineyards are cited.

Ag. 1 yr; *superiore* 2 yrs.

Accademia Torregiorgi
Elio Altare
Giacomo Ascheri
Fratelli Barale (Bussia)
Bera
Fratelli Brovia
Brezza
Cantina del Glicine
Cantina Vignaioli Elvio Pertinace
Cappellano
Fratelli Casetta
Castello di Neive (Santo Stefano)

Cavallotto
Ceretto (Piana-Brunate)
Fratelli Cigliuti (Serraboella)
Clerico
Cogno-Marcarini
Confratelli di San Michele
Aldo Conterno (Conco Tre Pile)
Giacomo Conterno (Cascina Francia)
Bruno Giacosa (Altavilla d'Alba)
Marchesi di Barolo

▶

Giuseppe Mascarello & Figli
(Ginestra)
Riccardo Fenocchio (Pianpolvere
Soprano)
Fontanafredda
Franco-Fiorina
Gaja (Vignarey)
Podere Rocche dei Manzoni
Parroco di Neive
Luigi Pelissero
Pio Cesare

Alfredo Prunotto (Pian
Romualdo)
Renato Ratti (Altavilla)
Rocche Costamagna
Roche
Paolo Scavino & Figli
Terre del Barolo
(Valdisera)
G.D. Vajra
Vietti (Rocche)
Voerzio

**Barbera d'Asti** DOC r. dr.  ☐ ★→★★★ ☐ 78 79 80 82 83 85 86
Robust and full-bodied, it tends to be less acidic and somewhat fruitier
and softer than Barbera d'Alba and, at its best (exemplified by Scarpa),
hard to beat. Most Barbera d'Asti is to drink fairly young, though in this
vast zone of heavy production it is hard to define a style. Some vintages
may improve for a decade or more. Worthy special vineyards are cited.
Ag. 1 yr; *superiore* 2 yrs.

Anforio – Premiovini
Antica Contea di Castelvero
Antonio Benso
Bersano (Cascina Cremosina)
C.S. Antiche Terre dei Galleani
C.S. di Canelli
C.S. di Cassine
C.S. di Castelnuovo Calcea
C.S. di Maranzana
C.S. Stazione Calamandrana
Cantine Bava
Giorgio Carnevale
Cascina Canova – Barbero
Cascina Castlèt (Malabaila)
Cascina Croce – Brema
(Impagnato)
Cascina La Spinetta – Rivetti
Cascina Pesce
Ca' Tesi della Pianca
Castello di Gabiano
Contratto
R. Cortese
Fassio

Granduca (Valle del Sole)
Marchesi Spinola
Moncucchetto – Biletta
Montetusa – Bertelli
Livio Pavese
Luigi Pia (La Badia)
Pinbologna
Podere Borlotto
Poderi Bricco Mondalino –
Gaudio
Pracalliano – Gremmo
Renato Rabezzana
Giuseppe Ratti
A.B. Ravetto
Ronco
Giovanni Rosso
Scarpa (Banin, Bogliona,
Cascina Possabreno)
Fratelli Spagarino
Tenuta dei Re
Tenuta Tenaglia – Quattrocolo
G.L. Viarengo & Figlio
Vignaioli Piemontesi

**Barbera del Monferrato** DOC r. dr. (fz.)  ☐ ★→★★★ ☐ 82 83 85 86
This Barbera from Monferrato hills N and S of Asti and Alessandria
may include up to 15% of Freisa, Grignolino, or Dolcetto, which tend to
make it lighter and suppler than Barberas of Asti and Alba. Often
*frizzante*, it is best in 1–4 years.
Ag. *superiore* 2 yrs.

Antica Contea di Castelvero
Balestrino & Vivalda
Bersano
Carlo Brema
Pietro Calvo
Renzo Campagnola
C.S. del Monferrato
C.S. Mombercelli
C.S. San Giorgio
Cantine Bava
Castello di Gabiano
Castello di Salabue – Cassinis
Castel Tagliolo
Amilcare Gaudio
Granduca-Duca d'Asti

Graziola
Enrico Imarisio
Ermenegildo Leporati
Dante Montiglio
Nuova Cappelletta
Livio Pavese
Podere Soria di Calosso
Giuseppe Ratti
Ronco
Tenuta Cannona
Tre Castelli
Tenuta Tenaglia – Quattrocolo
Valmosè
Zavanone di Mirabello

**Bardonè** r. dr. ★★ DYA
A mix of Barbera, Dolcetto and Nebbiolo vinified to be fresh, fruity and
youthfully light (11%) to drink within a year.
Fontanafredda

**Barilot** r. dr. 82 83 85 86
Following the trend, this Nebbiolo and Barbera aged in small oak barrels should prove interesting.
Granduca-Duca d'Asti

**Barolo** DOCG r. dr. **✶✶→✶✶✶✶** 70 71 74 78 79 80 82 83 85 86
"King of wine and wine of kings," as the Piedmontese define it, Barolo is indeed a regal wine, probably the most esteemed red of Italy. Made in the Langhe hills SE of Alba, it takes the name of the village of Barolo. It needs time to lose its initial tannic hardness (8 years or more from such vintages as '71, '78, '82 and '85) and it takes an experienced palate to master its complex grandeur. Barolo's austere robustness and intense concentration of fruit and extract can remain largely intact for well over a decade as color evolves from deep ruby garnet toward brick red, and bouquet becomes increasingly refined. Production of at most seven million bottles a year is centered in the villages of Castiglione Falletto, Monforte d'Alba, and Serralunga d'Alba (where the biggest wines are made), and Barolo and la Morra (from where the most graceful wines come). Regularly twinned with Barbaresco, Barolo can surpass it in size and longevity, if not in finesse and overall class. Most of Barolo's more than 400 producers have local reputations, but a few have built limited markets abroad for their wines, sometimes at lofty prices (notably Ceretto's Bricco Rocche). But in a day of preference for lighter, softer, standardized flavors, Barolo remains aloof, an anomaly, almost a cult wine. Special vineyard bottlings of proven worth are cited after the producer's name.

DOCG took effect with the '80 vintage and could be applied retroactively back to '77.
Ag. 3 yrs (2 in wood); *riserva* 5 yrs.

Accademia Torregiorgi
Giovanni Accomasso & Figlio (Rocchette)
Elio Altare (Arborina)
Anforio-Premiovini
Fratelli Anselma
Giacomo Ascheri
Fratelli Barale (Cannubi, Castellero)
Giacomo Borgogno & Figli
Serio & Battista Borgogno (Cannubi)
Gianfranco Bovio (Gattera)
Bricco Rocche-Ceretto (Bricco Rocche, Brunate, Prapò)
Brezza
Fratelli Brovia (Rocche)
Cantina della Porta Rossa
Cantina Mascarello
Cappellano
Giorgio Carnevale
Fratelli Casetta
Cavallotto (Bricco Boschis)
Ceretto (Zonchera)
Clerico (Ciabot Mentin Ginestra)
Colli Monfortesi (Ginestra)
Coluè
Aldo Conterno (Bricco Bussia Cicala, Colonello)
Giacomo Conterno (Cascina Francia, Monfortino)
Contratto
Paolo Cordero di Montezemolo (Enrico VI, Monfalletto)
Lorenzo Denegri
Luigi Einaudi
Riccardo Fenocchio (Pianpolvere Soprano)

Michele Fontana (Cannubi)
Saverio Fontana
Fontanafredda (Gattinera, La Delizia, La Rosa, La Villa, Lazzarito, San Pietro)
Franco-Fiorina
Maurizio Fracassi Ratti Mentone
Gemma
Bruno Ciacosa (Bussia, Rocche, Rionda)
Fratelli Giacosa
Granduca-Duca d'Asti
Grasso (Gavarini)
Graziola
Grimaldi (Groppone)
Marcarini (Brunate, La Serra)
Marchesi di Barolo
Giuseppe Mascarello & Figlio (Monprivato, Rionda, Villero)
Fratelli Oberto
Fratelli Oddero
Pio Cesare
E. Pira & Figli-Boschis
Podere Rocche dei Manzoni (D'la Roul, Vigna Big)
Alfredo Prunotto (Bussia, Cannubi, Ginestra)
Renato Ratti (Conca di Marcenasco, Rocche di Marcenasco)
Francesco Rinaldi & Figli
Giuseppe Rinaldi
Rocche Costamagna
Gigi Rosso (Arione)
Luciano Sandrone
Scarpa (Boscaretti di Serralunga, I Tetti della Morra)

▶

Alfonso Scavino
Paolo Scavino (Bric dël Fiasc)
Filippo Sobrero & Figli
Tenuta Carretta (Cannubi)
Tenuta Cerequio (Cerequio)
Tenuta Montanello
Terre del Barolo (Brunate,
　Rocche)

G.D. Vajra
Vietti (Briacca, Brunate,
　Bussia, Rocche)
Giacomo Voerzio (Ciabot
　della Luna, La Serra)
Roberto Voerzio
Basilio Zunino (Sori di
　Baudana)

**Barolo Chinato** r. dr. ★★★ NV
Barolo DOC permits production of a tonic made by steeping *china*
(quinine, the bark of the chinchona tree) in the wine until it takes on the
flavor. This fine *amaro* is found mainly in winemakers' homes.

**Bianco dei Roeri** w. dr. ★★ DYA
An unusual blend of light Arneis and dark Nebbiolo vinified off the skins
in a crisp, well-structured white.
Tenuta Carretta

**Boca** DOC r. dr. ┃★★→★★★┃ 78 79 82 83 85 86
Fine red from Nebbiolo (Spanna) at 45–70% with Vespolina and
Bonarda grown in the Novara hills near Boca. Robust and aggressive
when young, it grows smooth with 4–5 years, taking on a violet scent.
Ag. 3 yrs (2 in barrel).
Lorenzo Bertolo　　　　　　　Guido Ponti
Ermanno Conti　　　　　　　　Antonio Vallana & Figlio
Podere ai Valloni

**Brachetto**
The Brachetto grape usually makes pleasant, strawberry colored, sweet
bubbly wines in the Monferrato hills, sometimes not DOC. An
exception is Scarpa's Brachetto di Moirano, dry, still, ruby-violet and
enticingly drinkable in its youth.

**Brachetto d'Acqui** DOC r. s/sw. sw. fz. sp. ★★→★★★ DYA
Light red, either *frizzante* or sparkling, made from Brachetto grapes in
the Acqui Terme area. With delicate Muscat-like aroma and some
sweetness, it is served cool with pastry, fruit, and even sausages.
Antica Contea di Castelvero　　Giorgio Carnevale
Bersano　　　　　　　　　　　Livio Pavese
Braida-Bologna　　　　　　　　Marchesi Spinola
C.S. di Cassine　　　　　　　　Valmosè
C.S. di Maranzana　　　　　　　Villa Banfi – Strevi

**Bramaterra** DOC r. dr. ┃★★┃ 78 79 80 82 83 85 86
Recent DOC of Nebbiolo (Spanna) at 50–70% with Croatina,
Bonarda, and Vespolina, grown in Vercelli hills at village of
Bramaterra. Full-bodied and sturdy, it gains harmony and grace with
4–8 years.
Ag. 2 yrs. (in wood); *riserva* 3 yrs.
Luigi Perazzi　　　　　　　　　Sella Bramaterra

**Bricco del Drago** r. dr. ★★★ 78 82 83 85 86
Distinctive blend of Dolcetto with Nebbiolo grown near Alba in a rich,
ruby-violet wine, soft and attractive with its own sort of authority in 4–6
years, sometimes more.
Cascina Drago (De Giacomi)

**Bricco Manzoni** r. dr. ┃★★★→★★★★┃ 78 79 80 82 83 85 86
An ingenious mix of Nebbiolo and Barbera grown in the Barolo zone at
Monforte and aged in small barrels in a stylish red that matures sooner
than Barolo but shows similar depth and class.
Podere Rocche dei Manzoni-Valentino

**Bricco Uccellone** r. dr. ★★★→★★★★ 82 83 84 85 86
Like its patriarch Giacomo Bologna, this barrique-aged Barbera named
for a vineyard above Rocchetta Tanaro E of Asti is immense, strong,
warm, generous, filled with fantasy and humor, and though
immediately persuasive, is sure to stand the test of time. Bologna also
makes a lively Barbera called La Monella at his Braida cellars.
Braida-Bologna

**Briona** r. dr. ★★ 78 82 83 85 86
Nebbiolo with Bonarda grown in the Novara hills, this is a well

structured, finely dry but full-flavored wine of attractive bouquet, to drink in 4–8 years or more.
Antoniolo

**Cabernet Sauvignon**
Recent plantings of the Bordeaux vine in a region where it once thrived are promising wines of real interest. See Darmagi.

**Caluso Passito** DOC am. sw. ★★→★★★★ 74 78 79 82 83 85 86
From semidried Erbaluce grapes grown around Caluso and Ivrea NE of Turin, this is an exquisitely sweet, velvety dessert wine with a rich, intense nut-like flavor. Boratto's limited production is among Italy's finest dessert wines. The *liquoroso* is richer and stronger, capable of great age. Both versions go well with pastries and strong cheeses. See also Erbaluce di Caluso.
Ag. 5 yrs.
Vittorio Boratto                          Ubertini
Corrado Gnavi                            Macellio (Bianco)
Filiberto Gnavi                            Orsolani
Istituto Professionale Carlo

**Caramino** r. dr. ★★ 78 82 83 85 86
Intriguing red based on Nebbiolo from vineyards around the Caramino castle at Fara in the Novara hills. Similar to Gattinara, it can develop some depth of flavor and bouquet over 5–8 years.
C.S. dei Colli Novaresi                   Luigi Ferrando
Luigi Dessilani & Figli

**Carema** DOC r. dr. ★★→★★★ 74 78 79 80 82 83 85 86
Tiny, mountainous zone next to Valle d'Aosta in which vines are trained over trellises on rocky terraces. Made from Nebbiolo (here called Picutener or Pugnet), Carema is garnet-hued with somewhat less body and durability than other Nebbiolo wines, but cold climate and stony terrain account for unique refinement in bouquet and flavor developed through long barrel- and bottle-aging. Needs 5–6 years or more. Ferrando's black label and the Produttori's Carema dei Carema stand out.
Ag. 4 yrs (2 in barrel).
Lorenzo Bertolo                          Morbelli
Luigi Ferrando                            Produttori Nebbiolo di Carema

**Chardonnay** or **Chardonnay del Piemonte** w. dr. (sp.) ★★→★★★ 83 84 85 86
Recent plantings of this noble vine have brought new dimensions to Piedmontese whites, epitomized by Gaja's Gaia & Rey, aged in new French oak, in a style somewhere between Californian and French. The '85 and '86 promise ★★★★ with time. Fontanafredda is among other prominent producers issuing Chardonnay.
Fontanafredda                            Gaja (Gaia & Rey)

**Colli Tortonesi** DOC
Zone near the town of Tortona in SE Piedmont with two varietal wines.
– **Barbera** r. dr. ★→★★ 82 83 85 86
Lively, robust red from at least 85% Barbera. The *superiore* improves with 3–5 years.
Ag. *superiore* 2 yrs.
– **Cortese** w. dr. (fz.) (sp.) ★→★★ DYA
Pale, delicate, bone-dry, rather acidic white from Cortese. Good with seafood, it is sometimes bubbly.
Sergio Borasi                            Cantine Volpi
C.S. di Tortona                          Torricella-Bergaglio

**Cortese dell'Alto Monferrato** DOC w. dr. (fz.) (sp.) ★→★★ DYA
Crisp, pale, straw-green wine of at least 85% Cortese grown in a large area of the Alto Monferrato hills. Sometimes *frizzante* or sparkling.
C.S. di Cassine                          Oberto Pinelli Gentile
Cascina Pesce                            Tre Castelli
Contratto                                Vignaioli Piemontesi
Cossetti

**Cortese di Gavi**
See Gavi.

**Darmagi** r. dr. ***→**** 82 83 85 86
Angelo Gaja's entrée into the international Cabernet Sauvignon
sweepstakes was done with expected bravura. Already Darmagi, from
young vines planted in one of Barbaresco's best sites, has won prizes and
praise, setting off speculation about what it will be like when it comes of
age.
Gaja

**Dolcetto** or **Dolcetto del Piemonte**
DOC in seven zones, Dolcetto is sometimes sold as a generic *vino da
tavola*. Usually fairly tannic yet soft with a broad, grapy, mouth-filling
flavor, Dolcetto has been hailed as Piedmont's answer to Beaujolais,
though it is much too chauvinistic to follow a French lead.

**Dolcetto d'Acqui** DOC r. dr. *→*** 84 85 86
Among the softest and lightest of Dolcettos, from Acqui Terme. Villa
Banfi's barrel-aged Argusto is an exception.
Ag. *superiore* 1 yr.

| | |
|---|---|
| Argusto (Villa Banfi – Strevi) | Il Cascinone di Castel Rocchero |
| C.S. di Cassine | Francesco Poncini & Figlio |
| Castello d'Orsara | Marchesi Spinola |
| Castel Tagliolo | Vignaioli Piemontesi |

**Dolcetto d'Alba** DOC r. dr. **→*** 84 85 86
Steady improvements in technique have enabled producers in the Alba
zone to achieve Dolcetto of unequalled appeal; balanced, smooth,
gracefully grapy, mouth-filling wine to drink within 1–3 years. Special
vineyard bottlings of proven worth are cited after the producer's name.
Elvio Cogno's remarkable Boschi di Berri comes from ancient vines
unaffected by phylloxera.
Ag. *superiore* 1 yr.

| | |
|---|---|
| Accademia Torregiorgi | Riccardo Fenocchio |
| Giovanni Accomasso & Figlio | (Pianpolvere Soprano) |
| Elio Altare | Franco-Fiorina |
| Giacomo Ascheri | Gaja (Vignabajla) |
| Fratelli Barale (Costa di | Bruno Giacosa (Basarin, |
| Rose) | Plinet) |
| Borgà d'Arion | I Paglieri-Roagna |
| Serio & Battista Borgogno | La Spinona-Berutti |
| Gianfranco Bovio (Dabbene) | Marchesi di Barolo |
| Fratelli Brovia | Marchesi di Gresy (Monte |
| Cantina della Porta Rossa | Aribaldo, Palazzina) |
| Cantina del Glicine | Giuseppe Mascarello & Figlio |
| Cantina Vignaioli Elvio | (Boscareto, Gagliassi) |
| Pertinace | Fratelli Oddero |
| Cappellano | Pio Cesare |
| Fratelli Casetta | Podere Rocche dei Manzoni- |
| Castello di Neive (Basarin, | Valentino |
| Valtorta) | Alfredo Prunotto (Gagliassi, |
| Cavallotto | Mosesco) |
| Ceretto (Rossana, Vigna) | Renato Ratti (Ca' Colombè, |
| Fratelli Cigliuti (Serraboella) | Campetto Colombè, Colombè |
| Clerico | di Mango) |
| Elvio Cogno (Boschi di Berri, | Rocche Costamagna |
| Nassone, Panerole) | Gigi Rosso (Altavilla) |
| Aldo Conterno (Cascina | Luciano Sandrone |
| Favot) | Paolo Scavino |
| Giacomo Conterno (Cascina | Terre del Barolo |
| Francia) | G.D. Vajra |
| Paolo Cordero di | Sergio Vezza & Figlio |
| Montezemolo (Monfalletto) | Vietti (Bussia, Castelletto, |
| Redento Dogliotti & Figli | Pugnane) |
| (Campo Rosso) | Giacomo Voerzio |
| Drago | Roberto Voerzio |

**Dolcetto d'Asti** DOC r. dr. *→** 85 86
From the Monferrato hills in the province of Asti, an easy-drinking but
lightweight Dolcetto is made in limited quantity.
Ag. *superiore* 1 yr.

| | |
|---|---|
| Antica Contea di Castelvero | Carlo Brema & Figlio |
| Balestrino & Vivalda | C.S. di Canelli |

►

C.S. di Maranzana
Giorgio Carnevale
  (Della Rocchetta)
Cascina Pesce

Cossetti
La Gosa
Vincenzo Ronco & Figli
Vignaioli Piemontesi

**Dolcetto delle Langhe Monregalesi** DOC r. dr. ★★ 85 86
Made in minute quantities in the Langhe between Dogliani and
Mondovi. Though lighter than others, it is noted for special bouquet.
Not often seen in commerce.
Ag. *superiore* 1 yr.
Cascina La Meridiana

**Dolcetto di Diano d'Alba** DOC r. dr. ★★→★★★ 85 86
The Dolcetto from Diano is among the best, noted for its deep purple
color, smooth texture and grapy fragrance and flavor.
Ag. *superiore* 1 yr.
Anforio-Preniovini)
Sergio Casavecchia
Coluè (Vigna Tampa)
Fontanafredda (La Lepre)
Carlo Romana

Gigi Rosso (Moncolombetto)
Mario Savigliano
Terre del Barolo (Cassinotto)
Giovanni Veglio & Figli

**Dolcetto di Dogliani** DOC r. dr. ★★→★★★ 84 85 86
The Dolcetto vine reputedly originated at Dogliani, where it makes
wine of firm tone, depth and length of flavors, as exemplified by
Chionetti.
Ag. *superiore* 1 yr.
Celso Abbona & Figlio
Francesco Boschis
Cappellano
Quinto Chionetti & Figlio
  (La Costa, Sori Briccolero)
Mario Cozzo

Mario Devalle (Bric sur
  Pian)
Luigi Einaudi
Fabrizio Fabiani
Adalberto Schellino

**Dolcetto di Ovada** DOC r. dr. ★★ →★★★ 78 79 82 83 85 86
Dolcetto from hills around Ovada in SE Piedmont rivals the best of
Alba in class. Sturdy structure favors aging; some big vintages last a
decade.
Ag. *superiore* 1 yr.
C.S. Stazione Calamandrana
Giuseppe Poggio (Trionzo)
Giuseppe Luigi Ratto
Giuseppe Scazzola
Granduca-Duca d'Asti

Tenuta Cannona
Tenuta di Savoia
Terre del Dolcetto
Tre Castelli
Valmosè

**Erbaluce di Caluso** DOC w. dr. ★→★★ DYA
This light, dry white from Erbaluce grapes grown around Caluso and
Ivrea NE of Turin has not yet gone beyond the order of refeshing,
though insiders say the grape may have more to offer, possibly on the
order of Cortese for Gavi. See also Caluso Passito.
Colombaio di Candia
Luigi Ferrando
Corrado Gnavi
Filiberto Gnavi

Istituto Professionale Carlo
  Ubertini
Macellio (Bianco)
Orsolani

**Fara** DOC r. dr. ★★ 78 79 82 83 85 86
Red of noteworthy character from Nebbiolo, Vespolina, and Bonarda
grown in the Novara hills. Robust and nicely scented, it improves over
4–8 years, sometimes longer.
Ag. 3 yrs (2 in barrel)
Giuseppe Bianchi
C.S. dei Colli Novaresi
Giuseppe Castaldi

Luigi Dessilani & Figli
Luigi Ferrando

**Favorita** w. dr. ★→★★ DYA
New interest in this pale, acidic white wine from the once-forgotten
Favorita grown in the Roeri and Langhe hills has led to a modest
comeback. Bone dry and light, when well made it is not as simplistic as
it may seem on first sip.
C.S. del Nebbiolo
Cavallotto
Franco-Fiorina
Monticelli-Oliveri (La Corte)

Angelo Negro & Figli
Renato Rabezzana
Voerzio

**Freisa** or **Freisa del Piemonte** r. dr. (s/sw.) fz. sp. ★★→★★★ 85 86
Once popular in central Piedmont as a rustic bubbly wine with unique sweet-acidic flavor (something like lightly salted raspberries), Freisa has lost ground. But lately some producers, especially around Alba, have resumed making dry Freisa of good balance, whether *frizzante*, *spumante*, or still. With enticing ruby-cherry color and raspberry-like aroma, they show enough class to herald a revival.

| | |
|---|---|
| Cantina Sant'Uffizio | Fratelli Oddero |
| Fratelli Cigliuti | Pio Cesare |
| Aldo Conterno | Alfredo Prunotto |
| Giacomo Conterno | Scarpa |
| Redento Dogliotti & Figli | Tenuta Carretta |
| Drago-De Giacomi | Terre del Barolo |
| Franco-Fiorina | Vietti |
| Bruno Giacosa | Robert Voerzio |

**Freisa d'Asti** DOC r. dr. or s/sw. fz. sp. ★→★★ 85 86
Though DOC, Freisa d'Asti rarely equals the select unclassified Freisa of Alba. Dry or *amabile*, still, *frizzante*, or *spumante*, it has lively acidic flavor with a berry-like undertone and bright cherry-garnet color. Ag. *superiore* 1 yr.

| | |
|---|---|
| Antica Contea di Castelvero | Cascina Pesce |
| Bersano | Contratto |
| C.S. di Canelli | Moncucchetto-Biletta |
| Giorgio Carnevale | Vignaioli Piemontesi |

**Freisa di Chieri** DOC r. (dr.) s/sw. fz. sp. ★→★★ 85 86
Limited production from this zone at the doorstep of Turin is mostly consumed in the area. The *amabile* whether *frizzante* or *spumante* is preferred to the dry, still version.
Melchiorre Balbiano

**Gabiano** DOC r. dr. ★★ 74 78 79 82 83 85 86
DOC based on Barbera from the village of Gabiano in the Monferrato Casalese hills. Very limited, it is noted for extraordinary longevity.
Castello di Gabiano

**Gattinara** DOC r. dr. ★★→★★★ 70 74 78 79 82 83 85 86
Wine of ancient renown, Gattinara may be capable of greatness, though it rarely lives up to its name. At best, this red from Nebbiolo (Spanna) grown in the Vercelli hills approaches Barolo in dimensions, durability, style, and depth. But Nebbiolo, which may be mixed with 10% Bonarda, develops distinct nuances in the glacial moraine N of the town of Gattinara. There is a hint more of violets and tar on the nose, that slightly softer texture and sense of bitter almond at the finish that set it apart. Recent self-discipline has improved quality, but more consistency is needed in Gattinara's production of some 400,000 bottles a year. Ag. 4 yrs (2 in barrel).

| | |
|---|---|
| Antoniolo (Osso San Grato, San Francesco) | Umberto Fiore |
| | Le Colline (Monsecco) |
| Guido Barra & Figlio | Luigi & Italo Nervi |
| Agostino Brugo | Orsolani |
| Luigi Dessilani & Figli | Giancarlo Travaglini |
| Luigi Ferrando | Antonio Vallana & Figlio |

**Gavi** or **Cortese di Gavi** w. dr. (fz.) (sp.) ★★→★★★ 85 86
The most prestigious wines from Cortese grapes come from the hills around Gavi in SE Piedmont. One of Italy's most fashionable whites, it is noted for acute dryness and fresh, flinty acidity, which makes it excellent with fish. Standards of quality and price are higher than for most other Italian whites and the list of good producers is growing. La Scolca's Gavi dei Gavi was the standard-bearer for years, a white almost Burgundian in texture with unusual depth of aroma and flavors, but DOC rules forbid the use of that name. *Frizzante* and *spumante* are increasingly seen, though the best, La Scolca's "Pados", is not DOC.

| | |
|---|---|
| Balbiano | Castel di Serra |
| Balestrino & Vivalda | Castello di Tassarolo |
| Nicola Bergaglio & Figlio | Contratto |
| Bersano | R. Cortese |
| Ca' del Rosso | Fontanafredda |
| Cantina Produttori del Gavi | Luigi Gemme (La Merlina) |
| Giorgio Carnevale | Granduca-Duca d'Asti ▶ |

La Battistina
La Chiara
La Giustiniana
La Piacentina
La Raia
La Scolca-Soldati
Liedholm
Livio Pavese
Pio Cesare

Principessa Gavia-Banfi
Raggio d'Azeglio
Tenuta San Pietro
Valmosè
Villa Broglia (La Meirana,
   Vigna Fasciola)
Villa Costa
Villa Sparina

**Ghemme** DOC r. dr. ★★→★★★ 74 78 79 80 82 83
Among Nebbiolo-based wines of the Novara-Vercelli hills, Ghemme
ranks second to Gattinara in status but can surpass it in class. From
Nebbiolo at 60–85% with Vespolina and Bonarda, its sturdy, robust
qualities smoothen with age as it develops an elegant bouquet. Made in
limited quantity around the town of Ghemme.
Ag. 4 yrs (3 in barrel).

Antichi Vigneti di Cantalupo
   (Collis Breclemae)
Agostino Brugo
C.S. di Sizzano e Ghemme

Le Colline
Guido Ponti
G. Sebastiani & Figlio

**Grignolino**
Once widely planted, Grignolino has been reduced to secondary status
in Piedmont, a victim of shy yields. Its pale, delicate wines seem
strangely out of step in a region of bold reds, but local admirers of
"Grignè" (dialect for grin) find its almost rosy color and dry, vaguely
bitter, gritty flavor unmatchable at table. Some unclassified Grignolino,
from Portacomaro N of Asti in particular, show lovely freshness when
young, but the finest I've tasted is made by Riccardo Fenocchio in the
Barolo zone.

**Grignolino d'Asti** DOC r. dr. ★→★★★ 85 86
The largest DOC zone permits 10% of Freisa in light Grignolino to
drink young and fairly cool.

Balestrino & Vivalda
Bersano
Braida – Bologna
Carlo Brema & Figlio
C.S. Casorzo
Cantine Bava
Giorgio Carnevale
Cascina La Spinetta – Rivetti
Casaletto – Ronco
Aldo Cassina
Conte di Cavour
Contratto

R. Cortese
Bruno Giacosa
Marchesi Incisa della Rocchetta
Moncucchetto – Biletta
Pinbologna
Renato Rabezzana
A.B. Ravetto
Fratelli Rovero
Scarpa
Tenuta dei Re
G.L. Viarengo & Figlio

**Grignolino del Monferrato Casalese** DOC r. dr. ★→★★★ 85 86
Grown in the hills around Casale Monferrato, Grignolino (with 10% of
Freisa) is light ruby orange, refreshingly acidic, and sometimes quite
stylish. This is the classic Grignolino zone.

Renzo Campagnola
Fratelli Cantamessa
C.S. del Monferrato
C.S. di Vignale
C.S. Stazione Calamandrana
Cascina Belvedere
Castello di Gabiano
Castello di Lignano
Giorgio Cosseta
Franco-Fiorina
Bruno Giacosa
Granduca-Duca d'Asti

Ermenegildo Leporati
Nuova Cappelletta
Livio Pavese
Pio Cesare
Poderi Bricco Mondalino
   – Gaudio
Giuseppe Ravizza
Tenuta Tenaglia (Quattrocolo)
Tenute Riccardi Candiani
Valmosè
Vietti

**Lessona** DOC r. dr. ★★★ 78 79 80 82 83 85 86
Minuscule zone in the Vercelli hills makes refined red wine from
Nebbiolo with up to 25% Vespolina and Bonarda. Rich in bouquet and
flavor, robust, and lightly tannic, Lessona improves with 6–8 years,
sometimes more.
Ag. 2 yrs.

Ormezzano

Sella Lessona

**Malvasia di Casorzo d'Asti** DOC r. s/sw. sw. fz. sp. [**\*\***] DYA
Usually sweet and *spumante*, this cherry-hued wine comes from the
Malvasia Rossa vine grown around Casorzo NE of Asti. Appreciated
locally for its fragrant, grapy fruitiness.

Fratelli Biletta                       Francesco Morello di Cinzano
C.S. Casorzo                           Livio Pavese

**Malvasia di Castelnuovo Don Bosco** DOC r. sw. sp.  \*  DYA
This wine from the town of Castelnuovo Don Bosco near Turin is similar
to Malvasia di Casorzo but even harder to find.

Melchiorre Balbiano                    Giovanni Savio
Cantine Bava

**Mesolone** r. dr. [**\*\***] 78 82 83 85 86
Good red from Nebbiolo and Bonarda made at Brusnengo in the
Vercelli hills. It improves with 5–8 years or more.
Armando Beccaro & Figlio

**Moscato d'Asti-Moscato d'Asti Spumante** DOC
The DOC category for Moscato qualified as Asti Spumante is Moscato
d'Asti. Produced in quantity (more than 50 million liters a year) in the
Monferrato hills S of Asti between Alba and Acqui Terme from
Moscato Bianco or Moscato di Canelli grapes. DOC prescribes two
types of wine.

– **Asti Spumante** or **Asti** w. s/sw. sw. sp. \*\*→\*\*\* NV
Italy's most famous sparkling wine, noted for its seductive Muscat
aroma, refreshing sweetness, and moderate alcohol. The wine is usually
processed by *charmat* at low temperature in stainless steel tanks, only
rarely by *méthode champenoise*. Recent improvement in quality and
consistency is due to stricter self-control through their *consorzio* by large
firms, mainly at Canelli, with the resources to put Asti through its
complex production procedures. About 80% is exported, much to the
U.S.A.

Anforio – Premiovini               Filipetti
Antica Contea di Castelvero        Fontanafredda
Barbero                            Fratelli Gancia
Bera – Cascina Palazzo             Gaudenzio
Bersano                            Gilardino
Felice Bonardi                     Granduca-Duca d'Asti
Bosca                              Graziola
Calissano                          Clemente Guasti & Figli
C.S. Alice Bel Colle               Martini & Rossi
C.S. Canelli                       Morando
C.S. di Cassine                    Riccadonna
C.S. Dolcetto & Moscato            Tenuta Bertulot
Giorgio Carnevale                  Valfieri
Cinzano                            G.L. Viarengo
Cocchi                             Vignaioli di Santo Stefano
Contratto                          Vignaioli Piemontesi
Cora

– **Moscato d'Asti** w. s/sw. sw. fz. \*\*→\*\*\* DYA
This is the base wine. After filtration, the musts are fermented into a
wine with a high degree of residual sugar. Some of this is kept aside to be
sold as Moscato d'Asti, which is usually *frizzante* through fermentation
in tanks or (rarely) bottles. The best have exquisite Muscat fragrance, as
little as 5% alcohol (the rest is in residual sugar) and flavor so fresh it's
like biting into a ripe grape. (Not all wine from listed producers is
DOC.)

Angelo Arione                      Marenco
Bastian – Soria                    Vittorio & Giuseppe Mo
Bera – Cascina Palazzo             Giovanni Saracco
Braida – Bologna                   Tenuta Bertulot
Carlo Brema & Figlio               Traversa
Giorgio Carnevale                  Valmosè
Cascina La Spinetta – Rivetti      Vignaioli di Santo Stefano
Redento Dogliotti & Figli          Vignaioli Piemontesi
Fontanafredda                      Voerzio
Il Cascinone di Castel Rocchero

**Moscato di Strevi** w. s/sw. sw. fz. sp. \*\*→\*\*\* DYA
Strevi, a town near Acqui, is renowned for its Moscato, which is made
into wines, usually *spumante* or *frizzante*, of notable class.

F. Bruni  
Conti Valperga  
Domenico Ivaldi  

Domenico Mangiarotti  
Villa Banfi – Strevi  

**Möt Ziflon** r. dr. ★★ 78 82 83 85 86  
Dry red from Nebbiolo, Bonarda, and Freisa made at Suno in the
Novara hills. Medium in structure, it develops bouquet after 3–4 years.  
Luciano Brigatti  

**Nebbiolo** or **Nebbiolo del Piemonte**  
Generic name used for wines from Nebbiolo grapes not classified as
DOC or DOCG. These may range from ordinary to excellent and
include a range from light and frizzy to seasoned and bold. Several
prominent producers around Alba make such wines as lighter
alternatives to Barolo and Barbaresco.  

**Nebbiolo d'Alba** DOC r. dr. (s/sw.) (fz.) (sp.) ★★→★★★ 78 80 82 83
85 86  
Vineyards around Alba N of the Tanaro River in the Roeri hills and S
in the Langhe (but not in the Barolo or Barbaresco zones) produce this
often excellent but oddly varied DOC. It includes still, dry wines for
aging, as well as lightly sweet and/or bubbly wines to drink young. The
dry can show the nobility of more vaunted Nebbiolo wines with the
advantage of being softer, easier and less expensive. They often reach a
prime at 3–6 years, but from some vintages can last a decade. The new
Roero DOC applies to wines made in the Roeri, but producers can opt
for Nebbiolo d'Alba if they wish. Special vineyard bottlings of proven
worth are cited after the producer's name.  
Ag. 1 yr. (*secco*).  

Baracco de Baracho (San
  Tommaso)  
Fratelli Barale  
Fratelli Brovia  
Fratelli Casetta  
Ceretto (Lantasco)  
Colué  
Drago-De Giacomi  
Fontanafredda  
Franco-Fiorina  
Gaja (Vignaveja)  
Bruno Giacosa (Valmaggiore)  
Malvirà-Damonte  
Marchesi di Barolo  
Giuseppe Mascarello &
  Figlio (San Rocco)  
Angelo Negro & Figli  

Fratelli Pezzuto  
Produttori Montaldesi
  Associati  
Alfredo Prunotto
  (Occhetti)  
Renato Ratti (Ochetti)  
Roche (Mesdi)  
Mario Savigliano &
  Figlio  
Scarpa (Moirane, San
  Carlo)  
Tenuta Carretta (Bric'
  Paradiso, Bric' Tavoletto)  
Terre del Barolo  
Sergio Vezza' and Figlio  
Vietti (San Giacomo, San
  Michele)  

**Nebbiolo delle Langhe**  
Name used for *vini da tavola* by Barolo and Barbaresco producers for
second selection wines, some good, some ordinary. Successful examples
include Pio Cesare's Il Nebbio and Voerzio's Vigna Roscaleto in a light
vein. Occasionally such wine can match good Nebbiolo d'Alba in
quality.  

**Orbello** r. dr. ★★ 84 85 86  
Soft, fruity wine of good body from Nebbiolo with Bonarda, Vespolina
and Croatina grown at Bramaterra in the Vercelli hills. Drink in 2–4
years.  
Luigi Perazzi      Sella Bramaterra  

**Ornato** r. dr. 82 83 85 86  
Nebbiolo with Barbera aged in barriques, this experiment by Pio Boffa
showed real promise.  
Pio Cesare  

**Pelaverga** p. dr. ★★ DYA  
Prickly pale ruby wine with a scent of currants and spices made from the
few surviving vines of the Pelaverga variety, near Saluzzo and Verduno.  
Bel Colle      Castello di Verduno  

**Piccone** r. dr. ★★ 82 83 85 86  
Sturdy red, similar to Lessona but less imposing, from Nebbiolo,
Vespolina, and Bonarda grown at Lessona in the Vercelli hills.  
Sella Lessona

**Pinot** or **Pinot delle Langhe**
Both dark and light Pinot were once well known in Piedmont, but now
few vines can be found, mostly around Alba. New plantings should soon
result in interesting wines – red, rosé, white, still, and sparkling. Cascina
del Drago's Pinot Nero is smooth, fruity, something like a Rully in style,
to drink in 2–4 years. Fontanafredda's white Pinot delle Langhe is made
from Pinot Nero primarily with some Pinot Bianco and Grigio grown at
Serralunga d'Alba. Pale straw green, flowery with good fruit-acid
balance, it is best in a year or two. Fontanafredda's fine sparkling Brut
Gattinera and Contessa Rosa also originate there. See Spumante.

**Roero** DOC r. dr. 85 86
New category for red from Nebbiolo with 2–5% white Arneis grown in
the Roeri hills north of the Tanaro River near Alba. Growers may still
opt to produce Nebbiolo d'Alba (see) or Roero and since it was not yet
clear what the choices would be, producers are listed under Nebbiolo
d'Alba DOC. The zone, noted historically for Nebbiolo and Arneis,
makes enviously attractive red wines, good young, sometimes capable of
aging beyond 5–6 years.

**Rouchet**
See Ruchè di Castagnole Monferrato.

**Rubino di Cantavenna** DOC r. dr. ** DYA
Little-known DOC of Barbera with Grignolino and Freisa grown in the
Monferrato Casalese at Cantavenna. The wine is noted for its youthful
vigor and fresh flavor.
C.S. di Cantavenna

**Ruchè di Castagnole Monferrato** r. dr. **→*** 78 79 82 83 85 86
Rare and inimitable red from a vine of mysterious origin known as
Ruchè or Rochè or Rouchet grown in high vineyards above Castagnole
Monferrato. Producers have requested DOC. Scarpa's Rouchet is a
strong, ruby-violet wine with bold structure, blossomy bouquet and
peculiar elegance after 4–5 years.
Scarpa

**Sizzano** DOC r. dr. ⟦**⟧ 78 79 80 82 83 85 86
Limited production red from Nebbiolo at 40–60% with Vespolina and
Bonarda grown around Sizzano in the Novara hills. Robust, with fine
Nebbiolo bouquet, it lasts a decade from top vintages.
Ag. 3 yrs (2 in barrel).

| | |
|---|---|
| Giuseppe Bianchi | Guido Ponti |
| C.S. di Sizzano e Ghemme | Ercolina Zanetta |

**Spanna** r. dr. ⟦*→***⟧ 70 71 74 78 79 80 82 83 85 86
The name for Nebbiolo in the Novara-Vercelli hills is applied to many
unclassified wines, some mediocre, some superb, with life spans that may
range beyond 10 years to 30 or 40. Though these could be made of
Spanna alone, they most probably contain other wine from southern
regions that give body, strength, color, and longevity even to wines from
medium vintages. Indeed, the best Spanna can rival the best Gattinara
in every way – except authenticity. The exotically labeled Spanna
Campi Raudii and Traversagna bottlings of Antonio Vallana & Figlio
have provided unsurpassed bargains in aged wines, occasionally of
⟦****⟧ quality.

| | |
|---|---|
| Antoniolo (Santachiara) | Francoli |
| Guido Barra & Figlio | Luigi & Italo Nervi |
| Antonio Brugo | Ermanno Rivetti |
| Ermanno Conti | Travaglini |
| Luigi Dessilani & Figli | Antonio Vallana & Figlio |
| Luigi Ferrando | Villa Era |

**Spumante** non-DOC w. (p.) dr. (s/sw.) sp. **→****
Piedmont produces a dazzling array of sparkling wines beyond Asti
Spumante and other DOCs from Brachetto, Cortese, Malvasia and even
Nebbiolo. They are increasingly either *brut* or off-dry and whether made
by *charmat* or *champenoise* tend to favor Pinot and Chardonnay grapes,
often from Lombardy's Oltrepò Pavese or Trentino-Alto Adige.
Riesling and Sauvignon are also used. Results can be first rate, notably
those made by *méthode champenoise* – used for over a century in Piedmont
– and marked (m.c.).

- **Azzurra Blanc de Blancs, Bon Sec, Cinzano Brut (m.c.), Marone Cinzano Pas Dosé (m.c.), Pinot Chardonnay, Pinot Nature, Principe di Piemonte Riserva, Sauvignon Cremant**
Cinzano
- **Banfi Brut (m.c.), Banfi Brut Pinot**
Villa Banfi-Strevi
- **Bosca Anniversary (m.c.), Bosca Riserva del Nonno (m.c.)**
Luigi Bosca & Figli
- **Bruno Giacosa Extra Brut (m.c.)**
Bruno Giacosa
- **Brut Gattinera (m.c.), Contessa Rosa Brut and Rosé (m.c.), Nobel Sec, Pinot Spumante Brut**
Fontanafredda
- **Conte Balduino Extra Brut (m.c.), Nature de Pupitre Extra Brut (m.c.), President Reserve Extra Secco and Rosé, Riserva Privata Angelo Riccadonna (m.c.)**
Riccadonna
- **Calissano Brut (m.c.), Realbrut (m.c.)**
Calissano
- **Chardonnay Brut, Gancia di Gancia, Gancia Extra Brut, Gran Crémant Riserva Vallarino Gancia (m.c.), Gran Cuvé Carlo Gancia (m.c.), Pinot di Pinot, Sauvignon Brut**
Fratelli Gancia
- **Contratto Bacco d'Oro (m.c.), Contratto Brut (m.c.), Imperial Riserva Sabauda (m.c.), Reserve for England (m.c.), Riserva Novecento (m.c.)**
Contratto
- **Cora Brut, Royal Ambassador Brut Blanc de Blancs (m.c.)**
Cora
- **Gilardino Brut (m.c.)**
Gilardino
- **Granduca Brut (m.c.)**
Granduca-Duca d'Asti
- **La Giustiniana Nature (m.c.)**
La Giustiniana
- **Riesling Spumante, Riserva Montelera (m.c.)**
Martini & Rossi
- **Spumante Pados (m.c.)**
Soldati-La Scolca
- **Valentino Brut (m.c.), Riserva Elena Nature (m.c.)**
Podere Rocche dei Manzoni-Valentino

**Verbesco** w. dr. ** DYA
Recently conceived light white (10% alcohol) produced by five prominent firms from about two-thirds dark grapes (mainly Barbera) processed using modern low temperature techniques. The result is facile and fizzy.

Bersano                               Marchesi di Barolo
Contratto                             Volpi
Duca d'Asti

**Vermouth**
Piedmont is the world center of vermouth, which by law must contain at least 70% wine in intricate and often secret blends with herbs, spices and other natural flavorings. The industry, based in Turin, Asti, and Canelli, now usually employs wines from other regions.

**Villa Pattono** r. dr. *** 82 83 85
Renato Ratti's unique blend of Barbera with Freisa and Uvalino grown at Costigliole d'Asti, this is aged in small barrels of French oak into a special *vino da tavola*, freshly fruity and mouth filling but promising more graceful bouquet with 4–8 years of aging.
Villa Pattono (Ratti)

**Vinòt** r. dr. *** DYA
The first *vino novello* of Italy to be vinified using carbonic maceration – and arguably still the best in a crowded field. Made from Nebbiolo, it has fruity freshness with exceptional balance. Drink cool within 3 months.
Gaja

# Wine & Food

Piedmontese cooking, like robust red wine, comes into its own in the autumn. Hearty, almost chauvinistically traditional, it is refined country cooking that follows the seasons, and fall provides the bounty. There is game from the mountainsides; hams, cheeses and salame matured to perfection; and a bright array of garden vegetables augmented by what is found in woods and fields. The multitude of antipasto, the ample pastas and risottos, thick soups and stews, roast and boiled meats, is the kind of fare which requires generous red wines. But the heartiness can be deceptive, for Piedmontese cooking has touches of grace distinct from, but equal to, the artistry of the provincial cooking of Burgundy and Lyonnais. The ultimate luxury is the white truffle, sniffed out by mongrels in the Langhe and shaved raw over pastas, risottos, meats, and fondues. Some of the best Piedmontese restaurants are found where the best wines are, and the time to visit is when the grapes and truffles are coming in.

**Bagna caôda** "Hot bath" of oil, garlic, and anchovies bubbling over a burner into which raw vegetables – peppers, cardoons, fennel, celery, etc. – are dipped.
  ** Freisa *secco* or ** Barbera, young and sharp.

**Brasato al Barolo** Beef marinated and stewed slowly in Barolo.
  ***→**** Barolo, well aged.

**Bollito misto alla piemontese** Boiled veal and beef, including brains and tongue, with *bagnet piemontese*, a garlicky green sauce.
  ** Boca or ** Fara.

**Camoscio alla piemontese** Chamois in a savory stew.
  *** Carema or *** Lessona.

**Capretto arrosto** Richly seasoned roast kid.
  ***→**** Barbaresco.

**Finanziera** Leftover meat and poultry together in a type of stew.
  ** Nebbiolo or ** Dolcetto.

**Fonduta** Cheese fondue based on *fontina*, often used as a sauce for pasta or risotto, and sometimes topped with shaved truffles.
  *** Dolcetto d'Alba or *** Bricco del Drago.

**Fritto misto** or **fricia** Elaborate delicacies – brains, sweetbreads, lamb cutlets, chicken breasts, eggplant, zucchini, mushrooms, frogs' legs, sweet pastes, etc. – dipped in batter and fried.
  ** Barbera or ** Freisa *secco*.

**Insalata di carne cruda** Minced filet of beef marinated briefly with oil, lemon, and pepper, sometimes served with fine sliced mushrooms, Parmesan or truffles.
  *** Dolcetto or *** Nebbiolo.

**Lepre al sivè** "Jugged hare," marinated in wine and flavorings and stewed to rich tenderness.
  *** Gattinara or *** Carema.

**Panna cotta** Fresh cream molded with burned sugar like a crème caramel but more luxurious.
  *** Asti or *** Moscato d'Asti.

**Tajarin al tartufo** Hand-cut egg noodles with butter, Parmesan, and shaved truffles.
  **** Gavi dei Gavi.

**Tapulon** Ground donkey meat cooked with red wine, cabbage, and seasonings.
  *** Spanna or *** Ghemme.

**Tome** or **tume** Small, round sheep's milk cheeses from the Langhe, mild when young, sharp when aged.
  **→*** Dolcetto (young cheese), *** Nebbiolo (aged).

**Zabaglione** Egg yolks whipped with Marsala, other sweet wine or Barolo.
  *** Caluso Passito or *** Asti.

## Restaurants

Recommended in or near wine zones: **Alba-Langhe-Roero** *Cesare* at Alberetto Torre; *La Villa* at Guarene; *Bel Sit* and *Belvedere* at La Morra; *Il Giardino di Felicin* at Monforte; *La Contea* at Neive; *Al Castello* at Santa Vittoria d'Alba. **Asti-Monferrato** *Parisio* at Acqui Terme; *Gener Neuv* and *Il Vicoletto* at Asti; *La Torre* at Casale Monferrato; *San Marco* at Canelli; *Da Beppe* at Cioccaro di Penango; *Da Guido* at Costigliole d'Asti; *Il Cascinale* at Isola d'Asti. **Gavi-Ovada** *Cantine del Gavi* at Gavi; *Da Pietro* at Ovada; *La Pace* at San Cristoforo di Gavi. **Novara-Vercelli hills** *Pinocchio* at Borgomanero; *Due Camin* at Gattinara; *Al Soriso* at Soriso.

# Sardinia
## Sardegna

Off by itself in mid-Mediterranean, Sardinia has every reason to remain the most idiosyncratic of Italian regions. Its wines express the island's character to the letter. Several varieties are unique in Italy, brought by Phoenicians, Carthaginians, Romans, and Spaniards in particular. But over the centuries the climate (which is temperate rather than hot) and soil of the Mediterranean's second-largest island changed their nature while Sardinian concepts of taste gave them styles entirely their own.

Sardinian tastes have been changing, along with the methods which quickly revolutionized winemaking here. Though still a source of blending wines, Sardinia has become an increasingly noticed supplier of light, fresh, balanced vintages that appeal to contemporary palates. But novelties include too many punchless lightweights. Fortunately, change hasn't swept away all the old-style character. The most typical Sardinian wines, whether sweet, semisweet, or dry, are still strong in constitution: the Sherry-like Vernaccia di Oristano, Malvasia di Bosa, and Nasco di Cagliari; the Port-like Cannonau, Monica di Cagliari and Girò di Cagliari; and the aromatic Moscatos of Cagliari and Sorso-Sennori.

But the trend is irreversibly toward dry wines of moderate strength. Nuragus, introduced by the Phoenicians and named after the *nuraghe*, the island's prehistoric conical stone towers, is the most popular of DOC wines, though the modern neutrality of this white from Cagliari's fertile Campidano plains doesn't make

**Wine Zones**

1 Campidano di Terralba
2 Carignano di Sulcis
3 Girò di Cagliari
4 Malvasia di Bosa
5 Malvasia di Cagliari
6 Mandrolisai
7 Monica di Cagliari
8 Moscato di Cagliari
9 Moscato di Sorso-
   Sennori
10 Nasco di Cagliari
11 Nuragus di Cagliari
12 Vermentino di Gallura
13 Vernaccia di Oristano

it the most impressive. Vermentino, from northern Sardinia (from where most of Italy's corks come), has winning character, as does the non-DOC Torbato di Alghero. Among reds, the dry versions of Cannonau, Monica, and Carignano del Sulcis combine power with occasional finesse.

As elsewhere in the Mezzogiorno, wine production is centered in cooperatives, though here at least they seem to function. But the pacesetter remains Sella & Mosca, a privately owned firm at Alghero, one of Europe's largest wine estates. *L'Enoteca Cagliaritana* at Cagliari has a wide choice of the islands wines.

## Recent vintages

Few Sardinian wines require long aging, though Vernaccia di Oristano and other strong dessert or aperitif wines can last for years. Recommended vintages appear with each entry.

**Abbaia** r. dr.  **★★**  85 86
Vivid ruby table wine from Pascale di Cagliari and other grapes grown around Monti in NE Sardinia. Very dry, warm, and amply scented, it has attractive *gout de terroir* when young.
C.S. del Vermentino

**Anghelu Ruju** r. sw.  **★★★**  NV
From semidried Cannonau grapes grown near Alghero, this rich, authoritative dessert wine is named after a nearby *nuraghe*. Bright ruby-violet when young, it develops a garnet-brick color after 2–3 years in barrel and another 5 or more in bottle. It has a heady bouquet of berries and spices, and warm, lingering elegance with 18% alcohol.
Sella & Mosca

**Aragosta**
See Vermentino.

**Arborea** DOC r. p. w. (s/sw.) (fz.) 85 86
New and unproven DOC for red and rosé from Sangiovese and white from Trebbiano, the latter also possibly *frizzante* or *amabile*.

**Campidano di Terralba** DOC r. dr.  **★**  85 86
Ruby-crimson wine based on Bovale grapes grown in the Campidano plain S of Oristano around Terralba. Dry and soft, becoming round and tasty within 2 years.
C.S. del Campidano                    C.S. di Arborea

**Cannonau**
Non-DOC wines from Cannonau abound in Sardinia under various names, dry or sweet, usually red, but also rosé and even white. Some dry reds don't qualify as DOC because they have been kept less than the required year in wood or are held under 13.5%. Some of Sardinia's best Cannonau are not DOC: Anghelu Ruju (see above), Cannonau del Goceano, Cannonau del Parteolla, Cannonau di Alghero, Cannonau Marmilla, Le Bombarde, Perda Rubia, and Rosso di Dorgali.

**Cannonau di Sardegna** DOC r. p. dr. s/sw.  **★→★★★**  82 83 85 86
Many-faceted DOC from Cannonau grown throughout the region. The basic red *secco* must have 13.5%; it can be drunk after the required year in barrel when it is richly robust, warm, and complete. With 3–6 years of age, the red (whether *riserva* or not) can show considerable grace as a classic *vino da arrosto*. Despite its strength, Cannonau is not generally aged very long. The *superiore* must have 15% and can be either *secco*, *amabile* or *dolce*, depending on residual sugars. *Liquoroso*, fortified with wine alcohol, must have 18% whether *secco* or *dolce naturale*. Sweet versions can show notable, Port-like class. Cannonau from Oliena (near Nuoro) and Capo Ferrato (in SE Sardinia) may carry those subdenominations.
Ag. 1 yr in barrel; *superiore* 2 yrs; *riserva* 3 yrs.

C.S. di Dorgali                        C.S. Sorso-Sennori
C.S. di Jerzu                          Cossu (Casa della Vernaccia)
C.S. di Oliena                         Fratelli Deiana
C.S. Dolianova                         Sella & Mosca

**Carignano del Sulcis** DOC r. (p.) dr. ★→★★  82 83 85 86
Red and rosé from Carignano grown on the isles of Sant'Antioco and
San Pietro and the SW corner of the main island called Sulcis by the
Carthaginians. The *rosso* is good young or, if *invecchiato*, aged 3–6 years.
Both are fairly robust, garnet-hued wines, amply scented, dry, warm,
generous, and spicy. Sardus Pater of C.S. di Sant'Antioco is a superior
*rosso*. The *rosato* is smooth and balanced when young.
Ag. *invecchiato* 1 yr.
C.S. di Calasetta                C.S. di Sant'Antioco

**Girò di Cagliari** DOC r. dr. sw.  ★★  85 86
Rare, usually sweet red from Girò grown in the Campidano N of
Cagliari. The four versions – *secco* and *dolce* of 14–14.5%, and *liquoroso
secco* and *liquoroso dolce* of 17.5% – are used much as Port is. Bright ruby,
warm, and smooth, it is best in 2–3 years.
Ag. *riserva* 2 yrs (1 in barrel).
Vini Classici di Sardegna        Zedda Piras

**Malvasia di Bosa** DOC am. dr. s/sw. sw.  ★★→★★★  78 83 85 86
Prized dessert wine from Malvasia di Sardegna grown in coastal hills
near Bosa in W Sardinia. The best – Salvatore Deriu Mocci's *secco* – is
golden amber, suave in bouquet, with a flavor which is dry but rich and
has a toasted-almond finish. *Secco* and *dolce* must have 15%, *liquoroso secco*
and *dolce* 17.5%. Dry versions make fine aperitifs; the sweet are for
sipping after dinner. Good in 3–5 years, sometimes much more, this
expensive wine is rarely found outside the zone.
Ag. 2 yrs.
Mercedes Cau Secchi              Salvatore Deriu Mocci
Donchessa                       Fratelli Porcu

**Malvasia di Cagliari** DOC am. dr. s/sw. sw.  ★★  83 85 86
From Malvasia di Sardegna grown in the Campidano, this is a good
aperitif and dessert wine. There are *secco* and *dolce* of 14% and *liquoroso
secco* and *dolce* of 17.5%. The *secco* is best young; the *dolce* and *liquoroso*
may be kept a few years.
Ag. 8 months, *riserva* 2 yrs.
C.S. di Serramanna              Vini Classica di Sardegna
C.S. di Dolianova              Zedda Piras
C.S. Marmilla

**Malvasia di Planargia** am. dr.  ★★★  83 85 86
Virtually identical to Malvasia di Bosa *secco* and grown in the same zone
of the Planargia hills, this aperitif wine shows some elegance in 2–4
years.
Emilio & Gilberto Arru

**Mandrolisai** DOC r. p. dr.  ★  83 85 86
Red and rosé from Bovale Sardo, Cannonau, and Monica grown
around Sorgono in central Sardinia. The *rosso*, ruby, dry, and well
scented with a light bitter finish, is good in 2–3 years; the *rosato* is best
young.
Ag. *superiore* (*rosso*) 2 yrs. (1 in barrel.)
C.S. di Samughero              C.S. di Sorgono Atzara

**Monica di Cagliari** DOC r. dr. s/sw.  ★→★★  83 85 86
From Monica grown in the Campidano, the wines are more often sweet
than dry. Light ruby, soft, and delicate in scent, the *secco* and *dolce* must
have 14% and 14.5%. The *liquoroso secco* and *dolce*, of pronounced aroma
and flavor, have 17.5%.
Ag. *liquoroso riserva* 2 yrs.
C.S. del Campidano            Zedda Piras
C.S. di Villacidro

**Monica di Sardegna** DOC r. dr. (s/sw.) (fz.)  ★★  82 83 85 86
Usually dry, this wine is made in quantity from Monica grown
throughout Sardinia. Bright ruby, supple, medium in body, its bouquet
develops in 3–4 years. *Amabile* and *frizzante* versions are permitted.
Ag. *superiore* 1 yr in barrel.
C.S. del Campidano            C.S. Dolianova
C.S. di Marrubiu             C.S. Marmilla
C.S. di Sant'Antioco         Cossu-Casa della Vernaccia
C.S. di Serramanna           Vini Classici di Sardegna
C.S. di Villacidro           Zedda Piras

**Moscato di Cagliari** DOC w. sw. *→** 82 83 85 86
Desert wines from Moscato grown in the Campidano. The *dolce* has
15%, the *liquoroso dolce* 17.5%. The latter has deeper golden color, more
pronounced Muscat aroma, and smoother, richer texture.
Ag. *liquoroso riserva* 1 yr.
C.S. Dolianova                     Vini Classici di Sardegna
C.S. Marmilla

**Moscato di Sardegna** DOC w. s/sw. sp. *→** DYA
Recent DOC for *spumante* from Moscato grown in designated vineyards
throughout Sardinia. Aromatic, fairly sweet, fruity, and bright straw
yellow, it bears a family resemblance to Asti. Moscato from Tempio
Pausania (or Tempio) and Gallura can use these subdenominations.
C.S. Gallura

**Moscato di Sorso-Sennori** DOC w. sw. ** DYA
Limited production Moscato grown around Sorso and Sennori N of
Sassari. Of golden hue, it is rich (15%) and luscious with full aroma,
especially pronounced in the fortified *liquoroso dolce.*
C.S. Sorso-Sennori

**Nasco di Cagliari** DOC w. dr. s/sw. sw. ** 85 86
From the ancient Nasco grown in the Campidano, this may be dry,
semisweet or sweet in both the normal (14–14.5%) and *liquoroso*
(16.5–17.5%) categories. It can resemble Sherry after wood-aging, but
it is most distinctive as a lighter, drier wine with some youthful
fruitiness.
Ag. *riserva* 2 yrs in barrel.
C.S. di Quartu Sant'Elena          C.S. Dolianova
C.S. di Villacidro

**Nièddera** r. dr. ** 83 85 86
From Nièddera grapes of the Tirso valley near Oristano, this rare red is
very dry, strong but smooth, and fruity, best in 3–4 years.
Contini                            Cossu-Casa della Vernaccia

**Nuragus di Cagliari** DOC w. dr. (s/sw.) (fz.) *→** DYA
Sardinia's dominant DOC (more than 3 million liters a year), Nuragus
prevails in the Campidano. Pale straw green, dry, and neutral in scent
and flavor, it is appreciated with fish. *Amabile* and *frizzante* versions are
permitted.
C.S. del Montiferru                C.S. Dolianova
C.S. di Marrubiu                   C.S. Il Nuraghe
C.S. di Santadi                    C.S. Marmilla
C.S. di Serramanna                 Vini Classici di Sardegna
C.S. di Villacidro

**Rosé di Alghero** p. dr. ** DYA
Consistently good pink from Cannonau and Sangiovese grown near
Alghero. Light, flowery, fresh and graceful, it is best inside a year.
Sella & Mosca

**Rosso di Berchidda** r. dr. ** 83 85 86
From Pascale, Cannonau, and others grown around Berchidda in N
Sardinia. Bright ruby, with well-rounded fruitiness and flowery
bouquet, it is good in 3–5 years. A *rosato* is made as well.
C.S. Cooperativa Giogantinu

**Torbato di Alghero** w. dr. (sp.) *** DYA
This table wine from Torbato grapes grown near Alghero is Sardinia's
finest white, in the Vigna Terre Bianche special vineyard bottling. Pale
straw green, fragrant, it has exceptional balance of fruit, acid and
alcohol and crisp, clean finish. A *spumante* is also convincing.
Sella & Mosca

**Vermentino**
Several of Sardinia's better whites are table wines from Vermentino.
Basically dry, styles vary from rather rich, golden-yellow wines aged to
full flavor and bouquet to pale, sprightly, youthful whites. The most
impressive are Vermentino di Alghero of Sella & Mosca, Aragosta of the
C.S. Riforma Agraria di Alghero and Giovanni Cherchi's Vermentino
di Usini.

**Vermentino di Gallura** DOC w. dr. ★→⭐⭐ DYA
From Vermentino grown on the Gallura peninsula and nearby areas. Traditionally strong, rich in flavor and low in acid, as exemplified by the *superiore* of 13.5%, the old style can be tasted in the Aghiloia of the C.S. del Vermentino and the *superiore* of the C.S. Cooperativa Giogantinu. The trend is toward lighter, fruitier, crisper wines to go with fish, as noted in the S'Éleme of the C.S. del Vermentino.

**Vernaccia di Oristano** DOC am. dr. (sw.) ★★→★★★ 71 74 75 77 79 81 83
The glory of Sardinia, this Sherry-like wine is made from overripe Vernaccia grapes grown in the Tirso River basin near Oristano. Vinification resembles the *solera* of Sherry, but Vernaccia's processing involves distinct steps that need at least 2 years to complete. The best Vernaccias are the *superiore* and *riserva*, which require long wood-aging. Unfortified but strong (15% or more), this natural Vernaccia is bone dry with hints of almond blossom on the nose and a lightly bitter, acidic, woody flavor with a long finish. It needs 5 years, or considerably more, of age. Contini's is exemplary. The fortified *liquoroso dolce* and *liquoroso secco* are richer and stronger (16.5%–18%) but not as refined as the others.
Ag. 2 yrs in barrel; *superiore* 3 yrs in barrel; *riserva* 4 yrs in barrel.

| | |
|---|---|
| Atzori | Josto Puddu |
| Silvio Carta | Sella & Mosca |
| Contini | Sardinian Gold-C.S. della |
| Cossu-Casa della Vernaccia | Vernaccia |
| Pietro Madau | Fratelli Serra |
| Produttori Riuniti | Fratelli Zoncu |

*Wine & Food*

Though the island's population has shifted from the hills to the coast in recent times, the "real" Sardinian cooking is that of the back country and the open hearth: sucking pig, lamb, kid, soups of fava beans and barley, the ravioli-like *culingiones*, the piquant *pecorino sardo* and, most of all, the breads. It has been said that every Sardinian village has a bread of its own. The most sung about is *pane carasau*, also known as "music paper," because, unleavened, it is that thin. Fish on the menu is a relatively recent exploitation of a source that was always there in the deep waters off the island's rocky coasts. Almost every Mediterranean species can be savored, sometimes together in the lavish fish soup known as *cassòla*.

**Agnello con finocchietti** Lamb stewed with onion, tomato, and fennel.
    ★★★ Cannonau di Sardegna *secco*
**Aragosta arrosta** Rock lobster grilled.
    ★★★ Aragosta or ★★★ Torbato di Alghero.
**Bottarga** Dried mullet eggs sliced thin on toast or in salad.
    ★★★ Vernaccia di Oristano *superiore* or *riserva*.
**Favata** Rich stew of fava beans and pork.

    ★★ Monica di Sardegna
**Malloreddus** Tiny gnocchi of semolina, dressed with meat or tomato sauce and grated *pecorino*.
    ★ Cannonau *rosato*.
**Porceddu** Sucking pig spit roasted slowly on an open fire.
    ★★★ Cannonau di Oliena.
**Sebadas** or **seadas** Pastry with cheese and bitter honey.
    ★★ Moscato di Sorso-Sennori.
**Su farru** Mint and barley soup.
    ★★ Vermentino di Gallura *superiore*

### Restaurants
Recommended: **North** *Al Tuguri* and *Rafel* at Alghero; *Da Franco* at Palau; *Il Senato* at Sassari; *Canne al Vento-Da Brancaccio* at Santa Teresa Gallura. **Center** *Sa Funtà* at Cabras; *Su Gologone* near Oliena; *Da Giovanni* and *Il Faro* at Oristano. **South** *Antica Hostaria*, *Dal Corsaro* and *Ottagono* at Cagliari; *Is Morus* at Pula; *Su Meriagu* at Quartu Sant'Elena.

# Sicily

Sicilia

The revolution in Italian wine has unfolded most dramatically in Sicily, where in 20 years, from a step beyond medieval, enology has leapt headlong into the future. But the regional program which has transformed vineyards and cooperative wineries beyond recognition could hardly be labeled a resounding success. Nowhere are surpluses more voluminous than in Sicily, where production reached 1.3 billion liters in 1983, the record for an Italian region. Less than 3% is DOC.

Still, wine drinkers have much to savor in Sicily's conversion. Not long ago, light, dry, fruity wines were the exception; now they're the rule. Even those potent dessert and aperitif wines, such as Marsala and Moscato, which have long been the island's forte, have improved remarkably. The most qualified products are awarded the region's Q for quality.

Production is concentrated in Sicily's westernmost province of Trapani, which turns out more wine than do most Italian regions. Besides three DOCs – Marsala, Alcamo, and Moscato di Pantelleria – Trapani generates awesome amounts of blending and table wines, which often end up in storage in the province's 50 cooperatives. One problem is that Sicilians drink less wine per

**Wine Zones**
1 Faro
2 Regaleali

capita (under 50 liters a year) than do other Italians, so markets are by definition distant.

Sicily, Italy's largest region and the Mediterranean's largest island, still bears the stamps of Greeks, Arabs, Normans, Spaniards, and all manner of other peoples who imposed their wills and ways here. The major Greek ruins are at Siracusa (Syracuse), Agrigento, Segesta, and Erice – all conveniently near wine zones. Palermo, the capital and busiest port, and nearby Monreale with its cathedral, are on the edge of the Marsala and Alcamo zones. The active volcano of Mt Etna has a DOC zone on its lower slopes. The volcanic Lipari or Aeolian Islands are also noted for wine.

The *Enoteca Miceli* in Palermo has an impressive array of wines.

## Recent vintages

Sicily's temperate to torrid climate permits fairly consistent harvests, though drought can be a problem in non-irrigated areas and high altitude vineyards can suffer from cold and damp. Recommended vintages appear with each entry.

**Ala** r.–am. sw. ★★★ NV
From semidried grapes of Nero d'Avola, Perricone, and Frappato vinified in an old way and fortified, it has intense aroma from barrels of bitter cherry wood. Warm, rich, with unique bittersweet flavor and amber-red color, its strength (19%) permits it to last for decades.
Duca di Salaparuta

**Alcamo** or **Bianco Alcamo** DOC w. dr. ★→★★★ DYA
Dry white based on Catarratto Bianco from a large zone of W Sicily with axis in the town of Alcamo. Pale straw green, neutral in odor and flavor, bone dry, yet rather soft. Better examples have a hint of fruit and crispness. Rapitalà and Rincione can show real character.

| | |
|---|---|
| Baronati Normanni-Rallo | Martinico & Figli |
| C.S. Paladino | Fratelli Montalto |
| Cooperative Agricola Aurora | Rapitalà-Conte de la Gatinais |
| Duca di Castelmonte-Pellegrino | Tenuta Rincione-Papè |
| Gebbia-D'Angelo Vini | Virzi-C.S. Sant'Antonio |

**Ambrato di Comiso** am. s/sw. sw.
Curious amber wine from Frappato di Vittoria and other grapes, strengthened by cooked musts that gave a caramel-like flavor and light sweetness. Once a DOC candidate, it now seems headed for extinction.

**Carboj** r. p. w. ★→★★ 83 84 85 86
Brand name for table wines from Sciacca in SW Sicily. Rosso di Sciacca is most impressive. From Barbera with Nero d'Avola and Nerello Mascalese, it is bright garnet, generous in scent and body with rustic goodness that improves with 2–5 years. Rosato di Sciacca, from the same grapes and the white Trebbiano di Sicilia are table wines to drink young.
C.S. Enocarboj

**Cerasuolo di Vittoria** DOC r. dr. ★★ 83 84 85 86
Cherry-red wine from Calabrese and Frappato grown around Vittoria in SE Sicily. Light red, almost rosé, it can take a few years of aging, though when drunk young and on the cool side it is fragrant with good body and balance despite strength (13% or more). Production is still very limited. See also Stravecchio Siciliano.

| | |
|---|---|
| Giuseppe Coria | Biagio Giudice |

**Cerdèse** r. p. w. dr. ★→★★ 83 84 85 86
Table wines made at Cerda near Palermo. The rosso, from Nerello Mascalese and Perricone, is the best of the trio, structured, rounded and refined in 3–4 years. The *rosato* and *bianco* are refreshing young.
Fontanarossa

**Corvo**
Brand name applied to several wines made by Duca di Salaparuta at Casteldaccia from grapes gathered in various parts of the island.
– **Corvo Bianco** w. dr. ★★→★★★ DYA
Made from the free-run musts of Inzolia, Trebbiano, and Catarratto, there are two versions. Marca Verde Prima Goccia has a light straw-gold color with medium body and refined, balanced flavor. Colomba Platino is more delicate in color, odor, and flavor – to drink very young. Though the grapes may not be the noblest, for consistency of results in Sicily's climate, Corvo whites are admirable.
– **Corvo Rosso** r. dr. ★★★ 78 79 80 81 82 83 84 85 86
From Nerello Mascalese, Perricone, and Nero d'Avola, this red is

remarkably consistent. Dark ruby with orange highlights, generous and smooth, with bouquet developing after barrel and bottle age.

**– Corvo Spumante** w. dr. s/sw. sp.  ** DYA
Good *charmat* sparklers from the same grapes as Corvo *bianco*. The Brut, dry and refreshing, makes a good aperitif. The Demi-sec, soft and lightly sweet, goes well with fruit.

**– Corvo Stravecchio di Sicilia** am. dr.  *** NV
Fortified wine from Inzolia, Catarratto, and Grillo aged for years in barrels to refined, dry, amber-gold richness with exquisite bouquet.
Duca di Salaparuta

**Donnafugata** r. p. w. dr.  **→***  85 86
Table wines from the Belice valley in central Sicily, the *rosso* is rather full and well balanced, suited to 5–6 years of aging. The *rosato* is light but stylish when young. The *bianco* is the best of the trio with a perfumed fruitiness and subtly refined flavor. The white Damaschino is delicately lively. Baronessa Anca and Gemme brands are also used.
Tenuta Donnafugata-Rallo

**Draceno** r. p. w.  *→ **  83 85 86
Table wines from the Belice valley near Partanna in W Sicily. The *rosso*, based on Perricone, is deep garnet, strong, amply scented, robustly dry with a bitter background, to drink in 3–5 years. The *rosato*, also from Perricone, is refreshing young. The *bianco*, from Catarratto, is delicately fruity yet vivacious, the most attractive of the trio.
C.S. Saturnia

**Eloro di Casale** r. dr.  **  82 83 84 85 86
Good red from Nero d'Avola grown at Noto in SE Sicily. Ample in body, fine in bouquet, its ruby-violet color turns garnet with age.
A. Modica di San Giovanni

**Etna** DOC r. p. w. dr  *→ ***  82 83 85 86
The three types of wine made in this zone on the E slopes of Mt Etna benefit from cool climate with plenty of sunshine. The *rosso*, from Nerello Mascalese, dominates production. Deep ruby tending to garnet, with 3–4 years or more it develops deep bouquet and warm, full-bodied flavor with sound equilibrium. The *rosato*, also from Nerello Mascalese, is a versatile meal wine. The *bianco*, from Carricante and Catarratto, is straw gold, fresh in scent, dry, and delicate. The *bianco superiore*, grown in the community of Milo and containing at least 80% Carricante, is fruitier, somewhat stronger, and more elegant. Only Villagrande makes *superiore*.

| | |
|---|---|
| Baronati Normanni-Rallo | Solicchiata-C.S. di Torrepalino |
| Berbero-Vignaioli Etnei | Villagrande |
| Linguaglossa-Le Vigne dell'Etna | Villa Iolanda |

**Faro** DOC r. dr.  ** 83 84 85 86
Red based on Nerello grown at the island's NE tip around Messina. Ruby taking on brick tones with 3–5 years, it develops lovely bouquet and finesse. Unfortunately, very little is made.
Ag. 1 yr.

| | |
|---|---|
| Bagni | Spinasanta |

**Faustus** r. p. w.  ** 82 83 85 86
Brand name for three wines made at Casteldaccia, E of Palermo, by Giuseppe Mazzetti. The *rosso*, from Nero d'Avola, Nerello Mascalese, and Perricone, is garnet, full-bodied, with attractive herb-like bouquet after 3–5 years. The *rosato*, from the same dark grapes with a little light Inzolia, is lively and fragrant. The *bianco*, from Inzolia, is pale greenish and dry.
Azienda Vinicola Grotta

**Frappato di Vittoria** r. dr.  ** 82 83 84 85 86
Rich amber-red wine from Frappato grapes grown at Vittoria in SE Sicily. Grapy and lively young, it transforms to a slightly maderized aperitif wine with age.
Giordano

**Grecanico di Sicilia** w. dr.  ** DYA
From Grecanico grapes grown in the Marsala zone, this bright, straw-yellow table wine is faintly scented, clean, and dry, good young.

| | |
|---|---|
| Fratelli Montalto | Carlo Pellegrino |

**Grottarossa** r. p. w. dr. ** DYA
Table wines from the Colli Nesseni near Caltanissetta designed to drink
within a year or two. The red is sturdy and smooth, the white and rosé
fruity, zesty, refreshing.
C.S. Enopolio di Caltanissetta

**Inzolia di Samperi** sw. *** NV
Elegant white from Inzolia grown around Marsala, barrel aged to a
refined, velvety sweetness that retains more flowery freshness and fruit
flavors than its more elaborate neighbors.
De Bartoli

**Libecchio** w. dr. ** DYA
Recently conceived and highly publicized white from Trebbiano and
Inzolia made at Menfi. The truly distinguishing feature of this light,
crisp, blossomy wine is the label by Renato Guttuso.
Barone di Turolifi

**Luparello** p. dr. ** 84 85 86
Dark pink table wine from Calabrese grown near Pachino in SE Sicily.
Aged 2 years in oak, it is rich in nuance with hints of bitter and sweet.
Azienda Vitivinicola Luparello

**Malvasia delle Lipari** DOC am. s/sw. sw. ***→****
From local clones of Malvasia grown on the Lipari or Aeolian isles N of
Messina, this exquisite golden to amber wine comes in moderately
sweet, *passito* and *liquoroso* versions. The Capo Salina of Carlo Hauner is
in a class by itself with its Mediterranean floral sensations hinting at
apricots and citrus-worth sailing to the isle of Salina to experience.
Capo Salina (Hauner)                          Martingana

**Mamertino** am. s/sw. * NV
Antique wine of Messina, now made from semidried Catarratto,
Inzolia, and Grillo. Lightly sweet with a raisiny aroma and old-gold
color.
Spinasanta

**Marsala** DOC
Created for the English market in 1773 by John Woodhouse, Marsala
has since had its ups and downs. Recently its fortunes have revived
through new DOC rules to eliminate the flavored versions (with egg,
cream, coffee and other syrups) from the rolls and put the emphasis on
*superiore* and *vergine*, which can rank with the finest wines of their type.
These wines are increasingly prized for their heady wood-and-caramel
bouquets and luxuriantly rich, smooth, slightly burnished flavors,
whether bone dry or lusciously sweet. Most Marsala has an old gold to
amber color and is made from white Catarratto, Grillo and Inzolia
grapes grown in a vast zone of W Sicily in the provinces of Trapani,
Palermo and Agrigento. The new rules also permit the use of red
Perricone, Calabrese and Nerello Mascalese for ruby-amber colored
wines. The industry is based in the port of Marsala. Processes vary from
firm to firm, but often the natural wine is blended with *sifone* (sweet
wine and wine alcohol) and/or *cotto* (cooked down musts). Production of
some 20–35 million liters annually is not all sold as DOC. The five
categories take in some of the old commercial names and initials. Most
aging takes place in locally made wooden barrels.
– **Marsala Fine** am. (r.–am.) dr. s/sw. sw. *→*** NV
The common grade of 17% is made by blending base wine with more
*cotto* than *sifone*. Old names include Italy Particular (IP).
Ag. 1 yr.
– **Marsala Superiore** am. (r.-am.) dr. sw. **→**** NV
Regaining its lofty past reputation, this takes in the traditional Superior
Old Marsala (SOM), London Particular (LP), and Garibaldi Dolce
(GD). With 18% alcohol, it is blended by house formulas and can last
for decades. The sweet is rich and luscious, the dry is very dry with
aromas of wood, nuts, citrus and spices and a velvety yet austere flavor.
Ag. 2 yrs.
– **Marsala Superiore Riserva** am. (r.–am.) dr. sw. ***→**** NV
The same as the Superiore except that this is aged longer and can be
even more elegant.
Ag. 4 yrs.
– **Marsala Vergine** or **Soleras** am. (r.–am.) dr. ***→**** NV

The lightly fortified "virgin" product of 18% alcohol is the most prestigious. Dry to bone dry, it contains neither *sifone* or *cotto* but is blended from wines aged in barrels for different lengths of time, sometimes by the solera system of topping up the old with younger vintages though not necessarily. With its hues of amber and infinity of scents, it has the breed, tone and complexity to stand with the world's great aperitif wines. Some like it with strong or sharp cheeses. Ag. 5 yrs.

– **Marsala Vergine Stravecchio** or **Riserva** am. (r.–am.)
   dr.  \*\*\*→\*\*\*\* NV

Same as the Vergine or Soleras but aged longer and sometimes more refined. Wines for blending may be kept 20 years or more in barrels. Ag. 10 yrs.

| | |
|---|---|
| V. Giacalone Alloro & C. | Fratelli Mineo |
| Vito Curatolo Arini | Mirabella |
| De Bartoli | Fratelli Montalto |
| De Vita | Fratelli Oliva |
| Fratelli Fici | Carlo Pellegrino & C. |
| Florio & C | Diego Rallo & Figli |
| Ingham Whitaker & C. | Sala Spanò |
| Francesco Intorcia & Figli | Solero & Gill |
| Lilibeo | Woodhouse |
| Fratelli Martinez | |

**Moscato di Noto** DOC w. am. s/sw. sw. (sp.)  \*\* NV
From Moscato Bianco grown around Noto in SE Sicily, this dessert wine comes in three versions rarely seen in commerce. The basic Moscato is semisweet, fragrant, and golden, to drink young. The *spumante* is pale yellow, delicately sweet, and aromatic. The *liquoroso* of 22% is mellifluous and warm, with plush Muscat aroma.
Cantina Sperimentale di Noto

**Moscato di Pantelleria** DOC w. am. s/sw. sw. sp.  \*\*→\*\*\*\* NV
From Zibibbo (large Moscato) grapes grown on gnarled vines trained low in the volcanic soil of this island off the coast of Tunisia, Italy's most remote DOC zone. This most vaunted of Sicilian Moscatos has several styles. The basic Moscato di Pantelleria from normally ripe grapes has four types: *naturale* (softly sweet, fragrant, 12.5%), *naturalmente dolce* (richer, sweeter, 17.5%), *spumante naturale* (sparkling versions of the previous), and *liquoroso* (fortified with wine alcohol). Passito di Pantelleria from semidried grapes had three types: *naturalmente dolce* (14%), *liquoroso* (fortified to at least 21.5%), and *extra* (23.5%). All *passito* types are very sweet and rich. Much of the one million liter annual production is sold by the Agricoltori Associati cooperative whose *passito extra* is called Tanit and *spumante naturale* Solimano. De Bartoli's Bukkuram stands out.
Ag. *passito extra* 1 yr.
Agricoltori Associati di Pantelleria   Diego Rallo & Figli
Bukkuram-De Bartoli

**Moscato di Siracusa** DOC am. sw.
Why a DOC was granted to a wine no longer produced is puzzling. The zone comprises the community of Siracusa in SE Sicily where Moscato Bianco is prescribed for golden-yellow to amber, sweet wine of 16.5%.

**Moscato di Villa Fontane** w. sw.  \*\*
Dessert wine from Moscatello grown near Vittoria in SE Sicily. Golden, luscious, and richly aromatic, it can age a decade or more.
Giuseppe Coria

**Nerello Siciliano** r. dr.  \boxed{\*\*} 83 84 85 86
Generous, warm table wines from Nerello Mascalese grapes made in W Sicily become fairly smooth and refined with 3–5 years of age.
Marino                         Fratelli Montalto

**Pignatello** r. (p.) dr.  \*→\boxed{\*\*} 83 84 85 86
Table wines from the Pignatello (or Perricone) grape grown in W Sicily are usually red but sometimes rosé. The red can acquire an attractive bitter cherry aspect with 3–4 years of age.
Martinico & Figli            Carlo Pellegrino & C.

**Rapitalà**
See Alcamo.

**Regaleali** r. p. w. dr. ★★→★★★★ 78 79 80 81 82 83 84 85 86
Table wines firmly established among Sicily's elite originate in high
vineyards at Sclafani Bagni, SE of Palermo. The *rosso*, from Nerello
Mascalese and Perricone, is bright ruby, robust, soft, and scented after
3–4 years. The Rosso del Conte, a special reserve of the same grapes, is
more elegant and longer lived (a decade or more from some vintages),
perhaps Sicily's grandest red. The *rosato*, from the dark grapes, is
fragrant and classy when young. The *bianco*, from Catarratto, Inzolia,
and Sauvignon, is pale, clean, and as brisk and fruity as alpine whites.
The fine white Nozze d'Oro was created by owners Giuseppe and
Franca Tasca on their 50th anniversary.
Conte Tasca d'Almerita

**Rincione** r. p. w. dr. ★★ 83 84 85 86
Table wines from Calatafimi in W Sicily. The *rosso* and *rosato*, from Nero
d'Avola and Nerello Mascalese, are fine examples of their types. The
*bianco* is similar to Alcamo, but Trebbiano gives it more fruit and finesse.
Tenuta Rincione (Papè)

**Rosso di Menfi** r. dr. ★★ 83 84 85 86
Good red from Nerello Mascalese, Nero d'Avola and Sangiovese grown
near Menfi in S Sicily. Bright ruby, lightly scented, full and warm; best
in 2–5 years. The Settesoli cooperative also makes a Bianco di Menfi
and Feudo dei Fiori white of more than routine interest.
Bonera (C.S. Settesoli)

**Solicchiato Bianco di Villa Fontane** am. s/sw. ★★★
Unique dessert wine made near Vittoria in SE Sicily from light grapes
dried in the sun. After a year in barrel, it is golden, fruity, and
moderately sweet; after a decade it becomes amber and luxuriant.
Giuseppe Coria

**Solimano**
See Moscato di Pantelleria.

**Steri** r. w. dr. ★★→★★★ 80 81 82 83 84 85 86
Table wines from the Comarca di Naro E of Agrigento. The *bianco*, from
Trebbiano, Inzolia, and Vernaccia di San Gimignano, is light straw
yellow, mild in scent, and clean and fresh in flavor. The *rosso*, from Nero
d'Avola, Barbera, and Lambrusco, is bright ruby vermillion, soft, warm
and ample. Steri *riserva speciale*, from Lambrusco Salamino and Barbera,
is dense, rich in extract, and generous, singular among the island's reds.
Giuseppe Camilleri

**Stravecchio Siciliano di Villa Fontane** am. dr. ★★★ NV
Reserve wine from Cerasuolo grapes grown near Vittoria in SE Sicily is
aged 20, 30 years or more in casks, which makes it similar to very old dry
Sherry. A small quantity of wine from one barrel of this Stravecchio is
drawn off each year and replaced with new wine. This endless supply is
known as Perpetuo.
Giuseppe Coria

**Tanit**
See Moscato di Pantelleria.

**Vecchio Samperi** am. dr. ★★★→★★★★ NV
Practically a Marsala, made from the preferred Grillo grapes in the
DOC zone, but put through a personalized *solera* process that doesn't
conform to the norms (i.e., it is not fortified with alcohol). The Riserva
is a *solera* aged 20 years in wood.
De Bartoli

**Zibibbo**
This strain of large Moscato makes golden to amber dessert wines in
several parts of Sicily, notably Pantelleria.

*Wine & Food*

Sicily is the alleged cradle of all sorts of good things to eat, among
them pasta (unlikely, even if Italy's first such paste may have
been rolled here), innumerable sweets (including sherbet, thanks
to Etna's year-round snow), and various fish and vegetable

dishes. Fairly recent times have also witnessed the rise of the pizza (though Naples usually gets credit for that) and that other symbol of Italo-American culinary artistry, the meatball. The island's natural endowments of sunshine on fertile volcanic soil combined with the multitude of ethnic influences have left Sicily with an unrivalled heritage of foods. Sadly, many dishes are now neglected. But the basics are as flavorsome as ever: citrus fruit, olives, brilliant vegetables, herbs, spices, lamb, sheep's cheeses, grain for pasta, and a multitude of breads and pastries. Then there is the sea brimming full of fish, offering tuna, swordfish, and sardines, to name but a few. Sicily reigns as capital of Italian sweets, the encyclopedic array of which culminates in *cassata*.

**Beccaficu** Sardines either stuffed and baked or breaded and fried.
  ★★ Normanno *bianco.*

**Braccioli di pesce spada** Swordfish filets wrapped around a cheese-bread-vegetable stuffing and grilled.
  ★★★ Regaleali *bianco.*

**Caponata** Eggplant and other ripe vegetables in a rich stew.
  ★★ Cerasuolo di Vittoria.

**Cassata** The island's pride: opulent array of candied fruit and chocolate on a sponge-cake.
  ★★★ Moscato de Pantelleria.

**Cùscusu** Of Arab origin, couscous-style fish stew with semolina.
  ★★★ Rapitalà.

**Farsumagru** Braised veal roll stuffed with meat, cheese, and vegetables.
  ★★★ Regaleali *rosso.*

**Pasta con la Norma** Spaghetti with eggplant, basil, tomato, garlic, and cheese: a homage to Catania's Vincenzo Bellini and his opera *La Norma.*
  ★★ Etna *rosato.*

**Pasta con le sarde** Palermo's classic pasta flavored with sardines and wild fennel has become an island-wide speciality.
  ★★★ Corvo *bianco.*

**Peperonata** Peppers stewed with tomato, onion, and green olives.
  ★ Alcamo.

**Polpettone** The fabled meatballs, possibly even with tomato sauce on pasta.
  ★★★ Corvo *rosso.*

**Tonno alla siciliana** Fresh tuna cooked with white wine, fried anchovies, herbs, and spices.
  ★★★ Faustus *bianco.*

## Restaurants

Recommended in or near wine zones: **Etna** *Giova Rosy Senior* at Taormina. **Faro** *Da Alberto* and *Pippo Nunnari* at Messina. **Lipari** *Filippino* at Lipari. **Marsala** *Zio Ciccio* at Marsala. **Noto-Vittoria** *Alberto il Mago del Pesce* at Marina di Ragusa: *Al Sorcio* at Donnalucata; *Trattoria dei Due Mari* at Porto Palo. **Pantelleria** *Hotel Cossyra* at Pantelleria; *Le Lampare del Mursia* at Mursia. **Siracusa** *Jonico's Rutta e Ciali* at Siracusa.

# Trentino-Alto Adige

Trentino-Alto Adige

The northernmost point of Italy, with its perfumed white wines and German as an alternate language, can't avoid being compared with Alsace. They have numerous vines in common – Riesling, Sylvaner, Pinot Blanc, Pinot Noir, Pinot Gris (Tokay d'Alsace), and Muscat – and it is said that Traminer, a clone of which became Gewürztraminer in Alsace, took its name from the South Tyrolean village of Tramin. But the analogy should not be overdrawn, for Trentino-Alto Adige has distinctive styles in wines that carry over to a notable production of reds and rosés.

**Wine Zones**

1 Casteller
2 Colli di Bolzano
3 Meranese di Collina
4 Santa Maddalena
5 Sorni
6 Teroldego
7 Valle Isareo

Trentino (the southern province of Trento or Trent) and Alto Adige (the province of Bolzano or Bozen, also known as the South Tyrol) share a gorgeous region of Alps drained by the Adige River. Despite ethnic contrasts between the Italians and the German-speaking minority (the latter clings tenaciously to proud traditions), the region is a model of enological efficiency. Two records are unsurpassed: some 55% of wine is DOC and more than 35% of production is exported. Most exports depart from Alto Adige to Germany, Switzerland, and Austria – often labeled in German and even carrying the QbA (*Qualitätswein bestimmter Anbaugebiete*) in place of DOC. In the past, little found its way to other parts of Italy, though the demand, especially for white wines, has begun to reverse that pattern.

Vineyard space is confined (only 15% of the land can be cultivated). The cool climate is conducive to fruity, crisp whites and fragrant reds marked by a distinctly bitter undertone. The region is northern Italy's leading source of rosé. Fine as some wines are, experts feel that quality could be supreme if yields were lowered, irrigation were limited and more selection took place in the vineyards. Several winemakers are striving successfully to get more intensity and complexity and greater personality into their wines.

Most white varieties were imported long ago from France or Germany. The Pinots, with the increasingly noticeable Chardonnay, go into some of Italy's best sparkling wines. Outstanding Riesling, Müller Thurgau, Sylvaner and Sauvignon are also produced, notable for their fragance and uncanny capacity to retain freshness with age. Among reds, Schiava dominates in the popular Caldaro or Kalterersee and the renowned Santa Maddalena. Cabernet, Merlot, Pinot Nero, and the indigenous Teroldego, Lagrein and Marzemino further enhance the region's reputation for reds. Table wines from the region can carry the term Atesino

Trentino-Alto Adige with its towering Dolomites, glacier lakes and deep forests is one of central Europe's favorite vacation spots. Millions of tourists a year cross the Brenner Pass from Austria or venture up from Milan, Venice, Verona, and Lake Garda to ski, climb, and relax amidst the beauty of Gothic and Romanesque villages nestled into green mountainsides. Wine is a major attraction. The Adige valley is traversed by wine roads in both provinces, leading to an imposing array of wines. Among wine shops *Johnson* & *Dipoli* at Neumarkt/Egna and *Lunelli* at Trento are recommended.

## Recent vintages

1986  Snow destroyed vines in winter and early rot and hail took a toll, but results were good to excellent for reds and whites.
1985  Fine year for reds and for Chardonnay and Pinots, though some whites lacked acidity.
1984  Generally poor for reds, but some outstanding Sylvaner, Müller Thurgau and Riesling were made.
1983  Memorable for reds and whites from high altitude vines.
1982  Early optimism mostly faded for whites, but some reds were notable.
1981  Small crop of fair to good wines.
1980  Few wines were better than average.
1979  Large harvest of generally high quality.
Earlier fine vintages: '76, '75, '74, '71, '70, '69, '64.

*Note: Kellereigenossenschaft, German for cooperative winery, is abbreviated as K. in this chapter*

## Alto Adige (Südtiroler) DOC
This zone, which covers much of the vine land of Alto Adige through the Adige and Isarco valleys, boasts 19 types of wine. They include reds, rosés, and whites, mostly dry but also sweet – all varietals which must contain at least 95% of the grape – and *spumante*. Total production is about 13 million liters a year. Because the zone overlaps six others and part of a seventh, it is sometimes thought of as a catch-all, though it shouldn't be; some of Italy's best wines carry the appellation.

– **Cabernet** r. dr.  `**→***`  76 78 79 80 82 83 85 86
Cabernet Sauvignon and/or Cabernet Franc make appealing deep ruby wines, whether light and fruity or ample and complex. The bigger wines

can take from 4 to 10 years to mature as the early herb and bell pepper traits mellow. Cabernet Sauvignon from Margreid and Schwanburg are notable.
Ag. *riserva* 2 yrs.

**– Chardonnay** w. dr. ★★ → ★★★ 84 85 86
Some of Italy's best Chardonnay is made here, both in a fresh, young style exemplified by Tiefenbrunner and in the oak-aged complexity achieved by Lageder and Portico dei Leoni, which may near high Burgundy standards with age. The village of Buchholz and Mazzon and the valley vineyards of Margreid and Kurting are noted for quality.

**– Lagrein Dunkel (Scuro)** r. dr. ★★ → ★★★ 76 79 80 82 83 85 86
The South Tyrol's most distinctive native varietal, Lagrein from Gries (cited on labels as Grieser Lagrein) adjacent to Bolzano is esteemed locally. It can make a soft, easy Beaujolais-style red or a powerful, dark, intricated wine for aging up to a decade from certain vintages.

**– Lagrein Kretzer (Rosato)** p. dr. ★★ → ★★★ DYA
Delightful rosé from Lagrein: cherry pink, fragrant, and fruity, with balanced acidity.

**– Malvasia (Malvasier)** r. dr. ★ DYA
Malvasia Nera makes a ruby-garnet wine, well scented and generously mellow in its youth.

**– Merlot** r. dr.★ → ★★★ 80 82 83 85 86
Bright ruby, usually grapy with scent and flavor of herbs whether drunk young or aged for 3–5 years. Merlot from Siebeneich near Terlan can be first rate.
Ag. *riserva* 1 yr.

**– Moscato Giallo (Goldenmuskateller)** w. sw. ★★ DYA
Locally prized dessert wine from Moscato Giallo. Golden yellow, aromatic, sweet but not cloying, it is best very young.

**– Moscato Rosa (Rosenmuskateller)** r. p. s/sw. ★★ → ★★★★ 84 85 86
This rare *amabile* is as flowery and graceful as its pretty ruby-rose color indicates. Young, it makes a charming sipping wine; with some age it gets smoother and more elegant but loses some of its exceptional fruity fragrance. Graf Eberhard Kuenburg's Schloss Sallegg stands out.

**– Müller Thurgau** or **Riesling-Sylvaner** w. dr. ★★ → ★★★ 80 81 83 84 85 86
Though the popular style is for attractively tart whites to drink young, this Riesling-Sylvaner cross develops depth, fragrance and tone with age.

**– Pinot Bianco (Weissburgunder)** w. dr. (sp.) ★★ → ★★★★ 84 85 86
Pinot Grigio and Chardonnay win the popularlity contests, but there is more good, often excellent, Pinot Bianco here than any other variety. If convincing in *spumante* and young still wines, it can get even more impressive with age, retaining qualities of youth for a decade or longer.

**– Pinot Grigio (Ruländer)** w. dr. ★ → ★★★ 85 86
Though overtaxed due to public demand, the variety can produce admirable wines here, with more backbone and lasting power than the flowery but often fragile Pinot Grigio of Friuli. Usually vinified light, it has a pale bronze color, delicate fragrance and smooth texture.

**– Pinot Nero (Blauburgunder)** r. (p.) (w.) dr. (sp.) ★ → ★★★ 79 80 81 82 83 84 85 86
Though this rarely lives up to expectations, some producers manage soft, fruity wines of medium ruby color and a hint of mint in the bouquet after 2–3 years in bottle. A rare few achieve grander things, such as Hofstätter's '74 and '69, from Mazzon, which compare with good Burgundy. Grapes are also used for rosé, white and sparkling wines.

**– Riesling Italico (Welschriesling)** w. dr.★ DYA
Little of this wine is made, and probably just as well, for Riesling Renano is clearly superior here. Still, when young, it has a zestful, fruity charm.

**– Riesling Renano (Rheinriesling)** w. dr. ★★ → ★★★ DYA
The true Riesling thrives here at Buchholz, Margreid and Mazzon, as nowhere else in Italy. The normal style is very dry in straw-green wines, fresh, fruity, and finely scented. Some producers (Hofstätter, Bellendorf, Lageder, Tiefenbrunner) reach more impressive levels in wines that hold well with age.

**– Sauvignon** w. dr. ★★ → ★★★ 84 85 86
New interest in Sauvignon Blanc may lead to noble results. The small amount made is usually light and dry, with delicate gunflint scent.

– **Schiava (Vernatsch)** r. dr. ⌐★→★★⌐ DYA
The popular family of vines makes light, almondy, garnet-cherry hued
wines to drink young and cool. The best-known subvariety is Schiava
Grigia or Grauvernatsch. Many wineries issue a special house
Vernatsch.

– **Spumante** w. (p.) dr. ⌐★★⌐→★★★ DYA
Recently designated for DOC sparkling wines from the Pinots and
Chardonnay chiefly made by either *charmat* or *champenoise*. Many
producers do not specify the origin of their *cuvées*.

– **Sylvaner** w. dr. ★→⌐★★★⌐ 83 84 85 86
Though often made as a light, simplistic white, this can show
unexpected style from high altitude vineyards in wines that need 2–3
years or more to express the aromatic, fruity qualities. Tiefenbrunner's
stands out.

– **Traminer Aromatico (Gewürztraminer)** w. dr. ★→⌐★★★⌐ 85 86
Though it often lacks the weight of Alsatian Gewürz, the variety can do
enviably well around its home town of Tramin, where wines from the
high Söll vineyards excel. When young, it is straw-green and fruity.
Aged for 2 years, it tends toward gold as the aroma becomes opulently
spicy and the silky flavor gains length. Often confused with the
commoner Traminer, which makes lesser wines.

| | |
|---|---|
| Bellendorf | K. Tramin (C.S. Termeno) |
| Josef Brigl | Kettmeir |
| Castel (Schloss) Rametz | Klosterkellerei Muri-Gries |
| Castel (Schloss) Schwanburg | Alois Lageder |
| Della Staffa (Premiovini) | Laimburg |
| Anton Dissertori | Anton Lindner |
| Karl Franceschini | H. Lun (Sandbichler) |
| Alfons Giovanett | Karl Martini & Sohn |
| Glögglhof (Gojer) | Josef Niedermayr |
| Herrnhofer | Pfannenstielhof |
| Hirschprunn | Portico dei Leoni |
| Kehlburg | Hans Rottensteiner |
| K. Baron Di Pauli | Heinrich Rottensteiner |
| K. Girlan (C.S. Cornaiano) | Santa Margherita |
| K. Kaltern (C.S. Caldaro) | Schloss Sallegg (Kuenburg) |
| K. Margreid-Entiklar | Quinto Soini & Figli |
| (C.S. Magré-Niclara) | J. Tiefenbrunner (Schloss |
| K. Marling (C.S. Marlengo) | Turmhof) |
| K. Nals (C.S. Nalles) | Trattmannhof |
| K. St. Michael-Eppan (C.S. | Von Elzenbaum |
| San Michele-Appiano) | W. Walch |
| K. St Pauls (C.S. San Paolo) | Reinhold Waldthaler |
| K. Schreckbichl (C.S. Colterenzio) | |

*(Note: More than half the wines of Alto Adige are produced
by cooperatives and marketed by the Verband der Kellereigenossenschaften
Südtirols or Consorzio Viticoltori Alto Adige.)*

**Cabernet**
Both Cabernets Sauvignon and Franc are widely grown, as DOC Alto
Adige and Trentino, also in table wines with Merlot and others.

**Caldaro** or **Lago di Caldaro (Kalterersee)** DOC r. dr. ★→⌐★★⌐DYA
Alto Adige's *gemütlich* quaffing wine is better known in German-
speaking lands as Kalterersee than it is elsewhere in Italy. Made in
quantity (25 million liters a year) from Schiava Grossa, Gentile and
Grigia grown along the Adige valley, its name comes from the pretty
lake SW of Bolzano. Light garnet to almost pink, it has the noted
Schiava grapy fragrance and unusually refreshing verve and fluidity
with an almondy finish. It is best young – inside 2–3 years – and cool.
Wine from the original zone around the lake may be called *classico* or,
with 10.5% alcohol and some refinement, *classico superiore*. With 11%
alcohol, it may be called *scelto* or *Auslese*, suggesting it comes from late
harvested grapes.

| | |
|---|---|
| Ambach | Castel (Schloss) Schwanburg |
| Bellendorf | Gaierhof |
| Càvit | Hirschprunn |
| Cantina Produttori Mezzocorona | J. Hofstätter |
| Castel (Schloss) Rametz | K. Baron di Pauli |

▶

K. Girlan (C.S. Cornaiano)
K. Gries (C.S. Gries)
K. Kattern (C.S. Caldaro)
K. Margried-Entiklar
   (C.S. Magré-Niclara)
K. St. Michael-Eppan
   (C.S. San Michele-Appiano)
K. St. Pauls (C.S. San Paolo)
K. Schreckbichl (C.S. Colterenzio)
K. Tramin (C.S. Termeno)
Klosterkellerei Muri-Gries

Alois Lageder
Laimburg
Anton Lindner
Karl Martini & Sohn
Josef Niedermayr
Römigberg (Lageder)
Hans Rottensteiner
Schloss Kaltenburg (Brigl)
Schloss Sallegg (Kuenburg)
J. Tiefenbrunner (Schloss Turmhof)
W. Walch

**Castel San Michele** r. dr. ★★→★★★ 79 82 83 85 86
Fine Cabernet-Merlot from San Michele all'Adige N of Trento,
produced at the noted agricultural school. Deep ruby to garnet,
generous, and herby, its tannic harshness mellows in 5–6 years or more.
Istituto Agrario Provinciale San Michele all'Adige

**Casteller** DOC r. p. dr. ★ DYA
Trentino's everyday wine from Schiava, Merlot, and Lambrusco grown
in hills along the Adige from N of Trento S to the Veneto. Light ruby to
bright pink, vinous, dry, and light – drink inside 2 years.
Càvit                                   La Vinicola Sociale Aldeno
Lagariavini

**Chardonnay**
Though now DOC in Alto Adige and Trentino, Chardonnay has been
issued as a growingly fashionable table wine in Italy and abroad. Some
superior wines have emerged in both provinces – Pojer & Sandri and
Zeni in Trentino; Tiefenbrunner and Lageder in Alto Adige. But much
of the wine is aimed at the popular markets – Santa Margherita, Càvit
and Bollini, which sell well in the U.S.A., offer a light, fruity alternative
to the weightier, woodier California style. There are also questionable
products capitalizing on the name. (See also Spumante.)

**Colli di Bolzano (Bozner Leiten)** DOC r. dr. ★→★★ DYA
All-purpose Schiava from hills surrounding Bolzano. Light ruby-garnet,
soft and easy, it can be delightful young.
K. Gries (C.S. Gries)                   Alois Lageder
K. Terlan (C.S. Terlano)                Karl Martini & Sohn

**De Vite** w. dr. ★★★ 84 85 86
Exquisite white from Kerner, a cross between Riesling Renano and
Schiava (or Trollinger). Pale straw green and perfumed, it has
precocious charm which can extend a few years.
J. Hofstätter

**Feldmarschall**
See Müller-Thurgau.

**Foianeghe** r. w. dr. ★★ 79 80 82 83 85 86
Table wines from Isera near Rovereto. Foianeghe Rosso, in which
Merlot dominates Cabernet, is a deep ruby-garnet color, generous,
complex and poised. It develops bouquet over 4–5 years. Foianeghe
Bianco from Chardonnay and Traminer is full and fruity to drink
within 2 years.
Conti Bossi Fedrigotti

**Gewürztraminer** or **Traminer Aromatico**
DOC under Alto Adige, Trentino, and Valle Isarco, this variety named
for the South Tyrolean village of Tramin is growing in popularity,
though the noble Gewürztraminer is often confused with the common
Traminer.

**Goldmuskateller** w. dr. ★★★→★★★★ 83 84 85 86
This exceptional table wine from Moscato Giallo grapes grown near
Entiklar in Alto Adige is full of Muscat aroma but unexpectedly dry in
flavor. Its rich and complex bouquet improves in 3–4 years of age.
J. Tiefenbrunner (Schloss Turmhof)

**Grauvernatsch**
German for Schiava Grigia. DOC wines can carry the name under Alto
Adige Schiava.

**Kalterersee**
See Caldaro.

**Kolbenhofer** r. dr. ★★★ 85 86
From Schiava grown at the Kolbenhof vineyard above Tramin, this is
similar to Caldaro but more elegant. Garnet red and fragrantly fruity, it
is graceful and smooth inside 3 years.
J. Hofstätter

**Lagrein**
Admired variety of Bolzano now used for red and rosé throughout the
region. DOC under Alto Adige, Trentino, and Valdadige.

**Luna dei Feldi** w. dr. ★★★ 84 85 86
From an improbable mix of Chardonnay, Müller Thurgau and
Traminer grown in the Feldi vineyards at Rovere della Luna in N
Trentino, this is a sterling white with surprising breadth and depth of
flavors to support its full aroma.
Santa Margherita

**Malvasia (Malvasier)**
Red wine from Malvasia Nera is DOC under Alto Adige.

**Marzemino**
Native variety that thrives around Isera as a DOC under Trentino.

**Maso Lodron** r. dr. ★★→★★★ 79 81 83 85 86
Cabernet-Merlot from Nogaredo S of Trento. Deep ruby, herby in its full
aroma and flavor, it becomes smooth and deep with 4–6 years, or more.
Letrari

**Meranese di Collina (Meraner Hügel)** DOC r. dr. ★ DYA
Merano's local red from Schiava grown in the hills around the city.
Light ruby, lightly scented, easy, and tasty, it is best on the cool side in a
year or two. Wine from a small territory known as the Contea di Tirol
may qualify as Burgravio or Burggräfler.
Castel (Schloss) Rametz              K. Meran (C.S. Merano)
K. Algund (C.S. Lagundo)             Torggler
K. Marling (C.S. Marlengo)

**Merlot**
DOC as a varietal under Alto Adige, Trentino, and Valdadige, Merlot
is often blended with Cabernet in table wines.

**Mori Vecio** r. dr. ★★→★★★ 81 83 85 86
Cabernet-Merlot from Mori S of Trento. Ruby tending to garnet, with
5–6 years or more of age it is ample in structure and bouquet.
Lagariavini

**Moscato (Muskateller)**
Both Moscato Giallo (Goldenmustkateller) and Moscato Rosa
(Rosenmuskateller) are DOC under Alto Adige and Trentino. See
Goldmuskateller.

**Müller Thurgau**
Though DOC under Alto Adige, Terlano, Trentino, Valle Isarco and
Valdadige, Müller Thurgau has reached its grandest heights as a table
wine. In Trentino, Pojer & Sandri make a remarkably fragrant and
fruity version at Faedo. But the top-ranking (★★★★) Müller is
Tiefenbrunner's Feldmarschall, grown at 1,000 meters at Fennberg in
Alto Adige.
Pojer & Sandri              J. Tiefenbrunner (Schloss Turmhof)

**Navesel** r. dr. ★★→★★★ 82 83 85 86
Cabernet and Merlot blend from Trentino of solid middleweight
stature, reaching a prime in 3–6 years.
Armando Simoncelli

**Nosiola**
DOC in Trentino, this native variety is also the base of Vin Santo.

**Novaline Rubino** r. dr. ★★ 83 85 86
Cabernet-Merlot grown at Mattarello in Trentino vinified in a light
style that shows striking bouquet with 3–4 years.
Novaline

**Pinot Bianco (Weissburgunder)**
DOC in Alto Adige, Terlano, Trentino, and Valdadige. Much of what
was formerly believed to be Pinot Giallo has lately been identified as
Chardonnay and labeled as such.

## Pinot Grigio
DOC in Alto Adige, Trentino, Valle Isarco, and Valdadige, Pinot Grigio may also be a table wine, called Pinot Grigio delle Venezie or with some other vague geographical reference that doesn't signify authenticity. Still, along with the mediocre products designed to meet excessive demand, some good table wine is produced, though it is usually wiser to select DOC.

## Pinot Nero (Blauburgunder)
DOC under Alto Adige, Trentino, and Valdadige, Pinot Nero is also mixed with other varieties, sometimes in white, sparkling wines. Maso Cantanghel's non-DOC Pinot Nero from the heights at Civezzano near Trento combines youthful vigor with souplesse in one of Italy's best examples of the variety.

**Pragiara** r. dr.  ★★★  79 82 83 85 86
Minute production of Cabernet-Merlot aged in casks at Isera in Trentino to a robust, deep ruby-garnet wine that needs at least 5 years to attain elegance.
De Tarczal

**Quattro Vicariati** r. dr. ┌ ★★→★★★ ┐  79 81 82 83 85 86
From Cabernet and Merlot, this premium red of the region's largest cooperative group is selected vineyard by vineyard, then reselected before being aged 2 years in *barriques*. Deep, ruby, robust, and somewhat tannic but smooth, it needs 4–5 years to reach its best.
Càvit

## Riesling
Both Riesling Renano (Rheinriesling) and Riesling Italico (Welschriesling) are recognized as DOC under Alto Adige, Terlano, Trentino, and Valdadige. The Rieslings are also used for table wines.

**San Leonardo** r. dr. ┌ ★★★ ┐  78 79 80 81 82 83 85 86
Fine Cabernet-Merlot from San Leonardo vineyards in the Vallagarina, S of Trento. Rich in color and body, it needs 4–5 years for its noble tannin to mellow and bouquet of herbs and berries to develop. Recent experiments with *barrique* aging point to even better results.
Tenuta San Leonardo (Guerrieri Gonzaga)

**San Zeno** r. dr. ┌ ★★ ┐  82 83 85 86
Merlot dominates Cabernet in this table wine from Aldeno S of Trento. The result is a softer, lighter, somewhat earlier-maturing wine than most other Bordeaux-style blends.
La Vinicola Sociale Aldeno

**Santa Maddalena (St Magdalener)** DOC r. dr. ┌ ★★→★★★ ┐  85 86
Once the region's premier red, Santa Maddalena is still adored in Bolzano and neighboring German-speaking nations, though it hardly rates as one of Italy's three great wines (along with Barolo and Barbaresco) as determined under Mussolini in 1941. Made in quantity (4 million liters a year) from various Schiava grapes in a hilly zone above Bolzano, it ranges from dark ruby to garnet with pronounced almond and violet bouquet typical of Schiava. Dry, round, at best velvety with an enticing bitter background, it reaches peaks in a year or two, though it can last longer. *Classico* (or *Klassisches Ursprungsgebiet*) applies to a restricted area around the village of Santa Maddalena.

| | |
|---|---|
| Bellendorf | K. Terlan (C.S. Terlano) |
| Josef Brigl | Kettmeir |
| Castel (Schloss) Rametz | Klosterkellerei Muri-Gries |
| Castel (Schloss) Schwanburg | Alois Lageder |
| Glögglhof (Gojer) | H. Lun |
| J. Hofstätter | Karl Martini & Sohn |
| K. Gries (C.S. Gries) | Pfannenstielhof |
| K. St. Magdalena (C.S. | Henrich Plattner |
| Santa Maddalena) | Hans Rottensteiner |
| K. St. Michael-Eppan | Heinrich Rottensteiner |
| (C.S. San Michele-Appiano) | W. Walch |

## Sauvignon
DOC under Alto Adige and Terlano. This noble vine is gaining favor.

## Schiava (Vernatsch)
By far the most heavily planted vine here in Schiava Gentile, Grigia,

Grossa, Media, Piccola, and Tschaggeler. DOC under Alto Adige and Valdadige, it is the base of DOC Caldaro, Casteller, Colli di Bolzano, Meranese di Collina, Santa Maddalena, and Sorni *rosso*.

**Sorni** DOC r. w. ★→**★★★** DYA
DOC from around village of Sorni N of Trento. The *rosso*, from Schiava, Teroldego, and Lagrein, is light ruby, subtly perfumed, soft, and eminently quaffable when young. The *bianco*, based on Nosiola, is pale straw and subtly scented with fresh, soft flavor when very young. White of 11% may be called *scelto*. Maso Poli's wines stand out.
C.S. Lavis-Sorni-Salorno                Moser
Maso Poli

**Spumante** w. (p.) dr. (s/sw.) sp. **★★→★★★**
Though DOC *spumante* is prescribed under Alto Adige and Trentino, many producers opt to issue their wines under individual names. Some of Italy's finest *champenoise* is made here from Chardonnay, Pinot Bianco, Pinot Nero and Pinot Grigio mainly. There are also some good *charmat* wines. Numerous producers of *champenoise* in Trentino, including Ferrari, long a leader in the field, have formed the Consorzio Spumante Trento Classico to promote wines. Good small independent producers work here as well. Wines not marked (m.c.) for *champenoise* are presumably made by *charmat*.
– **Abate Nero Gran Spumante (m.c.)**
Asput
– **Arunda Brut (m.c.), Arunda Extra Brut (m.c.), Vivaldi Brut (m.c.)**
Arunda/Vivaldi
– **Brut del Concilio (m.c.), Brut Rosé del Concilio (m.c.), Grand Bleu**
Lagariavini
– **Castel Monreale (m.c.), Schloss Konigsberg Brut (m.c.)**
Castello (Schloss) Rametz
– **Cesarini Sforza Blanc de Blancs (m.c.), Cesarini Sforza Brut Riserva dei Conti (m.c.)**
Cesarini Sforza
– **Équipe 5 Brut Riserva (m.c.), Équipe 5 Brut Rosé (m.c.)**
Équipe Trentina Spumante
– **Ferrari Brut (m.c.), Ferrari Brut de Brut (m.c.), Ferrari Brut Rosé (m.c.), Ferrari Nature (m.c.), Riserva Giulio Ferrari (m.c.)**
Ferrari-Fratelli Lunelli
– **Firmato (m.c.), Graal Ducale (m.c.), Gran Càvit Brut, Gran Càvit Brut Brut, Novella Fronda Chardonnay Brut**
Càvit
– **Gran Le Brul (m.c.), Le Brul Rosé (m.c.)**
Le Brul
– **Haderburg Brut (m.c.), Haderburg Nature (m.c.)**
Haderburg-Ochsenreiter
– **Kettmeir Brut Grande Cuvée**
Kettmeir
– **Alois Lageder Brut**
Alois Lageder
– **Novaline Brut (m.c.)**
Novaline
– **Pojer & Sandri Brut (m.c.)**
Pojer & Sandri
– **Spagnolli Brut (m.c.)**
Cantine Spagnolli

**Sylvaner**
The chief varietal of Valle Isarco (Eisacktaler) DOC, it is also classified under Alto Adige, Terlano, and Valdadige.

**Terlano (Terlaner)** DOC
The zone in hills along the Adige NW and SW of Bolzano comprises seven white wines. Limited production is centered in the towns of Terlan, Nals and Andrian, where wines may be called *classico*.
– **Müller Thurgau** w. dr. **★★** DYA
The small amount made is crisp, light, and refreshing when young.
– **Pinot Bianco (Weissburgunder)** w. dr. **★★→★★★★** 84 85 86
The prevalent variety, Pinot Bianco (with some Chardonnay) can rival

the finest of Alto Adige.

– **Riesling Italico (Welschriesling)** w. dr. ★→ **\*\*** DYA
Good workaday white which occasionally rises above the ordinary.

– **Riesling Renano (Rheinriesling)** w. dr. **\*\*→\*\*\*** 84 85 86
Fruity, finely scented wine of straw-green color; though light it shows distinctive varietal character.

– **Sauvignon** w. dr. **\*\*→\*\*\*\*** 84 85 86
Though limited in quantity, Sauvignon Blanc does as well here as anywhere in Italy, achieving the characteristic *fumé* in its spicy aroma with a gunflint bite in its long, fruity flavor. The C.S. Terlano is consistently admirable and Lageder achieves heights from the steep Lehen-Montigl vineyards.

– **Sylvaner** w. dr. ★→ **\*\*** DYA
Though it doesn't reach heights here, it can be an amply scented wine of more than everyday appeal.

– **Terlano (Terlaner)** w. dr. ★→ **\*\*** 85 86
Light sipping wine from at least half Pinot Bianco with any or all other varieties. Pale straw, fruity, refreshingly acidic.

| | |
|---|---|
| Josef Brigl | (C.S. San Michele-Appiano) |
| Castel (Schloss) Schwanburg | K. Terlan (C.S. Terlan) |
| K. Andrian (C.S. Andriano) | Klosterkellerei Muri-Gries |
| K. Gries (C.S. Gries) | Alois Lageder |
| K. Nals (C.S. Nalles) | Anton Lindner |
| K. St. Michael-Eppan | Hans Rottensteiner |

**Teroldego Rotaliano** DOC r. p. dr. **\*\*→\*\*\*\*** 79 83 85 86
Wine from this vine, found only in the gravelly plain known as the Campo Rotaliano where the Noce River joins the Adige between Mezzolombardo and San Michele all'Adige, can stand with the most distinctive reds of NE Italy. Dark ruby violet to garnet, depending on vintage, it is generous, robust, and slightly tannic, with a bitter undertone and splendid bouquet of flowers and berries after 2–3 years or, from rare vintages, up to a decade of age. C.S. Mezzolombardo and Foradori excel. A vivacious *rosato* is included in production of some 2 million bottles a year.
Ag. *riserva* 2 yrs.

| | |
|---|---|
| Barone De Cles | Foradori |
| Cantina Cooperative Rotaliano | Gaierhof |
| C.S. Mezzolombardo | Istituto Agrario Provinciale San |
| Càvit | Michele all'Adige |
| Conti Martini | Lechthaler |
| Fratelli Delana | Maso Donati |
| Fratelli Dorigati | Zeni |

**Traminer**
See Gewürztraminer.

**Trentino** DOC
The zone covers much of the vineyard territory of Trentino, through the Adige, Sarca and Avisio valleys, where more than 6 million liters a year are produced. Recently expanded, Trentino DOC applies to 20 types of wine, mainly varietals but also Bianco, Rosso, and Vin Santo.

– **Bianco** w. dr. (sp.)
Though not seen much yet, the combination of Chardonnay and Pinot Bianco should result in first-rate white wines, both still and sparkling.

– **Cabernet** r. dr. ★→ **\*\*\*** 79 80 82 83 85 86
Usually a blend of Cabernet Franc and Cabernet Sauvignon, this can be among Italy's most consistent Cabernets with an unmistakable herbaceous aspect and a bitter finish, the local *gout de terroir*. Tenuta San Leonardo makes a classic.
Ag. *riserva* 2 yrs.

– **Cabernet Franc** r. dr. 85 86
Producers can specify this dominant subvariety, but I haven't seen one yet.
Ag. *riserva* 2 yrs.

– **Cabernet Sauvignon** r. dr. 85 86
Favored among new plantings, this subvariety might show more elegance than the Franc.
Ag. *riserva* 2 yrs.

– **Chardonnay** w. dr. (sp.)   ★★→★★★   85 86
Growingly prominent, more producers should start to show the noble potential of the Chardonnays from Pojer & Sandri and Zeni.
– **Lagrein** r. p. dr.   ★★→★★★   79 80 82 83 84 85 86
Both the persuasive *rosso* and the fragrant *rosato* can rival all but the finest Lagrein of Bolzano.
Ag. *riserva (rosso)* 2 yrs.
– **Marzemino** r. dr.   ★→★★★   82 83 84 85 86
This Trentino native can show Beaujolais-like charm when young, though its full-bodied, grapy softness evolves toward a deeper, richer, almost aristocratic tone accented by an almondy bite. The best comes from Isera where Battistotti, De Tarczal and Simoncelli excel.
Ag. *riserva* 2 yrs.
– **Merlot** r. dr.   ★→★★   82 83 85 86
Popular but rarely distinguished here, it seems better suited to blends with Cabernet. Usually light, herbaceous and not to keep.
Ag. *riserva* 2 yrs.
– **Moscato Giallo** w. am. s/sw. sw.   ★★   DYA
The yellow Muscat makes lightly sweet to sweet wines in limited quantities in S Trentino. Usually at its fragrant best young, the richer *liquoroso* version can take some age.
– **Moscato Rosa** p. s/sw. sw.   ★★   DYA
At its best flowery in fragrance and roseate color, it remains to be seen if it can match the fine Rosenmuskateller of Alto Adige. The *liquoroso* can age a bit.
– **Müller Thurgau** w. dr.   ★★→★★★   84 85 86
The potential of this Riesling-Sylvaner cross has already been shown by Battistotti and Pojer & Sandri.
– **Nosiola** w. dr.   ★★→★★★   DYA
Distinguished native traditionally used for sweet Vino Santo, it also makes a fine dry white with fruity aroma, smooth flavor and an exhiliratingly bitter background.
– **Pinot Bianco** w. dr. (sp.)   ★★→★★★   84 85 86
Though not considered as august as Chardonnay, Pinot Bianco here can stand proudly alongside its cousin as the source of some of the best whites of the region, exemplified by Zeni's special vineyard Sorti. Also a source of *spumante*.
– **Pinot Grigio** w. dr. (sp.)   ★→★★   DYA
Recently singled out, this could do as well as the more renowned Pinot Grigo of Alto Adige and Friuli. Also a source of *spumante*.
– **Pinot Nero** r. (p.) (w.) dr. (sp.)   ★→★★   82 83 84 85 86
Though it can make decent red and good rosé, Pinot Nero is usually best suited to white or pink sparkling wines.
Ag. *riserva (rosso)* 2 yrs.
– **Riesling Italico** w. dr.   ★   DYA
So far little evidence of worth.
– **Riesling Renano** w. dr.   ★★   DYA
Though not at the levels of Alto Adige's best, high vineyards could yield wines of similar class.
– **Rosso** r. dr. 85 86
If not yet in evidence, wines made under the auspices of this marriage of Cabernet (at 50–85%) with Merlot could include some of the province's better reds.
– **Traminer Aromatico**   ★★   w. dr. 84 85 86
If they rarely approach the class of Alto Adige's best Gewurztraminer, Traminers here can hold their distinct virtues for 3–4 years.
– **Vino Santo** am. sw.   ★★
Production of this locally prized sweet wine is concentrated in the Lake Toblino area. Made from semidried Nosiola grapes, after aging in sealed small barrels it becomes golden amber and aromatic, developing velvety texture with many years in bottle. There is also a fortified *liquoroso*.
Ag. 3 yrs.

| | |
|---|---|
| Barone De Cles | Cantina Produttori Mezzacorona |
| Riccardo Battistotti | C.S. di Isera |
| Conti Bossi Fedrigotti | C.S. di Mori |
| Conti Martini | C.S. Mezzalombardo |

Cantine Mezzacorona (Rotalvini)
*Càvit
De Tarczal
Fratelli Endrizzi
Foradori
Gaierhof
Istituto Agrario Provinciale
   San Michele all'Adige
Lagariavini
La Vinicola Sociale Aldeno
Letrari

Longariva
Novaline
Fratelli Pisoni
Giovanni Poli
Fratelli Rigotti
Armando Simoncelli
Società Agricoltori Vallagarina
E. Spagnolli
Tenuta San Leonardo (Guerrieri-
   Gonzaga)

> *\* Cavit groups most of Trentino's cooperatives and
> sells much of the select wines under its label.*

## Valdadige (Etschtaler) DOC

Though only *rosso* and *bianco* are specified under the terms of this zone, which follows the Adige from Merano S almost to Verona in the Veneto, varietals may also be mentioned on labels. Some 17 million liters of DOC wine flow annually from high-yield vineyards here, much of it to neighboring countries.

**– Bianco** w. dr. *→** DYA
Wine can derive from Pinot Bianco or Grigio, Riesling Italico, Müller Thurgau, Bianchetta Trevigiana, Trebbiano Toscano, Nosiola, Vernaccia, Sylvaner, and Veltliner alone, or in combinations. When varietal names appear separately, this indicates some personality. Valdadige is the source of growing amounts of Pinot Grigio.

**– Rosso** r. p. dr. * DYA
Nondescript red or rosé from various combinations of Lambrusco, Schiava, Merlot, Pinot Nero, Lagrein, Teroldego, and Negrara.

Barone Fini
Bollini
Cantina Produttori Mezzocorona
Cantine Mezzocorona

Càvit
Fratelli Delana
Gaierhof
Santa Margherita

## Valle Isarco (Eisacktaler) DOC

Small production of five white varietals grown at high altitude along the Isarco (Eisack) River NE of Bolzano in Italy's northernmost DOC zone. The subdistrict of Brixen or Bressanone may be cited on labels.

**– Müller Thurgau** w. dr. **→*** 84 85 86
Delicate and flowery, it is good young, but from some vintages develops grace over 2–4 years. It can be among the regions finest whites.

**– Pinot Grigio (Ruländer)** w. dr. *→** DYA
Well-rounded wine of pale roseate yellow color, fine scent, and fresh flavor.

**– Sylvaner** or **Silvaner** w. dr. **→*** 83 84 85 86
The local favorite, Sylvaner thrives here as nowhere else in Italy, achieving style similar to German Franken wines. Though some prefer it young when it is pale and snappy, with age it acquires opulently spicy aromas and flavors.

**– Traminer Aromatico (Gewürztraminer)** w. dr. ⟦**⟧ 85 86
Though similar in style to that of Tramin, here the wine develops ethereal aroma and a supple fragility when young.

**– Veltliner** w. dr. ⟦**⟧ 84 85 86
The small volume produced of this green-tinted wine – which is DOC only here – is light and appealingly fruity in scent and flavor.

K. Eisacktaler (C.S. della Valle
   d'Isarco)
Alois Lageder
Pacherhof (Huber)

Stiftskellerei Neustift (Abbazia di
   Novacella)
Karl Vonklausner

## Vinattieri Bianco w. dr. 84 85 86

Combines Pinot Bianco and Chardonnay selected in the South Tyrol in what would have been a classic Weissburgunder of blossomy, crisp fruity qualities when young, lengthening and broadening with age.
Vinattieri

# Wine & Food

The cooking of Trentino and Alto Adige derives from distinct heritages, one Italo-Venetian, the other Germanic-Tyrolean. But the intermingling of peoples drawing on shared resources along the Adige valley has taken the sharp edges off the contrasts. Something akin to a regional style of cooking has emerged. True, the Italian-speaking population still relies more heavily on polenta, gnocchi, and pasta, the German-speaking on wursts, black bread, and soups. But the fare found in *ristoranti* and *Gasthäusen* here has been enriched by the points in common. The *Knödel*, for example, has become *canederli* in Italian and savored just as avidly. The same can be said for *sauerkraut* or *crauti*. Game, trout, *speck* (smoked bacon), and Viennese-style pastries are further evidence of a unity of taste that makes the long hours spent at table in the warm, wood-paneled *Stübe* so enjoyable.

**Biroldi con crauti** Blood sausages with chestnuts, nutmeg, and cinnamon, served with *sauerkraut*.
   ** Santa Maddalena.
**Canederli/Knödel** Among many dumplings, perhaps the tastiest are with calf's liver served in broth.
   ** Lagrein Kretzer.
**Gemsenfleisch** Chamois cooked Tyrolean style with red wine vinegar and served with polenta.
   *** Lagrein Dunkel
   or *** Cabernet.
**Gerstensuppe** Barley soup with bacon, onions, and celery.
   * Meranese di Collina (Meraner Hügel)
**Gröstl** Beef, potatoes, and onions, cooked together in a cake-like mold.
   ** Merlot or ** Pinot Nero.

**Blau Forelle** Alpine trout boiled with white wine and flavorings.
   **→*** Müller Thurgau.
**Krapfen Tirolese** Fried paste with marmalade and powdered sugar.
   **→*** Moscato Rosa
   or ** Moscato Giallo.
**Sauresuppe** Flavorsome tripe soup traditionally eaten at mid-morning on market days and holidays.
   * Colli di Bolzano (Bozner Leiten).
**Smacafam** Buckwheat cake with sausages, onion, lard, and cheese.
   ** Marzemino.
**Speck** Smoked bacon sliced onto black bread.
   ** Caldaro (Kalterersee).

## Restaurants

Recommended in or near wine zones: **Alto Adige** *Grief*, *Kaiser Krone* and *Tabasco* at Bolzano; *Elefante* and *Fink* at Bressanone (Brixen); *Forstlerhof* at Burgstall (Postal); *Johnson & Dipoli* at Egna (Neumarkt); *Tshafon* at Fiè allo Sciliar (Völs am Schlern); *Andrea* and *Hotel Villa Mozart* at Merano. **Trentino** *Concorde* at Calceranica al Lago: *Maso Cantanghel* near Civezzano; *All'Olivo* at Faver; *Da Valentino* at Padergnone; *Albergo Ristorante al Ponte* at Pergine; *Al Castello* at Rovereto; *Da Silvio* at San Michele all'Adige; *Castel Toblino* at Sarche; *Accademia* and *Chiesa* at Trento; *Doss Pules* at Verla di Giovo; *Andreas* at Vilpiano (Vilpian).

# Tuscany

## Toscana

Tuscany is identified as intimately with wine as it is with art, craftsmanship and ideas, all of which over the centuries it has exported prodigiously. This is the realm of Sangiovese, the hearty, sometimes aristocratic mainstay of every Tuscan classified red from Chianti to Brunello di Montalcino, Vino Nobile di Montepulciano, Carmignano, and less lofty appellations. Chianti might be the world's best known name in wine, even if, after six centuries of fluctuating fortunes, it is undergoing a painful transition to DOCG. Chianti's cheerful flask has been almost entirely replaced by standard bottles, but moving the nation's largest production up scale has proved to be a monumental task.

Chianti has a crisis of identity. Producers themselves seem undecided about the wine's personality and their differences in concepts, techniques and, most conspicuously, skills in winemaking are reflected in variable quality. Some Chianti, with its almost Bordeaux-like complexion, ranks with Italy's finest reds and leading values; other wine of the name is still too often coarse and cheap.

Chianti in its seven geographical units accounts for a major share of production among the region's 21 DOCs and, though output has been reduced by DOCG, it still makes up 12–15% of the national DOC total. Though Tuscany ranks only sixth among the regions in wine production, it is second to the Veneto in DOC with an average of 150 million liters a year.

Brunello and Vino Nobile, two of the original four DOCGs, have been gradually building both prestige and markets. But it is just as much the fashionable unclassified wines led by Sassicaia, Tignanello and a galaxy of newer stars that are showing how brilliant Tuscan reds can be. In this field Sangiovese increasingly shares the limelight with Cabernet, which has even worked its way into Chianti.

Tuscan whites are also resurging, as technicians strive to upgrade the status of working class natives Trebbiano and Malvasia while building new homes in the hills for the upper class immigrants Chardonnay, Pinots and Sauvignon Blanc. Among those moving to define the new styles is a group of producers who use the term Predicato for four elite types of wine.

Tuscan wine flows from vineyards that cover hillsides from the Tyrrhenian to the Apennines – a rural civilization shaped over centuries into a landscape of extraordinary harmony. Visitors who come to see the Florence of the Medici, the Palio of Siena, and the towers of Pisa and San Gimignano also tour the wine zones. The prime wine road is the Chiantigiana, which cuts through the enchanting heart of Chianti to link Florence with Siena (home of the *Enoteca Italica Permanente* – the national wine library – in the Medici fortress). Also worth visiting are the *enoteche* at Montalcino, Carmignano, and Terricciola in the Colline Pisane. Among shops recommended are *Enoteca Trinci* at Agliana (Pistoia), *Enoteca Nebraska* at Camaiore, *Bottega del Vino-Casanova* at Chianciano Terme, *Enoteca Murgia* in Florence, *Enoteca Mora* at Ponte a Moriano, *Enoteca Peri* at San Giovanni Valdarno and *Punto di Vino* at Viareggio. *Enoteca Gallo Nero* at Greve sells nearly all Chianti Classico. In Florence, the *Enoteca Pinchiorri* restaurant has an unrivaled collection of Italian and French wines.

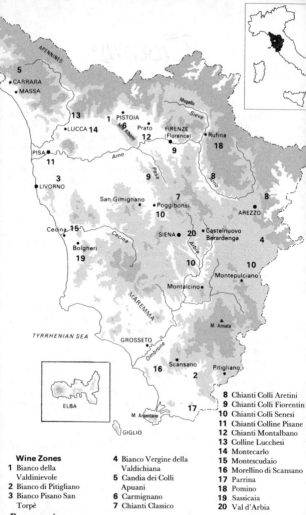

**Wine Zones**

1. Bianco della Valdinievole
2. Bianco di Pitigliano
3. Bianco Pisano San Torpè
4. Bianco Vergine della Valdichiana
5. Candia dei Colli Apuani
6. Carmignano
7. Chianti Classico
8. Chianti Colli Aretini
9. Chianti Colli Fiorentin
10. Chianti Colli Senesi
11. Chianti Colline Pisane
12. Chianti Montalbano
13. Colline Lucchesi
14. Montecarlo
15. Montescudaio
16. Morellino di Scansano
17. Parrina
18. Pomino
19. Sassicaia
20. Val d'Arbia

## Recent vintages

Chianti *riserva*, Vino Nobile, and Carmignano approach primes around 4–7 years, though some vintages favor aging of a decade or more. Brunello needs 6–10 years to begin opening up, and great vintages can last for decades.

1986 Splendid fall weather carried a questionable crop to unexpected peaks for reds and whites.

1985 Vies with '82 as this decade's "vintage of the century", though drought caused problems.

1984 A year of watered down lightweights.

1983 Extreme heat caused uneven ripening, but top producers made good to excellent wines with select grapes.

1982 Large, first-rate vintage of big, balanced red wines, perhaps the best in a string of favorable harvests.

1981 Reduced but in some cases very good; Brunello, Vino Nobile and Chianti from Siena province fared well.

| 1980 | Large, uneven crop, average quality with a few happy exceptions in Chianti and Carmignano. |
|---|---|
| 1979 | Record harvest of good to very good wines with average life spans, excepting Brunello for extended aging. |
| 1978 | Reduced, but some tannic, long-lived wines were made. |
| 1977 | Below normal in size but memorable for Brunello, Vino Nobile, and certain Chiantis. |

Earlier fine vintages: (Brunello) '75, '71, '70, '64, '61, '55, '45; (Chianti) '75, '71, '64, '62; (Vino Nobile) '75, '71, '67, '64, '58.

**Aleatico** r. sw. ★★→★★★
From the ancient Aleatico vine grown in the Maremma and on Elba where Enrico Tirloni's Aleatico di Lacona stands out for its soft, sweet, rich flavor with a bitter cherry finish. Though rare, Antinori will soon resume limited production.
Podere L'Isobella (Tirloni)

**Alicante** r. dr. ★★★ 81 82 83 85 86
From Alicante in the Grenache family (apparently via Spain as it is known locally as Tinto), this enticing red is bigger in bouquet and flavor than body, with a spicy, almost sweet, ethereal richness that reminds me of the best Sardinian Cannonau. Suited to medium aging.
Erik Banti

**Ansonica del Giglio** am. dr. ★ DYA
Curiosity from Ansonica grown on the isle of Giglio off the Argentario promontory. Amber, ample in scent, its rustically suave dryness makes it good with fish soup.
Le Cannelle

**Barco Reale** r. dr. ★★ 83 85 86
This new red wine named for the Medici park that covered the zone has become a lighter, fresher version of Carmignano, probably to serve as a second-tier DOC if Carmignano becomes DOCG. Producers are the same as for Carmignano.

**Bianco di Toscana** w. dr. (fz.) ★★ DYA
Table wines based on the ubiquitous Trebbiano and Malvasia are made throughout Tuscany in varying styles and with different degrees of success. Though such wines were customarily rather light, plain and fragile (if not sour), the addition of nobler grapes and the use of low temperature fermentation have brought out more fruit and aroma. Some have good balance with refreshing tone and occasionally a hint of *pétillance*. Since nearly every estate makes a white wine – but too often obviously to use up excess grapes – only a few of the better such *vini da tavola* are cited. See also Galestro.

- **Amorosa Bianco**
Amorosa
- **Bianco del Beato**
Fattoria dei Barbi
- **Bianco di Castellare**
Castellare di Castellina
- **Bianco di Coltibuono**
Badia a Coltibuono
- **Bianco di Volpaia**
Castello di Volpaia
- **Brolio Bianco**
Barone Ricasoli
- **Capannelle Bianco**
Capannelle

- **Capezzana Bianco**
Villa di Capezzana
- **Colline di Ama**
Castello di Ama
- **La Massa Bianco**
La Massa
- **Monte Vertine Bianco**
Monte Vertine
- **Sanpolo Bianco**
Castello di San Polo in Rosso
- **Vigneto della Rosa Bianca**
Podere Il Palazzino
- **Vin Brusco**
Montenidoli

**Bianco della Val d'Arbia**
See Val d'Arbia.

**Bianco della Valdinievole** DOC w. dr. (am.) (sw.) ★ DYA
Simple white from Trebbiano grown around Montecatini Terme and Pescia where most is consumed. Pale straw yellow, it is light with a hint of prickle. Vin Santo della Valdinievole is DOC but rarely seen.
Ag. Vin Santo 3 yrs.

**Bianco di Pitigliano** DOC w. dr. ★★ DYA
Trebbiano, Grechetto, and others combine in a neutral, clean,

sometimes fruity white from Pitigliano in S Tuscany best expressed by La Stellata's Lunaia.

| | |
|---|---|
| C.S. Cooperativa di Pitigliano | Lunaia-La Stellata |
| Il Bargaglino-Bargagli | Podere Scansanaccio |

**Bianco Pisano San Torpè** DOC w. dr. ★→ ★★ DYA
Recent DOC of Trebbiano, Canaiolo Bianco, and Malvasia grown SE of Pisa in a zone overlapping Chianti Colline Pisane. Straw green, lightly fragrant, dry, round, and slightly bitter at the finish. Vin Santo is also permitted.
Ag. Vin Santo 3 yrs.

| | |
|---|---|
| Badia di Morrona (Gaslini) | Fattoria di Piedivilla |
| Barone Hostini di Sant'Ermo | Fattoria Usigliano del Vescovo |
| Cosmiano-Aldobrandini | Fratelli Salvadori |
| Fattoria di Gello | San Giacomo |

**Bianco Vergine della Valdichiana** DOC w. dr. ★→ ★★ DYA
From Trebbiano chiefly with Malvasia and Grechetto grown in the Chiana valley between Arezzo and Chiusi. Straw yellow, it is usually soft and dry with hints of both sweet and bitter. Avignonesi's fragrant, fruity version, with its hints of almonds and honey, rates plaudits.

| | |
|---|---|
| Avignonesi | Fattoria Santa Vittoria |
| Baldetti | Luca della Robbia |
| C.S. Colli Aretini | Molino della Vecchia |
| C.S. di Cortona | Poliziano |
| Aldo Casagni | Tenuta di Vitereta |
| Fattoria delle Maestrelle | Vecchia Cantina di |
| Fattoria di Manzano | Montepulciano |

**Bolgheri** DOC p. w. dr. ★→★★ DYA
Recent DOC for rosé and white wines from Bolgheri SE of Livorno. The *rosato*, from Sangiovese and Canaiolo, is exemplified by Marchesi Antinori's Vigneto Scalabrone which includes 15% of Cabernet. The *bianco*, from Trebbiano and Vermentino, is not yet clearly identifiable. Sassicaia (not DOC) is grown nearby.

| | |
|---|---|
| Vigneto Scalabrone-Antinori | Podere Grattamacco |

**Borgo Amorosa** r. dr. ★★★ 83 85 86
From Sangioveto grown around the lovely country inn of Amorosa in the Colli Senesi, this pure Sangioveto is aged a year in small barrels of French oak, which tame its youthful tannic aggression into what shows all the signs of becoming a Tuscan aristocrat.
Amorosa

**Borro Cepparello** r. dr. ★★★→★★★★ 82 83 85 86
Pure Sangiovese selected in the Isole e Olena vineyards in Chianti Classico and aged in *barriques* by winemaker Paolo De Marchi. The amply structured '82 ranks as one of the finest new-style Tuscan Sangiovese reds to date.
Isole e Olena

**Brunello di Montalcino** DOCG r. dr. ★★→★★★★ 70 71 75 77 78 79 80 81 82 83 85 86
This long-lived red from Brunello (a clone of Sangiovese) grown in the community of Montalcino S of Siena has emerged relatively recently as one of Italy's most prized and, from some estates, most expensive wines. Powerfully structured, it matures in cask and bottles into an austere, warm, amply favored wine of deep ruby to brick red color and richly complex bouquet. Brunello is capable of grandeur with great age (notably from Biondi-Santi which originated the wine a century ago and still has bottles from 1888 and 1891), but rapid expansion has confused production among more than 100 registered growers or wineries. Output of some 3.5 million liters is 15 times greater than in the late 1960s. Still as vines mature, techniques improve and DOCG tightens the discipline, general quality is coming into line with great expectations. Though established methods prevail, many producers oppose the $3\frac{1}{2}$-year aging in cask required by DOCG. And here, as elsewhere, there is new interest in avant-garde table wines. Traditional producers Biondi-Santi and Fattoria Barbi have drawn criticism for recent vintages, while more progressive estates such as Il Poggione, Tenuta Caparzo and Altesino, as well as the prodigious Villa Banfi, have won high praise for what might be considered more contemporary styles of wine. See also Rosso di Montalcino.

Ag. 4 yrs. (3½ in casks); *riserva* 5 yrs.

| | |
|---|---|
| Altesino | La Casa-Caparzo |
| Argiano | La Chiesa di Santa Restituta |
| Biondi Santi-Il Greppo | La Fortuna |
| Camigliano | La Gerla |
| Canalicchio-Lambardi | Lisini |
| Canalicchio di Sopra-Pacenti | Mastrojanni |
| Capanna | Pertimali |
| Caprili | Pian di Conte-Talenti |
| Casale del Bosco-Nardi | Poderi Emilio Costanti |
| Casanova | Poggio Antico |
| Case Basse | San Carlo |
| Castelgiocondo | San Filippo dei Comunali |
| Castiglione del Bosco | Tenuta Caparzo |
| Col d'Orcia | Tenuta Il Poggione |
| Colombaio di Montosoli | Tenuta di Sesta |
| Fattoria dei Barbi-Colombini | Tenuta Valdicava |
| Il Casello-Franceschi | Val di Suga |
| Il Greppone Mazzi-Ruffino | Villa Banfi |

**Bruno di Rocca** r. dr. 83 85 86
From equal parts of Sangioveto and Cabernet Sauvignon grown near
Greve in Chianti Classico, and aged in small French barrels, this limited
edition from the '83 vintage was issued in late 1986 with all the signs of a
**★★★★** rating over time.
Vecchie Terre di Montefili

**Brusco dei Barbi** r. dr. **★★→★★★** 82 83 85 86
Special wine from Brunello grapes of Montalcino processed by *governo*
(refermentation induced by semidried grapes) to be ready sooner than
Brunello, though it has similar size and livelier character. Usually to
drink inside 4–5 years, but it can age.
Fattoria dei Barbi

**Ca' del Pazzo** r. dr. **★★→★★★** 82 83 85 86
An innovation of winemaker Vittorio Fiore, blending declassified
Brunello with Cabernet Sauvignon aged 6–7 months in small, new oak
barrels. Though initially impressive, early bottlings raised questions
about aging capacities.
Tenuta Caparzo

**Cabernet**
Cabernet Sauvignon (and some Franc) seems to have a bright future in
Tuscany as a varietal and in blends. After the pioneering of Sassicaia,
others have followed suit: Antinori with Solaia, Castello dei Rampolla
with Sammarco, Capezzana with Ghiaie della Furba (Cabernet-
Merlot), Villa Banfi with Tavernelle. Antinori's Tignanello started
another trend of Sangiovese with Cabernet, now found in many table
wines, as well as Chianti. See also Predicato.

**Cabreo**
Ruffino brand name. See under Predicato.

**Candia dei Colli Apuani** DOC w. dr. **★** DYA
From Vermentino and Albarola grown above Massa and Carrara in
NW Tuscany, this obscure DOC is straw colored, lightly aromatic, and
dry but soft with a hint of bitterness.

**Capannelle Rosso** r. dr. **★★★** 81 82 83 85 86
From pure Sangiovese grown above Gaiole in Chianti Classico and aged
briefly in barriques and then in casks, this is Raffaele Rossetti's premier
red. Early versions were elegant but light, though recent vintages
promised weight to go with style.
Capannelle

**Carmignano** DOC r. dr. ★★★→★★★★ 75 77 78 79 80 81 82 83 85 86
Recognized as one of the world's first wine zones of controlled name and
origin by the Grand Duchy of Tuscany in 1716, Carmignano is noted
chiefly for its aristocratic red. Recently the tiny zone W of Florence was
expanded to take in *rosato* and Vin Santo. The red is similar to Chianti,
but with Cabernet at 6–10% for a touch of elegance, Carmignano is
bright and ruby tending to garnet and orange with age. Its smooth, dry,
complex flavor and flowery bouquet show finesse similar to wines of the
Haut Médoc, in particular those of Contini Bonacossi with Tenuta di

Capezzana, Villa di Capezzana (*riserva*) and Villa di Trefiano. Though well expressed after 4–10 years, certain vintages (Villa di Capezzana 1931, for example) hold admirably for decades. Some 300,000 liters a year of Carmignano red show the most consistency of any Tuscan DOC, because only wines approved by experts at an annual tasting can carry the name. (See also Barco Reale.)
Ag. 18 months (1 yr in barrel); *riserva* 3 yrs (2 in barrel).
**– Rosato** p. dr. (fz.) (sp.)  **\*\* DYA**
Lovely rosé often called Vin Ruspo from Carmignano grapes processed in a special way to attain youthful freshness. Flowery and fruity, it can be *frizzante* or even *spumante*.
**– Vin Santo** am. dr. s/sw.  **\*\* → \*\*\***
Some of the best Tuscan Vin Santo originates in this zone, where it is now confirmed as DOC. Aged several years in small barrels, it can age 5–10 years in bottle.

| | |
|---|---|
| Fattoria Ambra | Podere Le Poggiarelle |
| Fattoria di Artimino | Podere Lo Locco |
| Fattoria di Bacchereto | Tenuta di Capezzana |
| Fattoria di Calavria | Villa Capezzana |
| Fattoria Il Poggiolo | Villa di Trefiano |
| Fattoria Le Farnete | |

**Cetinaia** r. dr.  **\*\*\*\*  81 82 83 85 86**
Cesare and Katrin Canessa decided to make an alternative to Chianti Classico from dark grapes only, but bucking the *barrique* trend, aged their "cru" in traditional Slavonian oak casks. The result may be less complex, less durable, less French than the competition, but Cetinaia is complete, opulent, joyously drinkable – a notion of what in an ideal world Chianti might be.
Castello di San Polo in Rosso

**Chardonnay** or **Chardonnay di Toscana** w. dr.  **\* → \*\*\*  83 84 85 86**
The preferred vine for white wine being planted in Tuscany now, Chardonnay has already begun to live up to its promise. Villa Banfi with Fontanelle, Villa di Capezzana and Ruffino with Cabreo Vigneto La Pietra are wood-aged wines sold internationally and noted for their style. Tenuta Caparzo's Le Grance Avignonesi's Marzocco and Castello di Ama's Colline di Ama joined the ranks with the '85 vintage. Other wineries were preparing their versions, though sometimes in a light, almost Trebbiano-like vein that may do well in Italy, probably not elsewhere.

**Chianti** DOCG
Italy's most renowned wine is produced in seven zones of central Tuscany in the historic hills extending from around Florence to well south of Siena between the coastal range and the Apennines. Recently promoted to DOCG which lowered grape yields and, in theory, upgraded standards, Chianti has reduced its output from the record 180 million liters of 1979 to about half that but remains the most voluminous of Italy's classified wines. DOCG also modified the grape formula, nearly eliminating the white Trebbiano and Malvasia from the blend with Sangiovese (or the small-berried Sangioveto) and Canaiolo and allowing in their place such outsiders as Cabernet, Merlot or Pinot Nero. The mandate is for deeper, richer, more structured Chianti with greater aging capacity, though many producers make both a *riserva* and a younger, lighter wine to sell within a year or two. Nearly forgotten is the straw-based *fiasco* that brought the world those light-hearted reds freshened by *governo* (a refermentation induced by adding semidried grapes to the new wine). But even the new Chianti from dark grapes alone has no semblance of a uniform personality. Each zone has distinct terrains and microclimates and since there are some 7,000 registered vineyards and hundreds of producers who tend to express individual attitudes and styles, Chianti is not one wine but many. Some can be as big and bold as a Pomerol or Saint-Emilion, others as subtle and refined as a Pauillac or Saint-Julien, others as insipid as the lowliest Bordeaux Rouge. But since estates or communes are not classified by *cru* and since only a few properties have status recognized on the market, there is no clear signal to the consumer of Chianti's type, style or value. Evidence of Chianti's lack of identity and uneasy standing are the new-style *vini da tavola* issued in growing numbers as the estates' most prized and pricey wines. Add to that the various rosé, white, bubbly and sweet bottlings

being offered and you'll see why in Chianti, as in Bordeaux, it could take a lifetime to get to know all the names, places and tastes. Still, the district names can have significance. Chianti Classico, the historic heartland, produces more good Chianti than any other zone, though the general quality level in the small Rufina district may be as high or higher. Throughout the zones there are fine producers whose wines can be exceptional values. In the listings I have marked with an * some whose wines have been consistently good in recent times, though I won't pretend to have cited all worthy producers. The consortiums of Chianti Classico (symbolized by a black rooster) and, for many producers elsewhere, Chianti Putto (symbolized by a cherub) supervise production and promotion, but not all the reliable wineries belong.
Ag. 5 months (8 months in Classico, Colli Fiorentini, Rufina); *riserva* (all zones) 3 yrs.

– **Chianti Classico** r. dr. ★★→★★★★ 75 77 78 79 80 81 82 83 85 86
The heart of Chianti between Florence and Siena, this picturesque zone includes Castellina, Radda, and Gaiole, where the original Chianti League was formed in the 13th century. Though character varies from sector to sector, quality is becoming more consistent. Much of the best, longest-lived *riserva* originates here. Most Chianti Classico is good in 2–5 years, *riserva* in 4–8, though some estates' wines can age well beyond a decade from good vintages.

*Aiola
*Aziano (Ruffino)
 Baccio da Gaiuole (Gittori)
*Badia a Coltibuono
*Berardenga-Felsina
 Bertolli
 Bibbiani
*Brolio-Ricasoli
 Caggiolo
 Campomaggio
*Capannelle
 Carobbio
 Casalgallo
 Casalino
 Casa Volterrani
*Casanuova di Nittardi
 Castagnoli
 Castelgreve
*Castellare di Castellina
*Castell'in Villa
*Castello dei Rampolla
*Castello di Ama,
   (Bellavista, San Lorenzo)
 Castello di Bossi
 Castello di Cacchiano
 Castello di Cerreto
*Castello di Fonterutoli
*Castello di Gabbiano
 Castello di Mugnana
*Castello di Querceto
 Castello di Rencine
*Castello di San Polo in Rosso
 Castello di Uzzano
 Castello di Verrazzano
*Castello di Volpaia
*Castello Vicchiomaggio
   (Prima Vigna)
 Castel Ruggero
 Castelvecchi
 Catignano
 Cellole
 Cennatoio
 Cerbaiola
 Chianti Geografico
*Cispiano
 Fattoria delle Corti
 Fattoria delle Lodoline

 Fattoria di Rosenanno
 Fattoria di Petroio
 Fattoria di Selvole
 Fattoria di Tizzano
 Fattoria di Vistarenni
*Fattoria Granaio (Melini)
 Fattoria La Pesanella
 Fattoria Le Pici
 Fattoria Montecchio
 Fattoria Poggiarello
*Fattoria Querciabella
 Filetta
*Fontodi
*Fossi
 Gaiello delle Filigare
 Grignanello
 I Sodi
 Il Campino di Mondiglia
 Il Guerrino
*Il Poggiolino
*Isole e Olena
 La Bricola
*La Loggia
*La Massa
*Lamole di Lamole
 La Pagliaia
 La Quercia
*La Selvanella-Melini
*Le Masse di San Leolino
 Le Piazze
*Lilliano
 Lo Spugnaccio
 Lornano
 Luiano
*Machiavelli-Serristori
*Melini
 Mocenni
*Monsanto (Il Poggio)
*Montagliari
*Montemaggio
 Montesassi
*Monte Vertine
*Montoro
*Nozzole
 Ormanni
*Pagliarese
 Palazzo al Bosco

*Peppoli-Antinori
Petroio alla Via della Malpensata
*Pian d'Albola-Zonin
*Podere Il Palazzino
*Podere Capaccia
Poggio alla Croce
*Poggio al Sole
Poggio Bonelli
*Poggio Rosso
Quercesola
Quornia
*Giorgio Regni (Valtellina)
Ricasoli
*Riecine
Riseccoli
*Rocca delle Macie
*Ruffino Riserva Ducale
San Cosma
*San Felice (Il Grigio)
*Santa Cristina-Antinori
Santa Lucia
Santo Stefano
San Vito in Berardenga

*Savignola Paolina
Straccali
Tenuta di Vignole
*Terrarossa-Melini
Terre di Melazzano
Tiorcia
*Tomarecchio & Miscianello
Valiano
*Vecchie Terre di Montefili
Vigna di Sorripa (Le Lame)
Vignamaggio
Vignavecchia
Vigneti di Poneta
*Villa Antinori (Riserva del
　Marchese)
Villa a Sesta
*Villa Banfi
*Villa Cafaggio
Villa Calcinaia
*Villa Cerna
Villa Giulia
Villa Montepaldi
*Villa Rosa

**– Chianti Colli Aretini** r. dr. ★→ ★★★ 82 83 85 86

Soft, well-scented Chianti from hills overlooking the Arno E of Chianti Classico. Most is of medium body to drink in 1—4 years, but some ages.

C.S. Colli Aretini
Castello di Montegonzi
Fattoria dell'Albereto
Fattoria di Chiaravalle
Fattoria di Marcena
Fattoria di Santa Vittoria
Fattoria La Trove
I Selvatici

*Monte Petrognano
San Fabiano
Sant'Elena
Savoia Aosta
*Villa Cilnia
Villa Fabbriche
*Villa La Selva

**– Chianti Colli Fiorentini** r. dr. ★→★★★★ 75 77 78 79 81 82 83 85 86

Source of much of the flask Chianti consumed in Florence, this zone in hills S and E of the city and down along the Arno and Pesa valleys, also makes some of the finest estate-bottled *riserva*. The flask wine, still sometimes made by *governo*, is light, soft, and round when young. The aging wine, of ruby-garnet color, later takes on amber-orange highlights; it can be robust, austere, aristocratic, and complete in bouquet and flavor, to drink in 5–10 years. Producers include several from the fringes of the zone with the right to call their wine Chianti.

Bracciolino
Ottorino Buti
Casalbosco
*Castello del Trebbio
Castello di Poppiano
Chianti Pillo
Collazzi
Conti Lucchesi Palli
Dianella Fucini
Fattoria Cabbiavoli
*Fattoria dell'Ugo
Fattoria di Loro
Fattoria di Mandri
Fattoria di Poggio Capponi
Fattoria di Sammontana
Fattoria Gigliola
*Fattoria Il Corno
Fattoria Il Palagio
Fattoria La Tancia
*Fattoria Lilliano
Fattoria Montellori
*Fattoria Pagnana
Fattoria Terranova

*Fattorie Giannozzi
Granaiolo & Coiano
I Golli
La Marta
*La Querce
La Tassinara
Le Torri a Mosciano
Montegufoni
Nardi-Dei
*Pasolini Dall'Onda Borghese
Passaponti
Poggio Romita
San Vito in Fior di Selva
*Tenuta Corfecciano
*Tenuta Il Monte
*Tenuta Ribaldaccio
*Torgaio di San Salvatore-
　Ruffino
*Torre a Decima
*Torre di Brugnano-Guicciardini
Uggiano
Ugolino
Villa dell'Olmo

**– Chianti Colli Senesi** r. dr. ★→ ★★★ 75 77 78 79 81 82 83 85 86

This zone, the largest, is split into three sectors: one around Montalcino, one around Montepulciano, and the rest in an arc S of the Classico zone from San Gimignano eastwards past Siena and Castelnuovo Berardenga. Chianti here ranges from some of the most elegant and long-lived down to the wine factory variety with price to match quality (that industry is centered in Poggibonsi and Castellina Scalo). Variations in conditions and techniques result in a wide range of styles.

*Amorosa
*Avignonesi
*Castel Pietraio
Castello di Montauto
*Castelpugna
Cecchi
Cercignano
*Chigi Saracini
*Riccardo Falchini
Fanetti
Farneta
*Fassati
Fattoria Casabianca
*Fattoria del Cerro
Fattoria di Monte Oliveto
Fattoria di Pancole
*Fattoria di Pietrafitta
Fattoria di Santo Pietro
*Fattoria Il Paradiso
Fattoria La Torre

Il Macchione
Il Palagetto
*Il Poggiolo-Bonfio
La Foce Castelluccio
*La Muraglia
*La Suvera
*Le Portine-Bonfio
Majnoni Guicciardini
*Montenidoli
Podere Santa Croce
*Poderi Boscarelli
*Poderi Emilio Costanti
*Poliziano
Rosso di Casavecchia
*Tenuta La Lellera
Fratelli Vagnoni
*Villa Cusona (Guicciardini Strozzi)
Villa Montemorli

– **Chianti Colline Pisane** r. dr. ★→★★ 82 83 85 86
From hills around Casciana Terme SE of Pisa, this zone has a mild maritime climate and its Chianti is the lightest, softest and, as a rule, the shortest-lived, though its round fruitiness makes it a versatile meal wine.

Badia di Morrona-Gaslini
Barone Hostini di Sant'Ermo
Benagotti
Cantina delle Colline Pisane
Cittadella

Fattoria Cempini Meazzuoli
Fattoria di Piedivilla
Tenuta di Ghizzano
Usigliano del Vescovo
Vino del Caratello-Salvadori

– **Chianti Montalbano** r. dr. ★→★★★ 82 83 85 86
The Montalbano balcony of hills W of Florence and S of Pistoia is more noted for Carmignano, but Chianti can also reach admirable levels here, usually in soft, fruity wines to drink in 1–5 years.

*Bibbiani
Fattoria Belvedere
Fattoria di Artimino
*Fattoria di Bacchereto

Fattoria di Montorio
*Fattoria Il Poggio
*Tenuta di Capezzana
*Tenuta di Lucciano-Spalletti

– **Chianti Rufina** r. dr. ★★→★★★★ 74 75 77 78 79 80 81 82 83 85 86
The smallest zone, in hills above the Sieve River E of Florence, produces some of the most grandiose Chianti. Rufina's vineyards lie at a relatively high altitude, which can be sensed in the rarefied bouquet and lingering elegance of well-aged wines, notably Selvapiana, Fattoria di Vetrice, Castello di Nipozzano and the special vineyard Montesodi.

Antiche Fattorie
Busini
Camperiti
*Castello di Nipozzano-Frescobaldi
Fattoria Altomena
Fattoria di Bossi
*Fattoria di Vetrice
Fattoria Parga

Grignano
*Montesodi-Frescobaldi
Petrognano
*Poggio a Remole-Frescobaldi
*Poggio Reale (Spalletti)
*Selvapiana
*Tenuta di Poggio
*Villa di Ponte

**Colline Lucchesi** DOC r. w. dr. ★→ ★★★ 82 83 85 86
Rosso delle Colline Lucchesi, a good Chianti-style red grown in the hills around Lucca, now shares its zone with a white based on Trebbiano. The red can be soft and lively to drink in a year or two or, in some cases, as durable and elegant as a fine Chianti. The white is an unknown entity.

Alberto Bertolli
Fattoria Bruguier
Fattoria di Forci
Fattoria di Fubbiano

Fattoria I Tre Cancelli
Maionchi
Tenuta Maria Teresa

**Coltassala** r. dr.  ★★★→★★★★  80 81 82 83 85 86
A special vineyard red from Sangioveto and Mammolo grown at
Volpaia high in Chianti Classico and seasoned in small, new oak
barrels. Rich yet refined, it has enviable complexity of bouquet and
flavors with a soft elegance deriving from high altitude vines.
Castello di Volpaia

**Concerto** r. dr.  ★★★  81 82 83 85 86
From Sangiovese with Cabernet and other varieties aged in *barriques*,
this fine red made by Lapo and Filippo Mazzei should take its place in
the front ranks of Chianti Classico's alternative wines.
Castello di Fonterutoli

**Elba** DOC r. w. dr. (sp.)  ★→|★★★|  81 82 83 85 86
The island where Napoleon encouraged viticulture during his brief exile
is noted for iron-rich soil which lends vigor to wines. The *rosso*, from
nearly the same grapes as Chianti, is usually bright ruby and grapy, an
all-purpose wine to drink young, though the red of Tenuta La Chiusa
stands out for its full body, depth, and bouquet, reaching peaks of
elegance in 4–8 years. The *bianco*, from Procanico (Trebbiano) chiefly, is
light straw gold, delicately scented, dry but rather full-bodied, and soft,
though the best have a crisp finish. A *spumante* is also permitted.
Azienda Agricola di Mola             Tenuta Acquabona
M. Gasparri & C.                     Tenuta La Chiusa
Podere La Pianella                   Vinicola Elbana

**Elegia** r. dr.  ★★★  83 85 86
From Prugnolo Gentile grapes grown near Montepulciano, this is
Federico Carletti's deft variation on the time-worn theme of Vino
Nobile. The '83, after a year in small barrels, was still emerging three
years later, but with immense power and depth that promise an
illustrious future.
Poliziano

**Flaccianello della Pieve** r. dr.  ★★★★  81 82 83 85 86
Perhaps the most acclaimed of the new-style Tuscan reds from pure
Sangiovese, Flaccianello comes from a vineyard at Panzano in Chianti
Classico. After nearly a year in *barriques* and a few months more in casks,
it reaches a graceful harmony in bottle, a tribute to the skill and
patience of Dino and Domiziano Manetti.
Fontodi

**Fontanelle**
See Chardonnay.

**Galestro** w. dr.  ★★  DYA
New-style white backed by a consortium of producers equipped to vinify
this basically simple but technologically advanced product. Based on
Trebbiano with other grapes grown in central Tuscany, it puts to
profitable use the excess of white wine in Chianti. It was the first Italian
wine to have a maximum alcohol grade (10.5%) and must be processed
and bottled entirely at low temperature. The result is a light, dry, pale,
modern wine, attractively fresh and fruity and made in volume with
exemplary consistency.
Agricoltori di Chianti Geografico    Marchesi Antinori
Barone Ricasoli                      Marchesi de' Frescobaldi
Cecchi                               Rocca delle Macie
Fattoria Fonti                       Ruffino
Fattorie Giannozzi                   Teruzzi-Puthod (Ponte a
Il Raccianello                         Rondolino)
Le Chiantigiane

**Ghiaie della Furba** r. dr.  ★★★  78 79 81 82 83 85 86
Established red of Cabernet Sauvignon and Cabernet Franc with
Merlot grown in low-lying, gravelly vineyards near Carmignano.
Recent vintages of this racy, Bordeaux-style wine are still immature, but
with time promise to reinforce the estate's lofty status.
Villa di Capezzana

**Granato di Scarlino** r. dr.  |★★|  82 83 85 86
Tasty red in the Chianti mold at Scarlino near Grosseto. Of
bright ruby-garnet color, it has full bouquet and lively warm flavor after
3–4 years, sometimes more.
Righetti-Lancione

**Grattamacco** r. w. dr.  ★★→★★★  81 82 83 85 86
Inspired wines made by Piermario Meletti Cavallari near Castagneto
Carducci in coastal hills SE of Livorno. The *rosso*, from Colorino,
Sangiovese, and light varieties, has irresistible berry-like goodness in its
youth. The *bianco*, of Trebbiano, Malvasia and others, is fruity, zestful,
as poised as whites of supposedly nobler breed. The estate is also
preparing a red based on Cabernet and aged in new oak that promises
to be a worthy neighbor of Sassicaia.
Podere di Grattamacco

**Grifi** r. dr.  ★★★→★★★★  81 82 83 85 86
Growingly admired blend of Prugnolo Gentile with a localized clone of
Cabernet grown near Montepulciano and aged by winemaker Ettore
Falvo in new *barriques*. This should reach peaks of splendor in 5–8 years
from the harvest.
Avignonesi

**Grosso Senese** r. dr.  ★★★→★★★★  81 82 83 85 86
From pure Sangiovese grown in a privileged area of Chianti Classico
near Brolio, this big-bodied red, after aging in *barriques* and larger casks,
has found a place in the elite of Tuscany's new-style wines.
Podere Il Palazzino

**I Coltri** r. dr.  80 81 82 83 85 86
Recently issued blend of Sangiovese and Cabernet from the Granaio
vineyard in Chianti Classico, this is Melini's entry in the *nouvelle vague* of
Tuscan reds. Aged at least a year in *barriques*, early vintages were
difficult to assess but left no doubt that a promising future awaits more
recent efforts.
Melini

**I Sodi di San Niccolò** r. dr.  ★★★→★★★★  79 80 81 82 83 85 86
In the new wave of single-vineyard Tuscan reds aged in new French
oak, this has moved quickly to the fore. From Sangioveto, Canaiolo and
Malvasia Nera grown near Castellina in Chianti, it has the depth and
complexity to improve for 6–8 years or more.
Castellare di Castellina

**Il Lucomone** r. dr.  ★★  81 82 83 85 86
This table wine based on Sangiovese grown near Chiusi has the
elements – color, body, fruit – to rival the best of neighboring Vino
Nobile, if it only had a touch more finesse.
Villa Peraio

**La Corte** r. dr.  ★★★  78 79 81 82 83 85 86
A special vineyard Sangiovese grown in Chianti Classico, aged in
*barrique* and fined in bottle. The early vintages from this progressive
estate were delicate and finely tuned like a Pauillac.
Castello di Querceto

**Le Pergole Torte** r. dr.  ★★★→★★★★  77 78 79 81 83 85 86
Sergio Manetti created Tuscany's original new-style pure Sangiovese in
1977 and has kept it ahead of the competition in prestige and price
since, though it no longer stands alone. Manetti's Il Sodaccio is similar
and he has recently opted out of the Chianti Classico ranks and sells his
fine basic red as Monte Vertine. One innovation, named "M" (a barrel-
aged white from Trebbiano and Malvasia) missed the mark, however,
unless you like liquid oak.
Monte Vertine

**Le Vignacce** r. dr.  82 83 85 86
From equal portions of Brunello, Cabernet Sauvignon and
Montepulciano d'Abruzzo grown on the outskirts of Arezzo, this
*barrique*-aged invention of winemaker Giovanni Bianchi has so far
promised more than it's delivered. But the idea seems worth working on.
Villa Cilnia

**Logaiolo** r. dr.  ★★  82 83 85 86
This warmhearted red from dark grapes only grown at Vagliagli in
Chianti Classico and aged in traditional chestnut casks, needs 3–4 years
to reach a prime of drinkability.
Aiola

**Malvasia**
The ancient vine has many clones grown in Tuscany, used in Chianti

(alas) but more suitably in white wines both dry and sweet (Vin Santo).
Though rarely noteworthy on its own, Avignonesi's Malvasia – dry,
smooth, silky – hints that better things might be coming.

**Maremma** r. p. w. dr. ★→★★★ 82 83 85 86
Wines from the coastal Maremma hills of Grosseto province have
attracted notice for their sound virtues. The *rosso*, from Sangiovese and
others, is bright ruby, fragrant, and round, good in 1–4 years. The
*rosato*, from dark grapes, is lively when young. The *bianco*, from
Procanico (Trebbiano), Ansonica, and Vermentino, is light and fruity,
ideal with fish inside a year. The newly conceived white Corniello and
red Ghimbergo from the Cornia valley bear watching, as does the
intriguing Ghibello from the town of Suvereto.

**Monte Antico** r. w. dr. ★→★★★ 78 79 81 82 83 85 86
Name applies to distinguished table wines from Monte Antico in hills
between Siena and Grosseto, adjacent to Montalcino. The *rosso*, from
Sangiovese, Canaiolo, and light varieties, is deep ruby tending to
garnet-orange with 5–6 years, dry, elegant with good bouquet and long
finish. The *bianco*, from Trebbiano and Malvasia is pale gold, soft, and
scented when young. Castello di Monte Antico red stands out.

Ardenghesca                         Fattoria La Pievanella
Castello di Monte Antico

**Montecarlo** DOC r. w. dr. ★★→★★★ 85 86
The zone E of Lucca is known for its white. Though based on
Trebbiano, the supplementary varieties – Sémillon, the Pinots,
Vermentino, Sauvignon, Roussanne – distinguish it and give producers
a chance to create styles. Bright straw, delicate and flowery, it is suavely
fruity and sumptuous with a crisp finish. Some vintages improve beyond
a year or two. DOC has expanded to include a red based on Sangiovese,
which shows promise (see Rosso di Cercatoia) even if it isn't established
yet.

Badia Pozzeveri                     Fattoria di Montecarlo
Buonasola                           Fattoria La Torre
Cerruglio-Tori                      Fattoria Manzini
Eredi di Carmignani                 Fattoria Michi
Fattoria del Buonamico              Romano Franceschini
Fattoria del Teso                   Poderi San Luigi

**Montescudaio** DOC r. w. dr. (am.) (sw.) ★→★★ 82 83 85 86
This hilly zone inland from Cecina in Pisa province has three types of
wine. The *rosso* from Sangiovese and light grapes, is bright ruby,
scented, and soft, good in 2–5 years. The *bianco*, based on Trebbiano, if
rarely inspiring can be tasty young. The rare Vin Santo, from semidried
light grapes, must be aged in small barrels in the traditional way and
have 17% alcohol, whether sweet or dry.
Ag. Vin Santo 3 yrs.

Fattoria San Giovanni              La Rinserrata
Fattoria Santa Maria               Podere Morazzano

**Montesodi** r. dr. ★★★→★★★★ 74 78 79 80 82 83 85 86
This excellent special vineyard red from Frescobaldi's Castello di
Nipozzano is DOC under Chianti Rufina.
Marchesi de' Frescobaldi

**Morellino di Scansano** DOC r. dr. ★★→★★★ 79 81 82 83 85 86
Up and coming DOC from hills SE of Grosseto around Scansano, this is
the only classified Tuscan red besides Brunello that may be made
entirely from Sangiovese. Deep ruby tending to garnet, it develops big
bouquet and dry, warm, austere, fairly robust balance with long finish
in 4–5 years, sometimes more. An appellation to watch.
Ag. *riserva* 2 yrs.

Banditaccia                         Fattoria Coltiberto
Erik Banti                          Fattoria Le Pupille
Bargagli                            Ezio Montellassi
C.S. del Morellino di Scansano      Poggiolungo
Fattoria Palazzaccio                Sellari Franceschini

**Mormoreto** r. dr. 83 85 86
From Castello di Nipozzano in Chianti Rufina, this blend of two-thirds
Cabernet Sauvignon with Sangioveto will be issued by Frescobaldi
under the Predicato di Biturica grouping (see). Though too young to

evaluate fully, the '83 showed signs of developing into a leader in the field.
Marchesi de' Frescobaldi

**Moscadello di Montalcino** DOC w. s/sw. sw. fz. ★★ DYA
Of ancient renown, this sweet Moscato from Montalcino has been revived as a DOC, thanks largely to the American giant Villa Banfi and its heavy investment in a futuristic winery and vast vineyards. Though aimed at the U.S. market, Moscadello should find admirers elsewhere, for its Muscat fragrance, clean sweetness and bubbles seem to be in vogue. There is also a still and sweeter *liquoroso* version (rarely seen).
Tenuta Il Poggione                    Villa Banfi

**Palazzo Altesi** r. dr. ★★★→★★★★ 81 82 83 85 86
Though made entirely from Brunello grapes grown near Montalcino, this is the most voluptuously Burgundian of the new Tuscan reds, probably because winemaker Angelo Solci does a French-style maceration with whole grapes and ages the wine in barrels direct from the Cote d'Or. Immediately soft and seductive, but it has enough backbone to benefit from years of aging.
Altesino

**Parrina** DOC r. p. w. dr. ★★ 82 83 84 85 86
Tiny zone in hills E of the Argentario promontory in S Tuscany. The *rosso*, based on Sangiovese, is bright ruby, fruity, neatly dry, balanced, and tasty in 2–4 years. The *riserva* can show class for longer. The *rosato* can be bright in its youth. The *bianco*, from Procanico (Trebbiano), is light golden and grapy with a bitter undertone, good young.
Ag. *riserva* (*rosso*) 3 yrs.
Fattoria del Chiusone                    Fattoria La Parrina

**Pinot Bianco**
Popping up here and there as a table wine, this fine variety shows promise as an alternative to Chardonnay and a complement to Trebbiano.

**Pinot Grigio** w. dr. ★★→★★★ 84 85 86
The Pinot Grigio craze in N Italy influenced planting here for wines that, though still rare, show unexpected class. Banfi's perfumed San Angelo from Montalcino can match most anything from the Venezie, and Castello di Ama's barrel-aged Vigna Bellaria ended my doubts that Pinot Grigio and oak can go together.
Castello di Ama (Vigna Bellaria)    Villa Banfi (San Angelo)

**Pinot Nero**
Though Tuscans aren't mounting any threats to Burgundy, Pinot Nero is gaining favor in the region, so far for blending, but planting in high, cool places indicates more novelties on the horizon.

**Pomino** DOC r. w. dr. (s/sw.) ★★→★★★ 82 83 85 86
New DOC for red, white and Vin Santo made in one of the oldest recognized wine areas of Tuscany in the Chianti Rufina area. The *rosso*, from Sangiovese with Canaiolo, Cabernet and Merlot, is enticingly smooth and round, to enjoy in 2–6 years, sometimes considerably more. The *bianco*, already renowned from Frescobaldi, is based on Pinot Bianco and Chardonnay with Trebbiano. Pale golden, flowery, smoothly dry with polish, it has the stuff to last several years. A special reserve bottling known as Il Benefizio is barrel fermented, rounded out in *barriques* to give an oaky, richly scented wine that can rate ★★★★ when it mellows into form. The Vin Santo from raisined grapes follows traditional standards.
Ag. 1 yr; *riserva* (*rosso*) 3 yrs; Vin Santo 4 yrs in barrels.
Marchesi de'Frescobaldi

**Predicato** or **Alto Predicato**
Though still in the early stages, several key Tuscan producers led by Ambrogio Folonari of Ruffino have created a system for classifying new-style Tuscan wines under what has been proposed as a DOC for Vini dei Colli della Toscana Centrale. Members' wines approved by an expert tasting commission may carry the term Predicato (or eventually Alto Predicato for highest quality) under four categories:

– **Predicato del Muschio** for white based on either Chardonnay or Pinot Bianco with up to 20% Riesling permitted. Ruffino's Cabreo Vigneto La Pietra wood-aged Chardonnay was the first on the market, from '83 (★★★) with even more impressive vintages aging.
– **Predicato del Selvante** for white wines based on Sauvignon Blanc.
– **Predicato di Biturica** for red wines based on blends of Cabernet (at 30% minimum) and Sangiovese. Ruffino's Cabreo Podere il Borgo '82 (★★★★) is one of the classiest expressions to date of this felicitous mix.
– **Predicato di Cardisco** for red based on Sangiovese with up to 10% of other red grapes, excepting Cabernet or Merlot.
By late 1986, several other producers – including Frescobaldi, Melini, San Felice and Giovanni Bianchi's Villa Cilnia – had wines approved for release.

**Querciagrande** r. dr. ★★★ 83 85 86
Pure Sangioveto from a vineyard on the Podere Capaccia estate near Radda in Chianti Classico. Selected in better years and aged in oak casks, the wine has the size and depth to indicate excellence with age.
Podere Capaccia

**Rosato** or **Rosé**
Many rosés are made in Tuscany, usually from Sangiovese blended with other varieties. Most popular is Ruffino's simplistic Rosatello. Antinori's Vigneto Scalabrone (Bolgheri DOC) and Frescobaldi's Villa di Corte show blossomy class. Impressive rosés have been issued in Chianti Classico by Badia a Coltibuono and Castello di San Polo in Rosso. Among the artisanal-style rosés, two from the Montescudaio zone stand out: Rosato da Morazzano and Rosato La Rinserrata. Vin Ruspo, now Carmignano DOC as *rosato*, is also noteworthy.

**Rosso delle Colline Lucchesi**
This long-standing DOC now comes under Colline Lucchesi.

**Rosso di Cercatoia** r. dr. ★★→★★★★ 79 81 82 83 85 86
Fine red made at Montecarlo near Lucca from Sangiovese and other varieties selected in top vintages and aged in oak casks. Deep ruby-garnet, over 3–6 years it develops rich bouquet and, from Fattoria del Buonamico, the velvety texture of good red Burgundy. This may now qualify as Montecarlo Rosso DOC.
Fattoria del Buonamico

**Rosso di Don Giovanni** r. dr. ★★ 82 83 85 86
From Sangiovese with some Cabernet grown in the Colline Pisane this is pleasant, even refined, but not as persuasive as its operatic namesake.
Principi Aldobrandini

**Rosso di Montalcino** DOC r. dr. ★★→★★★★ 83 84 85 86
New appellation for red wine from Brunello grapes of Montalcino not aged long enough to qualify as Brunello di Montalcino and serving as an alternative to DOCG. Though lacking the austere, tannic complexity of aged Brunello, this Rosso can make eminently delightful drinking at much lower cost. Generous in color, bouquet and body, round, complete, even noble – some prefer this style to Brunello, which has been criticized for having too much cask age. Good young, some versions could age. Tenuta Il Poggione's Rosso is consistently among Italy's best wines for the price. Chrysler's Lee Iacocca, who owns a villa nearby, exports to the U.S.A. under the Villa Nicola label.

| | |
|---|---|
| Altesino | La Chiesa di Santa Restituta |
| Argiano | La Fortuna |
| Camigliano | La Magia |
| Campogiovanni | Lisini |
| Capanna | Mastrojanni |
| Casanova | Poggio Antico |
| Castelgiocondo | San Filippo dei Comunali |
| Castiglione del Bosco | Tenuta Caparzo |
| Centine-Villa Banfi | Tenuta Il Poggione |
| Col d'Orcia | Val di Suga |
| Colombaio di Montosoli | Villa Nicola-Iacocca |
| Il Casello | |

**Rosso di Montepulciano** r. dr. ★★ 85 86
*Vini da tavola* are sold under this name proposed as a DOC alternative to
Vino Nobile di Montepulciano DOCG.

**Rosso di Toscana**
The generic term for Tuscan red *vini da tavola* applies to many of the
region's finest wines along with lesser products. Sangiovese or
Sangioveto is also often used.

**Rubizzo** r. dr. ★★ DYA
Youthful, light ruby wine from red grapes for Chianti vinified under a
modern *governo* method that leaves it soft, fruity, full of brio – "the
perfect wine for spicy food," as estate owner Italo Zingarelli, who adores
spicy food, puts it.
Rocca delle Macìe

**Sammarco** r. dr. ★★★★ 80 81 82 83 85 86
Owner Alceo Di Napoli reversed the formula and let Cabernet
Sauvignon dominate Sangiovese from his vineyards below Panzano in
Chianti Classico. A big wine, in its youth it hints more at California's
North Coast than Bordeaux, but time brings out a princely grandeur to
which only a chosen few Italian Cabernets could aspire.
Castello dei Rampolla

**San Giocondo** r. dr. ★★ DYA
Italy's most popular *vino novello*. Like Beaujolais *nouveau* its sprightly,
grapy freshness is best within 3–4 months.
Marchesi Antinori

**Sangioveto di Coltibuono** r. dr. ★★★→★★★★ 80 81 82 83 85 86
Badia a Coltibuono's old vines of Chianti Classico's true Sangioveto
make wine of great authority but stubborn disposition, demanding years
beyond the *barrique* aging before it softens its tannins and reveals its
noblesse. But Sangioveto should easily outdistance the field of parvenus.
Badia a Coltibuono

**Santa Costanza** r. dr. ★★ DYA
Banfi's *nouveau* from Montalcino not only hits the market before
Beaujolais but, being an infant Brunello, may still be pleasantly plump
months after the flower children of Gamay have withered. Winemaker
Ezio Rivella recommends it aged – i.e. at 6–12 months.
Villa Banfi

**Sassicaia** r. dr. ★★★→★★★★ 75 76 77 78 79 80 81 82 83 84 85 86
This Cabernet Sauvignon from the Tenuta San Guido at Bolgheri SE of
Livorno is a contemporary legend, admired in Italy and abroad
("Perhaps Italy's best red wine" – Hugh Johnson) despite limited
production of 50,000–60,000 bottles a year and increasing competition.
A curiosity in Tuscany, it often deviates from the vintage patterns for
other reds. Aged 2 years in *barriques*, this full ruby-garnet wine needs 5
years in bottle to bring out deep, herby bouquet and rich, velvety, warm
flavor with Bordeaux-like breed and California-like structure.
Marchesi Incisa della Rocchetta

**Sassolato** w. sw. ★★★ 83 84 85 86
A refreshing switch from the often plodding Vin Santo, this sleek *amabile*
from semidried Malvasia, Trebbiano, and Chardonnay grown outside
Arezzo shows harmony with elaborate tone lent by aging in new French
barrels, plus bouquet that would flatter more than a few Sauternes.
Villa Cilnia

**Secentenario** r. dr. ★★★★ NV
This special red was created from Sangiovese and Cabernet grown in
Chianti Classico and issued in some 16,000 magnums in 1985 only to
celebrate the Antinori 600th anniversary. A superb red with great aging
potential, it seemed to combine the best traits of Tignanello and Solaia.
Marchesi Antinori

**Ser Niccolò** r. dr. ★★ 79 80 81 82 83 85 86
From Sangiovese Grosso and Canaiolo grown in Chianti at
Sant'Andrea in Percussina where (Ser) Niccolò Machiavelli whiled
away his unhappy exile from Florence, this limited issue red has a solid

base but might be more intriguing if the old master were around to give
it a deft twist or two.
Conti Serristori

**Solaia** r. dr. ★★★→★★★★  79 82 85
Cabernet Sauvignon (in recent years with about 15% Sangiovese) from
the Solaia plot of Antinori's Santa Cristina estate in Chianti Classico,
this highly touted newcomer needs to grow a bit to live up to its
credentials, but with time it will bolster the house record for excellence.
Marchesi Antinori

**Solatio Basilica** r. dr. ★★★→★★★★  81 82 83 85 86
Winemaker Stefano Farkas fashioned this predominately Sangiovese
wine from old vines in a plot near Panzano in Chianti Classico. Deep,
dark, loaded with extract, it needs time to soften and expand, but it
should be one of the new wave wines to keep well over a decade.
Villa Cafaggio

**Spumante** w. dr. ★★→★★★  DYA
The trend toward sparkling wine is spreading through Tuscany, though
so far results are mixed. Antinori has been producing *méthode champenoise*
from northern Pinots and Chardonnay since early in the century and
recently Frescobaldi and Ricasoli have successfully followed suit. Others
use home-grown grapes: Capezzana Chardonnay and Pinot, Falchini
Vernaccia di San Gimignano. All wines cited are *champenoise* (m.c.).
Many charmats are also made.
– **Antinori Brut Nature (m.c.)**
Marchesi Antinori
– **Brut di Capezzana (m.c.)**
Villa di Capezzana
– **Falchini Brut (m.c.)**
Riccardo Falchini
– **Frescobaldi Brut (m.c.)**
Marchesi de'Frescobaldi
– **Ricasoli Brut (m.c.)**
Barone Ricasoli

**Tavernelle** r. dr. ★★★→★★★★  82 83 85 86
From Cabernet Sauvignon grown at Montalcino and aged in new
French oak, Tavernelle, though youthful and full of vigor from '82 and
'83, has been winning praise and prizes, a tribute to Ezio Rivella's
Italianized California style.
Villa Banfi

**Tignanello** r. dr. ★★★→★★★★  75 77 78 79 80 81 82 83 85 86
From Sangiovese grown in Chianti with about 20% Cabernet, this is
among the most admired and imitated reds of Italy, the brainchild of
Antinori enologist Giacomo Tachis and the inspiration for a whole new
breed of Tuscan winemakers. Despite the mixed background,
Tignanello has aristocratic grace with complexity – from aging in small
oak barrels – that normally reach a peak in 7–10 years.
Marchesi Antinori

**Torricella** am. dr. ★★★→★★★★  77 81
Extraordinary white made only in years when conditions were ideal
(recently '77 and '81) from partly dried Malvasia and Trebbiano grown
in a special plot at Brolio in Chianti Classico. Left briefly in oak casks
and then for many years in bottle, which heightens its golden amber
color, refined bouquet and aristocratically dry, lingering flavor.
Barone Ricasoli

**Trebianco** w. dr. ★★★  85 86
Bizarre combination of Chardonnay, Sauvignon Blanc and Traminer in
a wine as unconventional as its producers, the Di Napoli family, but as
fresh, full and tasty as any white of Chianti Classico.
Castello dei Rampolla

**Val d'Arbia** DOC w. dr. (s/sw.) ★→★★ DYA
New DOC for dry white and Vin Santo grown along the Arbia valley
between Radda in Chianti and Montalcino. Bianco della Val d'Arbia –
based on Trebbiano and Malvasia – is delicate, dry, clean and fruity
when vinified at low temperature. Vin Santo follows the usual lines.
Ag. Vin Santo 3 yrs.

| | |
|---|---|
| Aiola | Fattoria di Vistarenni |
| Barone Ricasoli | Pieve a Barca |
| Casale del Bosco | San Felice |
| Castell'in Villa | Tolomei |
| Castello d'Albola | Villa di Radi |

**Vermiglio**

The name used centuries ago for red (or vermilion) wines from Chianti has been proposed to describe new DOC wines from the zone as alternatives to Chianti DOCG.

**Vernaccia di San Gimignano** DOC w. dr. (sw.) (fz.) (sp.)
★→ ★★★ 85 86

Ancient white from Vernaccia grown around the towered hill town. For years made by traditional methods into a golden wine of some aging capacity (as typified by Pietrafitta), the trend is toward clean, pale, flowery wines to drink young. Leading producers are Falchini, with a smooth-textured style, and Teruzzi & Puthod, whose singular oak-aged *riserva* Terre di Tufo has brought out Vernaccia's too often hidden personality. Bubbly versions are increasing; the *liquoroso* seems nearly extinct.

Ag. *riserva* 1 yr.

| | |
|---|---|
| Castello di Montauto | Il Palagetto |
| Castello di Pescile | Guicciardini-Strozzi (Cusona) |
| Riccardo Falchini | Il Palagio |
| Fattoria della Quercia | Il Raccianello |
| Fattoria di Fugnano | La Quercia di Racciano |
| Fattoria di Monte Oliveto | Montenidoli |
| Fattoria di Pancole | San Quirico |
| Fattoria Il Paradiso | Teruzzi & Puthod-Ponte |
| Fattoria di Pietrafitta | a Rondolino |
| Fattoria La Torre | Fratelli Vagnoni |
| Fattoria Tollena | Vigna a Solatio |
| Giulio Frigeni | |

**Vigorello** r. dr. ★★★→★★★★ 79 80 81 82 83 85 86

From two clones of Sangiovese and 15% Cabernet grown in Chianti Classico, this vigorous red is aged in casks, *barriques* and bottles to attain notable depth and durability. The pride of the steadily improving San Felice estate near Brolio.
San Felice

**Villa Antinori Bianco** w. dr. ★★★ 85 86

Impeccable white from Trebbiano and nobler varieties grown on Antinori estates in Chianti Classico. Pale golden and delicate in scent, it has some of the refinement of a good, dry white Graves.
Marchesi Antinori

**Vin Ruspo or Vinruspo**
See Carmignano Rosato.

**Vin Santo** am. (r.) dr. s/sw. sw. ★★→★★★

This traditional sipping wine ("holy wine" probably refers to use in the Mass) is made all over Tuscany from grapes semidried on racks or by hanging from rafters, pressed, and sealed in *caratelli* (small barrels) in lofts for at least 3 years. Vintages vary intricately from place to place, though good Vin Santo can last for years. Most comes from Malvasia and Trebbiano, but dark grapes and red wine also figure. Whether sweet, semisweet or austerely dry, Vin Santo should be clear golden-amber, generously aromatic, strong (14–17%), and velvety. At best (the maximum ★★★★ is Avignonesi's luxuriant Vin Santo), it can be one of Italy's great dessert wines. But too often it is crudely improvised, oxidized, unpleasant. Industrial imitations (often from S Italian Moscato) are widespread. A regionwide classification has been delayed, but Vin Santo is DOC under Bianco di Valdinievole, Bianco Pisano San Torpè, Carmignano, Montescudaio, Pomino and Val d'Arbia, so producers in those zones are listed there. Every Tuscan farm has its own production, so only a choice few in commerce are cited.

| | |
|---|---|
| Avignonesi | Aldo Casagni |
| Badia a Coltibuono | Castell'in Villa |
| Brolio (Ricasoli) | Castellare di Castellina |
| Giovanni Cappelli | Castello di Uzzano |

Castello di Volpaia
Riccardo Falchini
Fattoria dei Barbi
Fattoria di Martignana
Guicciardini Strozzi (Cusona)
Marchesi Antinori
Marchesi de'Frescobaldi

Monte Vertine
Pagliarese
Poggio al Sole
San Giorgio a Lapi
Tenuta Il Poggione
Tenuta La Lellera

**Vinattieri Rosso** r. dr. 82 83 85 86
From Sangioveto and Brunello selected in Chianti and Montalcino and
aged in French oak by winemaker Maurizio Castelli, this new wave red
won't be rated since the author is involved in production.
Vinattieri

**Vino Nobile di Montepulciano** DOCG ★★→ ★★★★ 75 77 78 79 81
82 83 85 86
The hill town of Montepulciano in SE Tuscany is the home of this red
with the resounding name and the legend of having been described as
"king of all wines" by the poet Francesco Redi in the 17th century.
Though it can be splendid on occasion, production lacks consistency.
Still, the once habitual flaws in vinification and aging are less apparent
as professional winemakers come to the fore and DOCG helps weed out
inferior products. Vino Nobile resembles Chianti *riserva* in character and
grape content – Prugnolo Gentile, a clone of Sangiovese, dominates the
blend of red and white varieties. Deep ruby garnet tending toward brick
red with age, it is noted for a trace of violets in bouquet and an austerely
dry, somewhat tannic flavor, which can become truly noble after 3–4
years and stay so for over a decade. Paola De Ferrari Corradi's Poderi
Boscarelli has been the noblest in recent times, though other wineries
have also been bringing out the inherent class of this wine, notably
Avignonesi, Fattoria Del Cerro, Fattoria di Fognano, Fassati, Poliziano
and Valdipiatta. But some of the established names seem rather
stagnant. Production is about 1.8 million liters a year.
Ag. 2 yrs.; *riserva* 3 yrs.

Avignonesi
Fratelli Bologna Buonsignori
Buracchi
Cantine Baiocchi
Cantine Riunite Mario Contucci
Carletti della Giovampaola
Casella-Carpini
Fassati
Fattoria Casalte
Fattoria del Cerro
Fattoria di Fognano

Fattoria di Gracciano-
    Mazzucchelli
Il Macchione
Pantano
Poderi Boscarelli
Poggio alla Sala
Poliziano
Giuseppe Raspanti & Figli
Tenuta di Gracciano-Della Seta
Tenuta Sant'Agnese-Fanetti
Tenuta Valdipiatta

## Wine & Food

Contemporary Tuscan food is a triumph of nature: simplified
country cooking, it lacks imagination, but is an accurate
expression of the almost mystical equilibrium Tuscans maintain
with their land. The elaborations exported to France by the
Medici are long gone and mostly forgotten. Also vanishing,
sadly, are the inspired dishes that used to take cheerful Tuscan
mammas all morning to create. But the basics are still there:
bread and the emerald-green *extra vergine* olive oil that combine
so well in *bruschetta* and *panunto*; exquisite vegetables and greens
that make a *minestrone* easy (Tuscans have always been more
resourceful with soups than pasta); the rosemary, garlic, onion,
sage, basil, bay leaves, and tarragon that heighten flavor; and, of
course, the bean, so adored that when detractors couldn't think
of anything worse they called the Tuscans *mangiafagioli* (bean
eaters). Meat, simply grilled or roasted, is essential in the diet:
chicken, pork, duck, and Florence's highly rated *bistecca alla
fiorentina* (the hefty slab of beef from native Chianina steers).

Boar and game birds are also prized in this most wooded Italian region. Some of Italy's tastiest *pecorino* comes from sheep grazed in the stark *crete* hills of Siena province, notably around Pienza.

**Acquacotta** "Cooked water," soup of vegetables in season and mushrooms.
\*\* Parrina *bianco*.
**Arista** Pork loin roasted with rosemary and garlic.
\*\*\* Vino Nobile di Montepulciano.
**Bistecca alla fiorentina** Thick steak charred on the outside, pink inside, served with beans and oil.
\*\*\*→\*\*\*\* Chianti *riserva*.
**Cacciucco alla livornese** Piquant fish soup with garlic toast.
\*\* Montescudaio *rosso*.
**Cenci** Twists of fried dough with powdered sugar.
\*\* Vin Santo.
**Crostini di fegato** Breadcrusts with chicken liver paté.
\*\* Chianti young.
**Fegatelli di maiale** Pork livers spit-roasted with bay leaves.
\*\*→\*\*\* Morellino di Scansano.

**Gramugia** Ancient soup of Lucca with onions, artichokes, fava beans, asparagus, and bacon.
\*\* Montecarlo *bianco*.
**Panzanella** Stale bread soaked with water and crumbled with chopped tomatoes, onions, basil, oil, and vinegar in a sort of salad.
\*\*→\*\*\* Vernaccia di San Gimignano.
**Pappardelle alla lepre** Wide ribbon noodles with rich hare sauce.
\*\* Chianti Colli Aretini.
**Ribollita** Hearty *minestrone* with beans, black cabbage, and other vegetables, thickened at the end with bread.
\*\* Chianti Colli Senesi.
**Tordi allo spiedo** Spit-roasted wood thrush.
\*\*\*→\*\*\*\* Brunello di Montalcino or
\*\*\*→\*\*\*\* Carmignano.

## Restaurants

Recommended in or near wine zones: **Bolgheri** *Gambero Rosso* at San Vincenzo, *Il Biondo* at Sassetta. **Carmignano** *Da Delfina* at Artimino; *Cantina di Toia* at Bacchereto; *Erta del Moro* at Carmignano. **Chianti Classico** *La Torre* at Castellina in Chianti; *Badia a Coltibuono* and *Spaltenna* at Gaiole; *La Biscondola* at Mercatale Val di Pesa; *Montagliari* and *Villa Le Barone* at Panzano; *Antica Posta* at San Casciano Val di Pesa; *La Taverna* at Vagliagli. **Colli Aretini** *Castello di Sorci* at Anghiari; *Vicolo del Contento* at Castelfranco di Sopra. **Colli Fiorentini** *La Tavolozza* at Grassina; *Belvedere* at Impruneta. **Colli Senesi** *La Frateria di Padre Eligio* at Cetona; *La Casanova* at Chianciano Terme; *Il Patriarca* near Chiusi; *La Chiusa* at Montefollonico; *Il Pozzo* at Monteriggioni; *Antica Trattoria Bottega Nova* near Siena; *Locanda L'Amorosa* near Sinalunga. **Lucca-Montecarlo** *Forassiepi* and *La Nina* at Montecarlo; *Vipore* at Pieve Santo Stefano; *Trattoria La Mora* at Ponte a Moriano; *Solferino* at San Macario in Piano. **Montalcino** *Edgardo* and *Il Giglio* at Montalcino. **San Gimignano** *Le Terrazze* at San Gimignano. **Valdinievole** *Enoteca Giovanni* at Montecatini.

# *Umbria*

Umbria

Umbria's special aptitude for wine is not as widely noted as it might be. The only name of enduring fame is Orvieto, from the hill town where Etruscans mastered winemaking techniques two millennia before its golden nectar inspired Renaissance artists. After a lapse, Orvieto has bounded back as one of Italy's most exported whites. But the region's grandest *crus* flourish at Torgiano, though their reputations lag behind their remarkable class. The only other name known beyond the region is Colli del Trasimeno, wines from the basin of central Italy's largest lake.

Umbria is a treasure trove of local wines. Three promising DOCs have been added recently – Colli Altotiberini, Colli Perugini and Montefalco. But the rest, including some rarities, oddities, and antiquities, comprise a jumble of names and types, ranging from inspired, sometimes superb examples of wine-making skills down to the hit-and-miss results of the undying peasant tradition.

**Wine Zones**
1 Colli Altotiberini
2 Colli del Trasimeno
3 Colli Perugini

A startling variety of vines grows here. Besides the standard Sangiovese, Canaiolo, Trebbiano, and Malvasia, there are Grechetto, Montepulciano, Sagrantino, Verdicchio, and intriguing outsiders, some of which have been here since the last century, some just introduced: Merlot, Cabernet, Barbera, Tocai, Traminer, Garganega, Gamay, Nebbiolo, Dolcetto, the Pinots, Chardonnay, Riesling, and more. It will be fascinating to see what becomes of them as techniques improve.

Discovering Umbria's wines can be as exciting as exploring its ancient towns. Halfway between Rome and Florence, crossed by the *Autostrada del Sole* and other fast roads, the region mixes art and history with the bucolic attractions of a countryside noted as "the green heart of Italy." Enophiles should not miss the *Museo del Vino* at Torgiano, a model of the genre, or the *Enoteca Regionale* at Perugia. Interesting *enoteche* have also opened recently at Città di Castello and Orvieto. The *Enoteca Vino Vino* at Terni provides a sage selection.

## Recent vintages

Umbria has cool, damp winters and warm, dry summers, one of Italy's most consistently favorable climates for wine. For instance, from 1970 through 1986, Orvieto reported good to excellent harvests every year except 1972, 1976 and 1984. Torgiano was also weak in those years, but had good to very good results in other years, excellent in 1970, 1971, 1975, 1980, 1982, 1985 and 1986

**Assisi** r. p. w. dr. ★→★★ 82 83 85 86
The hills around the famous shrine have been producing good wines for years, recently consistent enough to aspire to DOC. Rosso di Assisi (Merlot and others) is deep purple, mellow, juicy and mouth-filling, best in 2–4 years. The *rosato*, from the same dark grapes, is fresh and tasty young. Bianco di Assisi, from Grechetto, Trebbbiano, Malvasia and others, can be round and smooth when young.
Sasso Rosso                                    Tili

**Bianco d'Arquata** w. dr. ★→ ★★★ 80 81 82 83 84 85 86
From Grechetto, Trebbiano, and others grown near Bevagna, S of Perugia. From good vintages, this light golden-green wine has perfumed, textured suavity and range of nuances that gain style over 3–4 years, sometimes more.
Adanti

**Cabernet Sauvignon di Miraduolo** r. dr. ★★★ 77 78 79 80 81 82 83 85 86
This Cabernet from Torgiano is deep garnet purple, generous in herby, berry-like bouquet, dry but fat, and still a touch assertive because Cabernet vines – and wines – need time to mature. With time, this could approach the glories of Torgiano Rubesco *riserva*.
Lungarotti

**Castel Grifone** p. dr. ★★ DYA
Brilliant pink from the same grapes as Torgiano *rosso* fermented at low temperature to crisp, fruity goodness.
Lungarotti

**Castello della Sala** w. dr. ★★★ 85 86
Antinori's savvy blend of traditional Orvieto grapes with Sauvignon Blanc and Pinot Blanc grown around the family castle. Fresh and fragrant yet distinctive enough to add a new dimension to local winemaking, its harmony should hold well for 2–3 years.
Marchesi Antinori

**Castello di Montoro** r. dr. ★★→★★★ 78 79 80 81 82 83 85 86
Winning composite of Sangiovese, Merlot, Barbera, and Montepulciano grown at Montoro di Narni near Terni. Ruby red tending to garnet, with 5–8 years, its subtle bouquet and warm, lingering flavor can show elegant complexity.
Marchesi Patrizi Montoro

**Cervaro della Sala** w. dr. ★★★ 85 86
This debuted from '85, an unprecedented blend of the worthy local Grechetto with Chardonnay, aged in French oak for several months. Though still a bit taut a year later, with 2–3 years in bottle this should fulfill its promise as one of central Italy's most distinguished white wines.
Marchesi Antinori

**Chardonnay di Miralduolo** w. dr. ★★★ 84 85 86
Impressive wood-aged Chardonnay from a special plot at Torgiano. Flowery and finely balanced, it has the structure to improve over 2–3 years. With time, this could become an exemplary Chardonnay.
Lungarotti

**Colli Altotiberini** DOC r. p. w. dr.  ★→★★★ 82 83 85 86
Recent DOC in the upper Tiber valley around Città di Castello applies
to three types, some well made, some decidedly countryish. The *rosso*,
from Sangiovese and Merlot, is ruby red, pleasantly vinous when young,
fairly robust, with enough tannin to take 3–4 years of age, sometimes
more. The *rosato*, from the same grapes, is bright roseate, clean, fragrant
and fruity within a year or two – notably from Colle del Sole and
Castello di Ascagnano. The *bianco*, based on Trebbiano, varies so much
that it is hard to define a style.

| | |
|---|---|
| Castello di Ascagnano | Panicale |
| Donini | Pie' di Murlo-Tondini |
| Enoagricola-Montone | Colle del Sole-Polidori |
| Roscetti | Fratelli Renzacci |
| Carlo Ferri | Tenuta di Montecorona |
| Silvio Nardi (Montione) | Antognolla |

**Colli del Trasimeno** DOC r. w.  ★→★★★ 82 83 85 86
This vast zone which surrounds Lake Trasimeno has two types of wine
and an emerging reputation. The *rosso*, from Sangiovese, Ciliegiolo, and
Gamay, is bright ruby tending to garnet with 2–6 years of age, with fine,
flowery scent and lively, fruity flavor. The *bianco*, from Trebbiano,
Malvasia, Verdicchio, and Grechetto, is light straw, subtle in scent, with
fresh, balanced crispness when young.

| | |
|---|---|
| Belvedere-Illuminati | Lamborghini (La Fiorita) |
| C.S. del Trasimeno | Morolli |
| Fattoria San Litardo | Po' del Vento-Anichini |
| Grifo di Boldrino (La | Sovrano Militare Ordine di Malta |
| Querciolana) | |

**Colli Perugini** DOC r. p. w. dr.  ★→★★★ 82 83 85 86
Umbria's latest DOC covers *rosso*, *rosato* and *bianco* grown in the hills
along the Tiber between Perugia and Todi. The fine *rosso* and *rosato* are
based on Sangiovese, the *bianco* on Trebbiano Toscano.

| | |
|---|---|
| Castello di San Valentino | Podere Collecorno |

**Corbara** or **Lago di Corbara** r. dr.  ★★ 82 83 85 86
Red wine based on Sangiovese and Montepulciano d'Abruzzo grown
near Lago di Corbara SE of Orvieto. Ruby, smooth, and lightly bitter,
it is best in 3–4 years.

| | |
|---|---|
| Barberani | Bigi |
| Barbi | |

**Decugnano dei Barbi Rosso** r. dr.  ★★★ 82 83 85 86
Winningly fruity red from Sangiovese and Montepulciano grown near
Lake Corbara. Deep ruby, fresh in bouquet and grapy in flavor, it has
the finesse of a fine Beaujolais with extra depth.
Decugnano dei Barbi

**Grechetto** or **Greco** w. dr. (sw.)  ★→★★ 85 86
Grechetto grapes make dry wines in several places S of Perugia, notably
around Foligno and Todi. Light golden green, seductively perfumed,
velvety, and fruity with a hint of both sweetness and bitterness, they are
good in 1–3 years. Grechetto from Adanti at Bevagna and Bigi in the
Orvieto zone (the latter seasoned in new oak) were being prepared for
release, promising ★★★ ratings with time. The variety is also used for Vin
Santo.

| | |
|---|---|
| Adanti | Enopolio di Foligno |
| Bigi | Fabbri |
| C.S. Todi | Tardioli |
| Caprai | |

**Merlot** r. dr.  ★→★★★ 81 82 83 85 86
Grown in Umbria for at least a century, Merlot is used in both varietals
and blends sometimes for wines of real interest, smooth and full for 4–5
years or more.

| | |
|---|---|
| Agraria Ponteggia | La Paciana |
| Castello di Ascagnano | Ruggero Veneri |

**Montefalco** DOC
Recent appellation comprises two distinct reds from hills around
Montefalco and Bevagna between Foligno and Todi.

– **Montefalco Rosso** r. dr.  ★→★★★ 82 83 85 86
From Sangiovese with some Sagrantino for mouth-filling tone, this is a

soft, ruby violet wine, its dryness rounded out by a mellowing sweet and bitter undertone. Adanti and Fongoli make impressive wine, usually to drink inside 4 years.

– **Sagrantino di Montefalco** r. dr. sw. ★★→★★★★ 81 82 83 85 86
From the venerable Sagrantino grape which was usually made into sweet *passito* wines, this full-bodied red is often dry. Both have a dark purple-garnet color, rich, berry-like scent and warm, rich, full flavor with a light bitter undertone. The *passito* is aromatic, strong and exquisitely *abboccato*. Both versions are best in 3–6 years. Adanti is the outstanding producer, but others are beginning to realize great potential.
Ag. *passito* 1 yr.

| | |
|---|---|
| Adanti | Angelo Fongoli |
| Colpetrone-Fabbri | La Paciana |
| Domenico Benincasa | Tardioli |
| Enopolio di Foligno | |

**Orvieto** DOC w. dr. s/sw. ★★→★★★ DYA
Umbria's renowned white comes from Procanico, Verdello, Grechetto and other white grapes grown in a large zone around the striking hill town of Orvieto (the classico area), extending N along the Paglia and S along the Tiber into Latium. Historically *abboccato*, most Orvieto is now dry, polished, but sometimes rather neutral in flavor due to modern processing. Yet the best bottlings of Orvieto Classico – Antinori, Barberani, Bigi's outstanding Vigneto Torricella and Decugnano dei Barbi – show enviable fruit and harmony. The *abboccato*, golden and softly textured in the past, has come back a bit paler and firmer in body, but balanced and silky with mouth-filling goodness in Bigi's Vigneto Orzalume, Dubini's Palazzone and Barberani's Vallesanta. Decugnano dei Barbi's *pourriture noble* is sold as an Orvieto, but its remarkable bouquet, rich flavors and velvety texture put it in a class by itself (★★★★) – reminiscent of renowned botrytis wines of Bordeaux and Germany. Of some 12 million liters of Orvieto a year, much is exported by Chianti firms. (Producers do not include all bottler and shipper brands, which could also be dependable.)

| | |
|---|---|
| Barberani | Melini |
| Barbi | Papini |
| Bigi (Vigneto Orzalume, Torricella) | Petrurbani |
| | Poggio Ciculetto |
| Vincenzo Cotti | Ruffino |
| Decugnano dei Barbi | Tenuta Le Velette |
| Dubini Locatelli (Palazzone) | Conte Vaselli |
| Marchesi Antinori | Villa Antica |

**Rosso d'Arquata** r. dr. ★★★ 81 82 83 85 86
Though the formula has varied from year to year, Adanti's winemaker Alvaro has recently blended Barbera with Canaiolo and Merlot in one of Umbria's most drinkable table wines. After aging in casks, it is fairly round and supple but with noteworthy depth and character to emerge over 3–5 years.
Adanti

**Rubesco**
See Torgiano *rosso*.

**Rubino** r. dr. ★★→★★★ 81 82 83 85 86
Fine red from Sangiovese, Merlot, and others grown near Umbertide in the Colli Altotiberini. With 4–7 years, more from top vintages, it develops deep bouquet, authority, and finesse, while its rich ruby color takes on hints of garnet.
Colle del Sole-Polidori

**Sagrantino**
See Montefalco.

**San Giorgio** r. dr. ★★★→★★★★ 77 78 79 80 81 82 83 85 86
A telling example of Giorgio Lungarotti's innovative spirit, this combines the basic Torgiano *rosso* varieties with 20–25% Cabernet Sauvignon. Bold, slightly aggressive in its youth, this will need years to mellow and perhaps a decade or more to reach its prime. Rich in bouquet, body and flavor, it shows distinctive class.
Lungarotti

**Solleone** am. dr. ✱✱✱ NV
Sherry-like aperitif wine from Trebbiano and Grechetto made by a
modified *solera* method. Light amber, bone dry, and strong (18%), its
ethereal bouquet of almonds and wood can last for many years.
Lungarotti

**Spumante** w. dr. sp. ✱✱→✱✱✱ DYA
The sparkling wine craze is spreading here, so far best expressed in
Decugnano dei Barbi's Brut *champenoise* from Chardonnay with Orvieto
varieties and Lungarotti's Brut based on Chardonnay.

**Torgiano** DOC r. w. dr. ✱✱→✱✱✱✱  70 71 73 74 75 77 78 79 80 81 82
83 85 86
The zone SE across the Tiber from Perugia is noted for both red and
white wines, particularly the *riserva* that carries Giorgio Lungarotti's
trademark Rubesco. The *bianco* (Lungarotti's is Torre di Giano), from
Trebbiano and Grechetto, is pale, flowery, with polished fruit-acid
balance – to drink young. The *riserva* Torre di Giano from the Vigna Il
Pino plot is aged briefly in wood and develops uncommon finesse with
3–4 years. The *rosso*, from Sangiovese, Canaiolo, Montepulciano, and
Ciliegiolo, is ruby red, round, and smoothly persuasive in 2–5 years.
Rubesco *riserva*, numbered from the Monticchio vineyard, is one of
Italy's most distinguished reds. It needs 6–7 years to develop opulent
bouquet and the aristocratic combinations of tastes and textures rarely
sensed outside the Haut Médoc. From great vintages, such as '71, '75,
'82 or '85, it needs a decade or more to reach prime as its color mellows
to rich garnet with a trace of *pelure d'oignon*.
Ag. *riserva* 3 yrs.
Lungarotti

**Vernaccia di Cannara** r. s/sw. sw. fz. ✱ DYA
*Simpatico* dessert wine from Cometta and Corvetta grown around
Cannara and Bevagna. Inky and fragrant, with thick, grapy sweetness,
usually *frizzante*, it is drunk locally, especially around Easter.

**Vin Santo** am. s/sw. sw. ✱→✱✱✱
Made nearly everywhere from Grechetto, Malvasia, Trebbiano and
other grapes semidried (preferably hanging from rafters near a fireplace
to pick up a smoky flavor) and aged in small, sealed barrels. Golden to
amber, aromatic, and fairly strong (14%), at best it is velvety and softly
sweet, capable of aging.
Adanti                                        Lungarotti

## *Wine & Food*

Umbrians can relate as humbly as Franciscans how they eat only
what their good earth provides. Granted, menus are spare,
repetitive, and orthodox – in other words, highly selective. Here
seasonal produce is prepared in streamlined ways by country
people without much time to spend in the kitchen – something
like *nouvelle cuisine*, except that it has scarcely changed since the
Middle Ages. Oil is so good it has been called Umbria's "liquid
gold," though it is never used so sparingly. There are thick soups
and exquisite pastas, including the always reliable home-
made *tagliatelle* strewn across oval platters and mixed with *ragù*
which often contains chicken livers. Meat and game are *di rigore*
in this landlocked region: prized Perugina beef, farm poultry,
wood pigeons, and lamb. Pork is so artfully prepared in the town
of Norcia that pork butcher shops throughout Italy are known as
*norcinerie*. Among things that grow, a special place is reserved for
cardoons, the artichoke-like thistles known here as *gobbi*. But the
most delicious irony of this region's "modest" cuisine is the truffle
– whether black or white it is so prolific that Umbria has become
the nation's (if not the world's) leading supplier.

**Anguille alle brace** Grilled eels from the Tiber or Lake Trasimeno.

   \*\* Colli del Trasimeno *rosso*.

**Cicerchiata** Carnival cake with honey, almonds, and candied fruit.

   \*\*\* Sagrantino di Montefalco *passito*.

**Gobbi alla perugina** Fried cardoons with meat *ragù*.

   \*\* Torgiano *rosso*.

**Mazzafegati** Piquant pork liver sausages, served around Christmas

   \*\* Colli Altotiberini *rosso*.

**Minestra di farro** Soup of semolina cooked with tomatoes, onions, etc., in broth of a *prosciutto* bone.

   \*\* Castel Grifone or \*\* Colli Altotiberini *rosato*.

**Palomba alla ghiotta** Spit-roasted wood pigeon with *ghiotta*, an intricate sauce of wine, vinegar, ham, livers, and herbs.

   \*\*\*\* Rubesco *riserva*

   or \*\*\* Castello di Montoro.

**Porchetta alla perugina** Whole young pig roast in a wood oven with wild fennel, rosemary, and garlic.

   \*\*\* Rubino.

**Spaghetti alla norcina** The sauce of sausages cooked with onions in cream may be topped with grated cheese or white truffles.

   \*\*\* Orvieto *classico secco*.

**Stringozzi** Short noodles dressed with garlic, oil, and sometimes tomatoes.

   \*\* Torgiano *bianco*.

**Torcolo** Sponge cake to be dipped in Vin Santo.

   \*\*\* Vin Santo.

### Restaurants

Recommended in or near wine zones: **Assisi-Montefalco** *Buca di San Francesco*, *Il Frantoio* and *Umbra* at Assisi; *Villa Roncalli* at Foligno. **Colli Altotiberini** *Castello di Ascagnano* at Ascagnano; *L'Enoteca* at Città di Castello. **Colli del Trasimeno** *Ottavi* at Corciano; *Sauro* on Trasimeno's Isola Maggiore; *Cacciatore da Luciano* at Passignano sul Trasimeno. **Colli Perugini-Torgiano** *Degli Angeli* and *Umbria* at Todi; *Le Tre Vaselle* at Torgiano. **Orvieto** *Vissani* at Civitella del Lago; *La Badia* and *Villa Ciconia* at Orvieto.

# Valle d'Aosta

## Val d'Aosta

Italy's smallest region, tucked into Piedmont's northwest corner with mountainous borders on France and Switzerland, has little space for vineyards amidst its massive Alps. Most vines grow over pergolas on terraces hewn out of stone on south-facing slopes along the Dora Baltea River, which flows from Mount Blanc's glaciers through the lone city of Aosta and on into Piedmont. Wine production of 3.5 million liters a year (Italy's lowest rate) isn't nearly enough to supply the region's 110,000 French-speaking people.

Valle d'Aosta's few wines are made by plucky and persevering *vignerons*, especially those who work Europe's highest classified vineyards at Morgex. They take in a little galaxy of *crus*, drawing some luster from Piedmontese and French varieties, though the most intriguing wines come from vines Aostans claim as their own: Blanc de Valdigne, Petit Rouge, the mutation of Pinot Gris known locally as Malvoisie and Vien de Nus.

In 1986 Italy's most comprehensive regionwide DOC was instituted. Known as Valle d'Aosta or Vallée d'Aoste, it takes in 15 types of wine with their names in two languages. But even if classified, Aostan wines could never be more than curiosities to be savored close to home by visitors who come to ski, climb or take in the dramatic scenery of castles and chalets amidst Europe's highest peaks.

## Recent vintages

Recommended years of wines for aging appear with each entry.

**Aymaville** r. dr. 83 85 86
From Petit Rouge and Fumin grown at Aymaville SW of Aosta, this bright ruby wine needs a couple years in barrel to develop fine, raspberry-like bouquet and lightly acidic but neatly balanced flavor that can last admirably for 2–5 years, sometimes more.
La Sabla-Charrère

**Blanc de Cossan** w. dr. ** DYA
Sprightly white from dark Grenache grown at Cossan outside Aosta. Light gold with rosy glints, its tart, fresh fruitiness is best very young. The Reserve du Prieur from the same grapes is semisweet with 15% alcohol.
Institut Agricole Régional Aoste

**La Colline de Sarre et Chesallet** r. dr. ⭐⭐ 83 85 86
Gamay and Petit Rouge combine W of Aosta in this bright garnet wine with Gamay nose and fresh, grapy flavor, good in 2–4 years.
Octave Vallet

**Malvoisie de Cossan** w. s/sw. ** 85 86
From Pinot Gris (here called Malvoisie) grown at Cossan, this golden-copper wine needs 2 years to develop soft bouquet and smooth, *abboccato* flavor with a light bitter undertone.
Institut Agricole Régional Aoste

**Sang des Salasses** r. dr. ** 82 83 85 86
From Pinot Noir grown at Cossan near Aosta, this ruby-garnet wine has a fruity scent and dry, round flavor with light bitter background, to drink in 2–5 years.
Institut Agricole Régional Aoste

**Valle d'Aosta (Vallée d'Aoste) DOC**
Taking in most of the region's recognized vineyards, including the two original DOCs of Donnaz and Enfer d'Arvier, the new appellation

applies to 15 types of wine. Most are rarities but a few have earned more than local reputations. Names and labels may be in Italian or French.

– **Arnad Montjovet** r. dr.

From at least 70% of Nebbiolo with Dolcetto, Pinot Noir or other varieties grown in SE around the towns of Arnad and Montjovet, this promises character similar to Donnaz.

Ag. *superiore/supérieur* 2 yrs.

– **Bianco (Blanc)** w. dr. (fz.)

From various white varieties grown along the Dora Baltea in the SE, this is designed to be light (9% minimum) and possibly fizzy.

– **Blanc de Morgex et de La Salle** w. dr. (fz.)  ✶✶  DYA

From the indigenous vine known as Blanc de Valdigne or Blanc de Morgex, this grows in steep mountain meadows at heights of more than 1,000 meters in places above the villages of Morgex and La Salle near Courmayeur. With rarefied aroma and delicately dry, crisp flavor, it may have some *pétillance*. Albert Vevey in certain vintages has made wine with enough personality to rate ✶✶✶.

– **Chambave Moscato (Muscat)** w. dr. (sw.)  ✶✶→✶✶✶  DYA

The basic version from Moscato grown around Chambave near St-Vincent is surprisingly dry, perfumed and grapy, to drink inside a year. The more vaunted Passito (or Flétri) comes from semidried Moscato grapes made into a richly aromatic, deep golden wine that has been known to keep for decades, becoming drier and increasingly suave. Ezio Voyat excels with both versions.

Ag. Passito (Flétri) 2 yrs. in barrel.

– **Chambave Rosso (Rouge)** r. dr.  ✶✶→✶✶✶  78 79 82 83 85 86

From Petit Rouge with other varieties grown around Chambave, this distinguished red has ruby-garnet color, dry, subtle flavor and bouquet taking on hints of violets with age. Ezio Voyat makes the classic.

– **Donnaz (Donnas)** r. dr.  ✶✶  78 79 82 83 85 86

Though established as a DOC from Nebbiolo grown around the village of Donnaz in the SE, this has never quite matched its Piedmontese neighbor Carema. Refined with understated Nebbiolo character but impressive bouquet, it can age well beyond 5–6 years.

Ag. 2 yrs.

– **Enfer d'Arvier** r. dr.  ✶✶  82 83 85 86

This long-standing DOC is based on Petit Rouge in restricted yields on a rocky mountainside at Arvier where occasionally torrid temperatures have prompted the reference to *l'Enfer*. Dark red to medium garnet in color, it has a rather sharp, bitter grape flavor that needs 3–5 years to soften.

– **Gamay** r. dr.  ✶✶  85 86

The Beaujolais grape puts on its alpine act here in hearty wines, a bit rustic and restrained in behavior, but with a likeable folksiness about them when they do have something to say.

– **Müller Thurgau** w. dr.

Called in for mountain duty from the foggy bottoms of the Rhine, this overworked half-breed may blossom nobly on the sunny side of the Alps.

– **Nus Pinot Grigio (Pinot Gris)** or **Nus Malvoisie** w. am. dr. sw.  ✶✶→✶✶✶

New norms call for both light dry and sweet Passito (or Flétri) wines from this strain of Pinot Gris known as Malvoisie in the village of Nus and considered autoctonous. The Passito, known as Malvoisie de Nus as made in minute quantities by Don Augusto Pramotton, the priest, has a reputation as a curio that lasts for decades. The dry is not yet proven.

– **Nus Rosso (Rouge)** r. dr.  ✶✶  82 83 85 86

From Vien de Nus with Petit Rouge and Pinot Noir, this should be a distinctive red if modeled after the Creme du Vien de Nus made by Don Augusto Pramotton in the parish vineyards.

– **Pinot Nero (Pinot Noir)** r. dr.  ✶✶  80 82 83 85 86

Designated as a varietal under DOC, scattered plantings have given promising results, such as Aldo Perrier's Pinot Noir de Charvensod and the Agricultural School's Sang des Salasses (see).

– **Rosato or Rosé** p. dr.

From red grapes grown along the Dora Baltea between Aosta and Piedmont this novelty remains to be seen.

– **Rosso (Rouge)** r. dr.

From the same base as the *rosato*, another unknown quantity.

– **Torrette** r. dr.  ✶✶→✶✶✶  78 79 80 82 83 85 86

Worthy red from Petit Rouge with other varieties grown along the Dora

Baltea on either side of Aosta, notably to the W at St-Pierre, Sarre and Aymaville. From Filippo Garin this graceful ruby red had bouquet that increased wondrously with age (sometimes over a decade) as the early robust flavor became more delicate. *Superiore* or *supérieure* needs 8 months of aging in barrels.

| | |
|---|---|
| Association des Viticulteurs- La Salle | Institut Agricole Regional Aoste |
| Cesarino Bonin | Gratien Montrosset |
| Caves Cooperatives de Donnaz | Aldo Perrier |
| Clos Gerbore | Don Augusto Pramotton |
| Co-Enfer | Marcello Quinson |
| Celestino David | Giuseppe Thomain |
| Luigi Ferrando | Alberto Vevey |
| Filippo Garin | Ezio Voyat |

**Vin des Chanoines** r. dr. ** 83 85 86
From Gamay grown near Aosta, this bright ruby wine has balance in light body and bouquet with flavor that improves for 2–4 years.
Institut Agricole Régional Aoste

**Vin du Conseil** w. dr. *** DYA
From Petite Arvine grown in the Vignoble de Prieuré de Montfleury outside Aosta, this is the pride of Joseph Vaudan, priest and director of the regional agricultural school. Aged briefly in barrel, it is bright straw yellow with seductive scent of pear and dry but mouth-filling fruitiness.
Institut Agricole Régional Aoste

## *Wine & Food*

Aostans thrive on rustic, generous fare; few specialities, but the dishes they share with Piedmont taste unmistakably Aostan. Pasta isn't at home here, but polenta, thick soups, rye bread and butter are. Meat is the essence of this hearty diet, with salami, sausages and cold cuts, such as mountain *prosciutto*, the rare *mocetta* (air-dried chamois meat), and the tasty stews and game dishes cooked with wine. The vaunted cheeses are *fontina* and *tome* (from ewe's milk). After cooked fruit and biscuits, each diner sips from the *grolla*, a pot with spouts filled with coffee and grappa.

**Boudins** Blood sausages, a speciality of Morgex.
　** Petit Rouge.
**Capriolo alla valdostana**
Venison stewed with vegetables, wine, grappa, and cream.
　*** Torrette.
**Carbonade** Salted beef cooked with wine in a rich stew served with polenta.
　*** Chambave Rouge.
**Costoletta alla valdostana**
Breaded veal cutlets with *fontina*, and possibly truffles.
　*** Donnaz.

**Polenta cùnsa** Polenta with *fontina*, *toma*, melted butter, and Parmesan.
　** Gamay.
**Tegole** Crunchy almond biscuits.
　*** Passito di Chambave.
**Trota** Trout from mountain streams cooked in butter.
　*** Vin du Conseil or ** Blanc de Morgex.
**Zuppa valpellinentze** *Fontina*, ham, black bread, cabbage, herbs, and spices, cooked in what could be defined loosely as soup.
　** Vin des Chanoines.

### *Restaurants*
Recommended in the region: *Cavallo Bianco* at Aosta; *Parisien* at Chatillon; *Le Vieux Pommier* at Courmayeur; *Maison de Filippo* at Entreves de Courmayeur; *Hôtel Bellevue* at Pré St Didier; *Casale* at St Cristophe; *Batezar-da Renato* at St Vincent; *Da Pierre* at Verres.

# Veneto

Veneto

Venice's region is leading Italian viniculture into the future, showing that wine can be a practical and profitable big business. The Veneto, though fourth in volume, leads all regions in DOC production with about 165 million liters a year. Much of the classified wine comes from Verona, where Soave ranks second to Chianti in prominence among DOCs with Valpolicella and Bardolino not far behind. The Veronese trio has far outdistanced Chianti in exports to become the most representative of Italian quality wines abroad. Efficient, modern production and astute marketing techniques lie behind the success of these three appealing, moderately priced wines for regular drinking. Verona also makes wines for special occasions, most notably Amarone, a limited-production red of dynamic dimensions.

The Veneto, which extends from the Austrian border S to the Po basin and from the Adriatic W to Lake Garda, is an enviably productive land. Vines flourish in its verdant hills and fertile flatlands. The range of grape varieties is remarkable. Among the natives are the light Garganega of Soave and the dark Corvina, Rondinella, Molinara, and Negrara of Valpolicella and Bardolino, as well as Piave's distinctive Raboso, Verduzzo, and

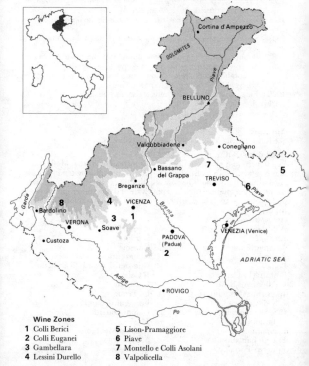

**Wine Zones**

1 Colli Berici
2 Colli Euganei
3 Gambellara
4 Lessini Durello

5 Lison-Pramaggiore
6 Piave
7 Montello e Colli Asolani
8 Valpolicella

Prosecco, the latter a source of growingly popular bubbly wines. The imports range even farther afield, from the aristocratic Cabernets, Pinots, Sauvignon and Merlot (the prevalent variety of the E Veneto) down to Clinton, an outlandish North American vine surviving here as an outlaw.

Quality covers the gamut from majestic estate bottlings to murky country wines to pasteurized products of assembly lines shipped all over Europe in outsized bottles with metal caps. It must be said, though, that industrial winemaking can be admirable here; some large houses make some of the best wine.

Visitors who wander into Venice's interior in quest of wine and some of Italy's finest food, will also find a heritage of art, architecture and history amidst landscapes that could still inspire Renaissance painters. Vinitaly, held each April in Verona, is the nation's premier wine fair. Wine roads lead through Verona's hills, as well as through Breganze, the Piave valley and the Marca Trevigiana north of Treviso. A local habit that tourists also take to is the little glass of wine called the *ombra* or *ombretta* sipped at intervals during the day. Impressive shops include the *Bottega del Vino* at Bassano, *Enoteca Angelo Rasi* at Padova, *Al Volto* at Venice, and *Istituto Enologico Italiano* at Verona.

## Recent vintages

Most Veneto wines are good young, though the Cabernets and Merlots of the E Veneto and Amarone take aging.

1986   Early signs pointed to one of the best of recent years, though dampness caused problems around Verona.
1985   Excellent in most places, though drought caused problems.
1984   Generally mediocre.
1983   Size was cut by hail and drought, though natural thinning led to a very good year all over.
1982   Bountiful crop, fine in the east, but disappointing for Amarone.
1981   Sharply reduced, especially in Verona, where quality was acceptable at best; results elsewhere were modest to good.
1980   Uneven; below average except for wine from select grapes.
1979   Fine, abundant harvest; reds of superior quality.
Earlier fine vintages: (Amarone) '78, '77, '74, '71, '70, '69, '67, '64, '62; (Cabernet-Merlot) '74, '71, '69, '67, '64.

**Amarone**
See Recioto della Valpolicella under Valpolicella.

**Bardolino** DOC r. p. dr. ★→★★★ 83 85 86
Popular red and rosé from Corvina Veronese, Rondinella, Molinara, and Negrara grown on SE shores of Lake Garda, most noted in *classico* zone behind Bardolino. The *rosso* is light ruby, grapy, dry, round, and balanced, sometimes with a hint of prickle and light bitter undertone – to drink in 4 years. The *chiaretto*, cherry pink, is lighter, more fragile, to drink in 2 years.
Ag. *superiore* 1 yr.

Aldegheri
Anselmi
Arvedi d'Emilei
Bertani
Bolla
Boscani (Le Canne)
Ca' Bordenis-Santi
Innocente Campostini
C.S. di Custoza
C.S. Veronese del Garda
Colle dei Cipressi
Eleonora
Fratelli Fabiano
Fraterna Portalupi

Rosino Ferri
Gardoni
Girasole
Gorgo (Bricolo)
Guerrieri-Rizzardi (Tacchetto)
Il Colle
Lamberti
Le Tende
Le Vigne di San Pietro
Gianni Lonardi
Masi
Antonio Menegotti
Montecorno
Montresor                    ▶

| | |
|---|---|
| Pallavicino Disertori | Fratelli Tedeschi |
| Fratelli Pasqua | Tenuta Ca' Furia |
| Pegaso-Premiovini | Tenute San Leone |
| Umberto Peretti | Eugenio Tinazzi & Figli |
| Pergreffi | Tommasi |
| Fratelli Poggi | Tre Colline |
| Luigi Rossi | Villa Girardi |
| Santa Sofia | Visconti |
| Sartori | Aldo Zanon |
| Taborro | Fratelli Zenato |

**Bianco di Custoza** DOC w. dr. (sp.) `**→***` DYA
Increasingly noticed white from a zone bordering on Lake Garda and
Lombardy. From a mélange including Trebbiano Toscano, Garganega,
and Tocai, when well made it is pale and flowery, with clean, dry, softly
fruity lines but crisp finish, capable of matching good Soave. A *spumante*,
usually *charmat*, is increasingly seen.

| | |
|---|---|
| Arvedi d'Emilei | Montecorno |
| Barbi | Albino Pezzini |
| C.S.di Custoza | Silvio Piona |
| C.S. Veronese del Garda | Santa Sofia |
| Cavalchina | Santi |
| Eleonora | Tenute San Leone |
| Fraterna Portalupi | Fratelli Tedeschi |
| Giarola | Eugenio Tinazzi & Figlio |
| Gorgo-Bricolo | Tommasi |
| Le Tende | Villa Girardi |
| Le Vigne di San Pietro | Villa Medici |
| Antonio Menegotti | Fratelli Zenato |

**Bianco Toara** w. dr. `**` DYA
From Gargenega grown at Toara in the Colli Berici, this light golden
wine is flowery and dry with refreshing almond finish.
Alessandro Piovene Porto-Godi

**Breganze** DOC
The glacial moraine of this zone N of Vicenza is well suited to vines, as
exemplified by the excellent modern wines of Maculan.
– **Bianco** w. dr. `*→***` 85 86
Based on Tocai Friulano, this is pale lemon yellow, delicate in scent,
smooth, and buoyantly good inside 2 years. Maculan's Breganze di
Breganze and the wood-aged Prato di Canzio rival the vaunted Tocai of
Friuli.
– **Cabernet** r. dr. `**→****` 78 79 80 81 82 83 85 86
From Cabernet Franc or, less likely, Cabernet Sauvignon, this is usually
a good, sturdy red, superb from Maculan with its Palazzotto and Fratta
special vineyard bottlings based on Cabernet Sauvignon. Rich yet
supple, grassy but harmonious, they rank among N Italy's finest
Cabernets, after 3–6 years of aging. *Superiore* must have 12% alcohol.
– **Pinot Bianco** w. dr. `*→***` 85 86
Light straw green, fresh and fruity, this can develop silky texture and
flowery fragrance in 2–3 years. *Superiore* if it has 12% alcohol.
– **Pinot Grigio** w. dr. `*→**` DYA
With a hint of copper in its pale straw color, it is limber and smooth.
– **Pinot Nero** r. dr. `*→**` 85 86
Light ruby, fruity, and dry with light bitter undertone, it can be labeled
*superiore* if it has 12% alcohol.
– **Rosso** r. dr. `*→***` 82 83 85 86
Based on Merlot, this most heavily produced Breganze wine is ruby red,
grapy and nicely rounded with a hint of tannin. Maculan's Brentino
becomes smooth and sumptuous in 2–3 years.
– **Vespaiolo** w. dr. `**` DYA
A local varietal, this is bright straw yellow, pleasantly scented, brisk,
almost lemony, with a hint of almond underneath. *Superiore* must have
12%.

| | |
|---|---|
| Cantina B. Bartolomeo | Villa Magna-Novello |
| Maculan | |

**Cabernet**
DOC under Breganze, Colli Berici, Colli Euganei, Lison-Pramaggiore,

Montello e Colli Asolani and Piave, Cabernet also makes table wines both as varietals and in blends with Merlot, Malbec and others. A cross of Cabernet-Prosecco known as I.M.2,15 or Cabernet Manzoni is also gaining favor.

**Campo Fiorin** r. dr. ★★★ 78 79 80 81 83 85 86
Basically a Valpolicella, it gains the body, color, and strength of a bigger wine by being refermented with the lees of Recioto Amarone. Deep ruby and ample in bouquet, its dry flavor is robust and warm, with bitter background and suave texture, impressive for 4–8 years, sometimes more.
Masi

**Capitel San Rocco** r. w. dr. ★★★ 81 83 85 86
Distinguished table wines from San Rocco vineyards at Pedemonte in Valpolicella. The *rosso*, like Campo Fiorin, is Valpolicella fermented with Amarone lees. The *bianco*, from Garganega with a touch of Durello, is more intricate than Soave, blossomy and fresh, steely dry with a long finish.
Fratelli Tedeschi

**Capo del Monte** r. dr. ★★ 82 83 85 86
Unique mix by winemaker Gianni Spinazzè in which the aggressive grass and pepper character of Cabernet is toned down by Marzemino in a wine of some stature to drink in 2–5 years, sometimes more.
Fattoria di Ogliano

**Cartizze** or **Superiore di Cartizze**
Special subdenomination of Prosecco di Conegliano-Valdobbiadene.

**Castello di Roncade-Villa Giustinian** r. dr. ★★→★★★ 71 78 79 82 83 85 86
This classic composite of Cabernet Sauvignon, Cabernet Franc, Merlot, Malbec, and Petit Verdot grown at Roncade in the Piave valley can be remarkably close in character to certain Bordeaux. The 1971 (which rated ★★★★ and hasn't been equalled since) combined extraordinary power with finesse – a complete, lingering, ruby-garnet wine with bouquet reminiscent of berries, tar, and flowers.
Barone Ciani Bassetti

**Castello Guerrieri** r. dr. ★★★ 82 83 85 86
Manifold varieties including Sangiovese and the Veronese red grapes go into this special house wine aged in Venetian oak casks by Cristina Guerrieri. Smooth and genteel, it needs only 2–3 years to express itself eloquently.
Guerrieri-Rizzardi

**Catullo** r. dr. ★★★ 83 85 86
From one of Verona's most respected houses comes this fine new example of the trend to *ripassare* Valpolicella with Amarone lees into a superior table wine.
Bertani

**Chardonnay**
DOC only in Lison-Pramaggiore, this coveted vine is being planted frantically throughout the Veneto, where it is used for sparkling and still wines, some of real promise.

**Clinton** r. (p.) dr. s/sw (fz.) DYA
Popular N American vine (barred because not *vitis vinifera*) makes simplistic wines in E Veneto of inky-violet color and strawberry-like aroma, usually dry with typically foxy flavor. Also pink and *frizzante*.

**Colli Berici** DOC
Zone historically noted for wine has seven DOC varietals, though some top producers leave theirs unclassified (see Costozza and Villa Dal Ferro).

– **Cabernet** r. dr. ★→★★★ 82 83 85 86
From Cabernet Franc, sometimes Cabernet Sauvignon, this bright ruby-garnet wine can show rich, herby bouquet over 3–7 years.
Ag. *riserva* 3 yrs.

– **Garganega** or **Garganego** w. dr. ★→★★ DYA
Pale yellow, subtly scented, the light, brisk, almondy traits of the zone's most popular wine are attractive when young.

**– Merlot** r. dr. ★→★★ 82 83 85 86
Fruity, full-bodied, and soft, from some producers it has enough stuff to show well for 4–5 years.
**– Pinot Bianco** w. dr. ★→★★ DYA
Pale greenish yellow and flowery, its dry, smooth flavor has zestful bite.
**– Sauvignon** w. dr. ★→★★ DYA
Pale straw with fine varietal scent, its refreshingly crisp, gunflint qualities are best young.
**– Tocai Italico** w. dr. ★ DYA
Pale lemon yellow and light, this doesn't match its Friulian namesake.
**– Tocai Rosso** r. dr. ★★ DYA
This native Tocai thrives here as a brilliant ruby-crimson wine, grapy with a hint of licorice and a cleansing tannic bite, refreshing young.

| | |
|---|---|
| C.S. dei Colli Vicentini | Alessandro Piovene Porto-Godi |
| Castello di Belvedere | Claudio Pozzati |
| Cornelio Fabbian | Nani Cav. Rizzieri & Figli |
| Fratelli Montagna | Franceschetto Rizzieri |
| Severino Muraro & Figli | |

**Colli Euganei** DOC
These dramatically sheer hills rising from the Po valley S of Padova have been noted for wine since Roman times. The list takes in 7 types.
**– Bianco** w. dr. (s/sw.) (sp.) ★→★★ DYA
From Garganega, Serprina, Tocai and Sauvignon, this straw-yellow wine is fruity in scent with dry, soft flavor, best young. An *amabile* is also made. Both may be *spumante*.
**– Cabernet** r. dr. ★→★★ 82 83 85 86
From Cabernet Sauvignon and/or Franc, this is a tasty red when young, taking on some class with age. *Superiore* must have 12.5%.
Ag. 1 yr.
**– Merlot** r. dr. (s/sw.) ★→★★ 82 83 85 86
Grapy, soft, to drink young – sometimes *abboccato*. *Superiore* must have 12%.
Ag. 1 yr.
**– Moscato** w. s/sw. sw. fz. (sp.) ★→★★ DYA
From Moscato di Canelli, this golden wine has aromatic sweetness, whether still or bubbly.
**– Pinot Bianco** w. dr. (s/sw.) ★→★★ DYA
This does well here as a dry wine. *Abboccato* is also permitted. *Superiore* must have 12%.
**– Rosso** r. dr. (s/sw.) (sp.) ★→★★★ 82 83 85 86
Based on Merlot with Cabernet, Barbera and Raboso, this singular red has a fresh, grapy bouquet, sturdy structure and smooth, mellow flavor that can improve for 3–6 years in the dry version. Villa Sceriman makes a good example. *Amabile* and *spumante* are also made. *Superiore* must have 12%.
**– Tocai Italico** w. dr. (s/sw.) ★ DYA
Newly designated white will make mostly dry but also semisweet wine. *Superiore* must have 12%.

| | |
|---|---|
| C.S. Cooperativa Colli Euganei | Luxardo de' Franchi |
| La Principessa | Villa Sceriman |

**Costa d'Olio** p. dr. ★★★ DYA
Exquisite "blush wine" from Pinot Nero grown in the Costa d'Olio vineyard near Breganze. With a hint of pink and fleeting floral aroma, it has bracing fruit-acid balance and youthful charm.
Maculan

**Costozza**
Eccentric Colli Berici estate-making non-DOC varietals from Cabernet, Pinot Nero, and Riesling.

**Durello**
See Lessini Durello DOC.

**Gambellara** DOC
The zone E of Soave in Vicenza province has three types of wine, all based on Garganega with a dose of Trebbiano di Soave.
**– Gambellara Bianco** w. dr. ★→★★ DYA
Almost a twin of Soave, it provides a fresh alternative. Light straw-gold,

somewhat fruity in scent, its dry, balanced softness has a nice hint of acid on the finish. *Superiore* must have 11.5%.

**– Recioto di Gambellara** w. sw. (sp.) **★★**
From slightly raisined grapes, this golden dessert wine is intense in aroma and flavor, whether still, *frizzante* or *spumante*.

**– Vin Santo di Gambellara** am. sw. **★★**
A rarity from semidried grapes. After aging in barrel it is amber, aromatic, sweet, smooth, and relatively strong (14%).
Ag. 2 yrs.

| | |
|---|---|
| C.S. di Gambellara | A. Menti & Figli |
| Fratelli Cavazza | Zonin |

**Grola** r. dr. **★★★** 82 85 86
Special vineyard bottling of a table wine from basic Valpolicella varieties semidried to build body, strength and character with grace over 3–6 years.
Allegrini

**Le Sassine** r. dr. **★★→★★★** 79 82 83 85 86
Special vineyard bottling of what is virtually a Valpolicella but with 10% of grapes from old vines added for character in this sturdy table wine that improves with 4–5 years of age, sometimes more. Owner Marta Galli also makes a bright young table wine known as Le Piane.
Le Ragose

**Lessini Durello** DOC w. dr. (sp.)
Newly approved zone in the Lessini hills adjacent to Soave and Gambellara for a white from the worthy Durello grape, which makes steely dry wines. Both still and sparkling, of sturdy texture and attractive tang. Destined for wider recognition.

**Lison-Pramaggiore** DOC
New DOC comprises the areas of Tocai di Lison and Cabernet and Merlot di Pramaggiore, expanding the wine list to 12 types. The zone, in E Veneto alluvial plains extends into Friuli.

**– Cabernet** r. dr. ★→**★★★** 79 80 82 83 85 86
New rules split Cabernet into 3, putting the old Cabernet di Pramaggiore in the "undecided" category. Warm, somewhat tannic, grassy, it can become stylish in 3–6 years.
Ag. *riserva* 3 yrs.

**– Cabernet Franc** r. dr.
The dominate subvariety may now be so labeled – if anyone chooses.
Ag. *riserva* 3 yrs.

**– Cabernet Sauvignon** r. dr.
Since the name has cachet, this will probably be seen more often.
Ag. *riserva* 3 yrs.

**– Chardonnay** w. dr. (sp.)
Why not? They're planting it everywhere else. Also sparkling.

**– Merlot** r. dr. ★→**★★** 83 85 86
With up to 10% Cabernet permitted, this Merlot can have a nicely grapy robustness when young, fleshing out over 2–4 years.
Ag. *riserva* 2 yrs.

**– Pinot Bianco** w. dr. (sp.)
Unproven. It may also be *spumante*.

**– Pinot Grigio** w. dr. (sp.)
Ditto.

**– Refosco del Peduncolo Rosso** r. dr.
This red should do as well as in neighboring Friuli's plains.

**– Riesling Italico** w. dr. (sp.)
Unproven. It may also be *spumante*.

**– Sauvignon** w. dr. (sp.) **★** DYA
Already appreciated locally as a substitute for lemonade.

**– Tocai Italico** w. dr. (sp.) ★→**★★** DYA
Established here as Tocai di Lison, with the right to be called *classico* if grown around town. Though light, it can be a fresh, clean satisfying wine of some character.

**– Verduzzo** w. dr. **★** DYA
Known hereabouts as bone dry with a bite, it can be zesty in summer.

| | |
|---|---|
| C.S. di Portogruaro (Gruarius) | Paolo De Lorenzi |
| Castello di Porcia | Dialma |
| Club Produttori Associati | Guarise |

►

| | |
|---|---|
| La Braghina | Santa Margherita |
| La Fattoria | Sant'Osvaldo |
| La Frassinella | Tenuta Sant'Anna |
| Morassutti | Torresella |
| Ruggeri | Villa Frattina |
| Russolo | |

**Lugana**
Part of the DOC zone is in the Veneto. See under Lombardy.

**Malbec** or **Malbeck** r. dr. ★→★★ 82 83 85 86
A native of Bordeaux, it makes varietals in E Veneto. Dark ruby to
cherry red with peculiar grapy-fruity scent, the tannic harshness
smoothens with 3–5 years, sometimes more.

| | |
|---|---|
| Bertoja di Ceneda | Sant'Osvaldo |
| Deroà | Tenuta Sant'Anna |

**Masianco** w. dr. ★★★ DYA
From Garganega, Trebbiano, and Durello grown in Valpolicella, this
straw-colored wine is among the most elegant whites of Verona, thanks
to masterful balance of fruit against ample acidity.
Masi

**Merlot**
DOC under Colli Berici, Colli Euganei, Lison-Pramaggiore, Montello e
Colli Asolani, Piave, Pramaggiore, and as Breganze *rosso*, the E Veneto's
most popular variety also makes table wines, often in the grapy, herby,
lissome style, but truly elegant from some.

**Montello e Colli Asolani** DOC
This zone in hills S of the Piave near Montebelluna has been long noted
for Palladian villas and wine, particularly Venegazzù (the finest reserve
of which is not DOC).

– **Cabernet** r. dr. ★→★★ 82 83 85 86
From Cabernet Sauvignon and/or Cabernet Franc, this ruby-garnet
wine is dry, warm, somewhat tannic, stylish in 3–6 years.
Ag. *superiore* 2 yrs (1 in barrel).

– **Merlot** r. dr. ★→★★ 82 83 85 86
Ruby-garnet, grapy, supple when young, it can take on some
refinement over 3–5 years.
Ag. *superiore* 2 yrs (1 in barrel)

– **Prosecco** w. dr. s/sw. fz. sp. ★★ DYA
This typical white of Treviso province is usually *frizzante* or *spumante*.
Pale straw to light gold, whether dry or lightly sweet, it has delicate fruit
in aroma and flavor and a refreshing nut-like undertone.

| | |
|---|---|
| C.S. La Montelliana e dei Colli | Tomasella |
| Asolani | Venegazzù (Loredan Gasparini) |
| C.S. Valdobbiadene | |

**Piave** DOC
Large zone on either side of the Piave extending through the alluvial
plains N of Venice, which have become a model of flatland viticulture.
The list takes in 8 varietals.

– **Cabernet** r. dr. ★→★★★ 82 83 85 86
Cabernet Franc and/or Sauvignon make a robust ruby to garnet wine
with bouquet and flavor gaining style over 3–6 years.
Ag. *riserva* 3 yrs.

– **Merlot** r. dr. ★→★★ 83 85 86
Soft, round and sapid when young, this can take on a persuasive
bouquet with 2–4 years. Up to 10 million liters a year are made.
Ag. *vecchio* 2 yrs.

– **Pinot Bianco** w. dr. ★→★★ DYA
Clean and pleasant at best.

– **Pinot Grigio** w. dr. ★→★★ DYA
Fair to good wines, if light.

– **Pinot Nero** r. dr. ★ DYA
The climate of Piave doesn't seem right for this difficult vine.
Ag. *riserva* 2 yrs.

– **Raboso** r. dr. ★→★★★ 82 83 85 86
Raboso is noted in Piave for warm, rich, tannic wines that need time to
mellow and develop bouquet of herbs, berries and warm earth.

– **Tocai Italico** w. dr. ★→ ★★ DYA
Pale and delicate, Tocai can develop some tone.

– **Verduzzo** w. dr. ★ DYA
A pale green lightweight, it can be snappily fresh when young.

| | |
|---|---|
| Abbazia di Busco-Liasora | Maccari |
| Bertoja di Ceneda | Marcello del Majno |
| Bianchi Kunkler | Rechsteiner-Stepski Doliwa |
| C.S. di San Donà | Santa Margherita |
| C.S. Ormelle | Silvestrini |
| Castello di Roncade | Tenuta Mercante |
| Enoteca Prof. Cescon | Torresella |

**Pinot Bianco**
DOC in Breganze, Colli Berici, Colli Euganei, Lison-Pramaggiore and
Piave, Pinot Bianco is also used for table wines and *spumanti* in the
Veneto.

**Pinot Grigio**
DOC only in Breganze, Lison-Pramaggiore and Piave, numerous table
wines labeled Pinot Grigio del Veneto, delle Venezie, or with other
vague allusions to origins are processed or bottled in the Veneto. The
vine is increasingly planted.

**Pinot Nero**
Planted in various places, Pinot Nero is DOC in Breganze and Piave as
a red wine. It is also used for rosé and both pink and white *spumante*.

**Pramaggiore**
See Lison-Pramaggiore DOC.

**Prosecco di Conegliano-Valdobbiadene** DOC w. dr. s/sw. sw. fz. sp.
★→ ★★★ DYA
The fortunes of this seductive white from the native Prosecco vine have
risen with the demand for light, bubbly wines. Grown in the Marca
Trevigiano hills N of the Piave between Conegliano and
Valdobbiadene, production has grown to about 12 million liters a year.
Some 750,000 liters of this are Superiore di Cartizze or simply Cartizze,
from a delimited area near Valdobbiadene where wines are noted for
finesse. Prosecco, whether still, *frizzante*, or *spumante*, is pale white to light
golden, with a hint of almond in its fruity scent. The *spumante* may be
*brut, demisec*, or *amabile*. It is not always sold as DOC.

| | |
|---|---|
| Adami | Carpenè Malvolti |
| Augusto Agostini | Fattoria di Ogliano |
| Antica Quercia (Riello) | Maschio |
| Walter Balliana | Museo del Vino (Cosulich) |
| Desiderio Bisol & Figli | Mario Rossi |
| Bortolomiol | Mionetto |
| Canevel | Orlando |
| Adamo Canel & Figli | Ruggeri |
| Cantina Club | Santa Margherita |
| Cantina Colli del Soligo | Tenuta Sant'Anna |
| C.S. di Valdobbiadene | Torre Collalto-Trevisiol |
| Cantine Nino Franco | Valdo |
| Cardinal | Pino Zardetto |
| Emilio Carnio | Zonin |

**Raboso**
The indigenous variety makes reds of some distinction in Piave, where it
recently became DOC.

**Recioto Bianco di Campociesa** am. sw. ★★★→★★★★ 78 79 80 81 82 83
From select semidried Garganega and Trebbiano of the Campociesa
vineyard at Valgatara N of Verona, this amber-gold dessert wine is rare
and exceptional. Amply perfumed of ripe fruit and flowers, it is warm on
the palate, silky, and exquisitely sweet.
Masi

**Recioto della Valpolicella, Recioto di Soave**
See under Valpolicella and Soave.

**Riesling**
Both Riesling Italico and Renano are grown in the Veneto, though only
the Italico is DOC in Lison-Pramaggiore. Good table wines are made
elsewhere.

**Ruzante** r. dr. fz. ** DYA
Impishly lively red table wine based on Refosco mixed with other dark
grapes of E Veneto. Crimson and grapy, it is best very young.
Santa Margherita

**Sauvignon**
DOC only in Colli Berici and Lison-Pramaggiore, Sauvignon is being
planted elsewhere in the Veneto, notably in well-drained vineyards
where its smoky bite is well expressed.

**Soave** DOC w. dr. (sp.) *→ ***  DYA
This basically simple, unpretentious wine, which not long ago was
Verona's "local" white, has enjoyed miraculous success in recent times.
Second in volume to Chianti among DOCs with 52 million liters a year.
Soave vies with Asti Spumante as Italy's best-selling DOC wine in the
U.S. and other nations. It shows that popular acclaim is worth more
than approval by experts, who tend to downgrade it for lack of
character. Though much mass-produced Soave is uninspiring, some
wine from the *classico* area in view of the town's castle can be remarkably
attractive in its youth. Pieropan's La Rocca consistently stands out, as
do Bolla's Castellaro and Vigneti di Frosca, Masi's Col Baraca and the
Capitel Foscarino of Anselmi, all limited-production *crus*. From
Garganega with up to 30% Trebbiano di Soave, it is straw yellow,
sometimes with green glints, lightly fragrant, dry, of medium body, and
delicately fruity – ideally with an acidic bite and a hint of almond at the
finish. A *spumante naturale* is also permitted. Soave of 11.5% may be
called *superiore* if aged 9 months.
 – **Recioto di Soave** w. or am. sw. **→*** 79 81 82 83
Dessert wine from semidried grapes for Soave, it is light golden to amber
and, after 2–3 years of aging, is moderately strong (14%), with raisiny
aroma, smooth, rich texture, and rather sweet flavor. This Recioto may
also be *spumante* or, if fortified with alcohol, *liquoroso*. (Producers do not
include all bottler and shipper brands, which could also be dependable.)

| | |
|---|---|
| Aldegheri | Masi (Col Baraca) |
| Anselmi (Capitel Foscarino, | Montresor |
| Monteforte) | Fratelli Pasqua |
| Bertani | Pegaso-Premiovini |
| Ottavio Bixio | Pergreffi |
| Bolla (Castellaro, Vigneti di | Pieropan (Calvarino, La Rocca) |
| Frosca) | Santa Sofia |
| Boscaini (Monteleone) | Santi (Monteforte) |
| G. Campagnola | Sartori |
| Cantina del Castello | Scamperle |
| C.S. Cooperativa di Soave | Fratelli Sterzi |
| Fratelli Castagna | Fratelli Tedeschi |
| Costalta | Tommasi |
| Fratelli Fabiano | Villa Girardi |
| Folonari | Fratelli Zenato |
| Guerrieri-Rizzardi (Costeggiola) | Zonin |
| Lamberti | |

**Spumante** w. (p.) dr. (s/sw.) sp. **→***
*Spumante* is permitted under several DOCs for such diverse wines as
Soave, Recioto della Valpolicella, Prosecco and Sauvignon. But the
emphasis is on sparkling wines based on the Pinots and Chardonnay
made by either *champenoise* or *charmat*, the latter now often by the long
method of contact with the lees. The base wines generally originate in
the Tre Venezie, but the sources are rarely clear. *Méthode champenoise* is
marked (m.c.).
 – **Accademia Brut**
Maculan
 – **Bisol Brut (m.c.), Bisol Brut Nature (m.c.)**
Desiderio Bisol & Figli
 – **Bolla Brut**
Bolla
 – **Cardinal Brut, Cardinal Brut Rosé**
Cardinal
 – **Carlo Santi (m.c.)**
Santi
 – **Carpenè Malvolti Brut (m.c.)**
Carpenè Malvolti

– **Extra Brut Champenois (m.c.), Pinot Brut, Pinot Rosé Brut**
Zonin
– **Maschio Metodo Classico (m.c.)**
Maschio
– **Primo Franco Brut**
Nino Franco
– **Santa Margherita Chardonnay Cremant, Pinot Brut, Rosé Brut**
Santa Margherita
– **Tenuta Sant'Anna Brut (m.c.)**
Tenuta Sant'Anna
– **Venegazzù Brut (m.c.)**
Conte Loredan Gasparini
– **Zardetto Brut**
Pinot Zardetto

## Tocai

The white Tocai Friulano or Italico is DOC under Colli Berici, Colli Euganei, Lison-Pramaggiore and Piave and is the base of Breganze *bianco*. The rare Tocai Rosso, DOC in Colli Berici, is occasionally grown elsewhere.

### Tocai di Lison
See Lison-Pramaggiore DOC.

**Torcolato** w. s/sw. ***→**** 77 78 79 80 82 83
From semidried Vespaiolo, Tocai, and others of Breganze which attain a trace of "noble rot", this superb dessert wine after aging in small oak barrels has a crystal-clear golden color, flowery aroma, and luscious *amabile* flavor with extraordinary balance of components and a long, clean finish. Some prefer it young when it is opulently fruity, others after 6–10 years when it develops an almost Sauternes-like mellow warmth.
Maculan

**Turà** w. dr. fz. * DYA
If the creators of this pop concoction (made from what seems to be leftover white grapes grown in the provinces of Treviso, Verona and Vicenza) had taken a step further down the scale, they might have invented the wine cooler.
Ca' Donini                    Lamberti
De Baj                        Santi
Della Torre

## Valdadige
Part of the DOC zone is in the Veneto. See under Trentino-Alto Adige.

**Valpolicella** DOC r. dr. *→ ★★★ 82 83 85 86
From Corvina Veronese, Rondinella, and Molinara grown in the lowest wave of Alpine foothills above where the Adige River swings E through Verona, Valpolicella is similar in composition to Bardolino but sturdier, deeper, and usually longer-lived. An all-purpose red of ruby to purple hue, solid to plump body, grapy odor and a ripe plum flavor with a bitter finish, it shows traits that can approach refinement from some producers. Usually best young – from 6 months to 3 years – some age it well beyond with debatable results. The trend, a return really, to refermenting the base wine with Amarone lees is building size in both Valpolicella and more expensive table wines. The *classico* zone, known historically as Valpolicella – around Sant'Ambrogio, Fumane, San Pietro in Cariano, Negrar, and Marano – tends to make the best wine. But the DOC zone extends E almost to Soave through the Valpantena (which may be cited on labels), Valsquaranto, Valmezzane, Val Illasi, and Valtramigna. With 30–35 million liters a year (including Recioto), Valpolicella is fourth behind Chianti, Soave, and Moscato d'Asti in DOC production.
Ag. *superiore* 1 yr.

– **Recioto della Valpolicella** r. s/sw. sw. (sp.) ★★→★★★ 78 79 80 81 83 85 86
Select grapes for Valpolicella semidried may be used either for this dessert wine or the dry Amarone (see next entry). The classic Recioto is deep purple tending to garnet red with ample bouquet and fat structure: rich, strong (14%), with concentrated semisweet flavor that has a bitter undertone, it is rather pulpy when young but becomes smoother with age. A *spumante* is popular locally. There is also a *liquoroso* of 16%.

– **Recioto della Valpolicella Amarone** or **Amarone** r. dr.
★★→★★★★  74 77 78 79 80 81 83 85 86
The most prized Veronese wine is widely appreciated for the way it combines raw power with an almost Burgundian softness. Dark ruby purple when young, it tends to garnet with 4–5 years of age as its aroma deepens and its youthful largesse becomes austere and ethereal, though still retaining the *amaro* (bitter) dry finish that gives it its name. Capable of lasting 20 years, some connoisseurs prefer it inside 5 years when its fruity buoyancy is unsuppressed. Bertani and Bolla have deserved international reputations; Masi, Quintarelli, Tedeschi and Allegrini are rated tops with smaller scale production. (Producers do not include all bottler and shipper brands, which could also be dependable.)

Aldegheri
Allegrini (Fieramonte, Fiorgardone)
Anselmi
Bertani
Bolla
Boscaini (Marano)
Brigaleara
Ca' del Monte-Zanconte
G. Campagnola
C.S. Valpolicella
C.S. Veronese del Garda
Fratelli Fabiano
Girasole
Guerrieri-Rizzardi
Lamberti
Le Ragose
Masi (Campolongo Torbè, Mazzano, Mezzanello)
Pegaso-Premiovini
Pergreffi
Giuseppe Quintarelli
Luigi Righetti
Santa Sofia
Santi (Castello d'Illasi)
Sartori
Scamperle
Serègo Alighieri-Masi
Fratelli Speri
Fratelli Sterzi
Fratelli Tedeschi (Capitel Monte Fontana, Capitel Monte Olmo)
Tommasi
Vantini (Tramanal)
Villa Girardi
Fratelli Zenato
Zeni

**Venegazzù della Casa** r. dr.  ★★→★★★★  78 79 80 82 83 85 86
Classic Bordeaux mix in ruby-garnet wines that needs 5–10 years of aging to show eloquent bouquet and austere breed, making them outstanding in their genre in Italy. Issued in two versions with light and dark labels, the wines differ in style from year to year.
Conte Loredan Gasparini

**Villa Dal Ferro**
Estate in the Colli Berici with distinguished varietals, each given a special name: Cabernet (Le Rive Rosse), Merlot (Campo del Lago), Pinot Bianco (Bianco del Rocolo), Pinot Nero (Rosso del Rocolo), Riesling Renano (Busa Calcara), and Tocai Friulano (Costiera Granda). The Merlot *vino da tavola* ranks with Italy's finest and the Pinot Nero isn't far behind.

**Vin de la Fabriseria** w. sw.  ★★★  78 80 81 83 85 86
Golden dessert wine from semidried Garganega and Trebbano di Soave grapes grown in Valpolicella Classico. Ample in bouquet, it has a rich, warm flavor with hints of spices and herbs in its sweet softness.
Fratelli Tedeschi

*Wine & Food*

Whether the setting is a smart *ristorante* on the Grand Canal or a country *trattoria* with a spit turning before an open fire in the *fogher*, dining in the Veneto is a civilized pleasure. No other region has such equilibrium in food sources – from fertile plains, lush hillsides, woods, lakes, streams and the Adriatic – and no other cooks combine them with such easy artistry. Dishes can be lavish, ornate, and/or exotic (the Venetians introduced spices to Italy), but the elements that bind the regional cooking are simple: rice, beans, polenta, sausages, salame, poultry, game, mushrooms, and mountain cheeses. Venice is the showcase, but the food is every bit as delicious in the interior provinces, in Verona, Vicenza, Padua, Belluno, Rovigo, and perhaps most of all in Treviso, which some consider the sanctuary of Italian gastronomy. Listed are but a few of the delights.

**Asparagi in salsa** Tender white asparagus of Bassano del Grappa with sauce of hard-boiled eggs chopped with vinegar and oil.
**** Breganze *bianco*.

**Bigoli con l'anara** Thick hand-made spaghetti with duck ragout.
**→**** Valpolicella.

**Fegato alla veneziana** Calf's liver cooked with onions and wine.
** Cabernet di Pramaggiore.

**Granseola alla veneziana** Spider crab with oil and lemon.
*** Bianco di Custoza.

**Pasta e fasioi** Soups of pasta and beans are popular in the Veneto.
** Merlot or ** Bardolino.

**Pastissada di manzo** Beef (or horse meat) stewed with wine and

served with gnocchi or polenta.
**** Venegazzù della Casa.

**Risi e bisi** Rice and peas cooked together Venetian style.
** Tocai di Lison.

**Risotto nero** The rice is cooked with squid, blackened by its ink.
*** Soave *classico*.

**Sopa coada** Thick soup – stew really – of pigeon meat, bread, wine, and vegetables.
**→*** Merlot del Piave.

**Torresani alla peverada** Spit-roasted pigeons with a sausage-liver-anchovy-herb sauce on a bed of polenta.
*** Raboso or
***→**** Amarone.

## Restaurants

Recommended in or near wine zones: **Breganze** *Al Sole* at Bassono del Grappa. **Colli Berici** *Da Remo* at Vicenza. Colli Euganei *La Montanella* near Arquà Petrarca; *Rifugio Monte Rua* at Torreglia Alta. **Montello e Colli Asolani** *Villa Cipriani* at Asolo; *Agnoletti* at Giavera del Montello; *Da Celeste alla Costa d'Oro* at Volpago del Montello. **Piave-Marca Trevigiana** *Tre Panoce* at Conegliano; *Da Paolo Zanatta* at Maserada sul Piave; *Da Gigetto* at Miane; *Miron* at Nervesa della Battaglia; *Relais Toulà* at Paderno di Ponzano; *Gambrinus* at San Polo di Piave; *Da Lino* at Solighetto; *Alfredo El Toulà* at Treviso. **Verona area** *San Vigilio* at Garda; *Groto di Corgnan* at Sant'Ambrogio di Valpolicella; *Al Cavallo* at Torri del Benaco; *12 Apostoli*, *Arche*, *Il Desco* and *Nuovo Marconi* at Verona.

# Index

Note: Wines from different regions/zones but bearing the same name occur throughout the text (e.g. Cabernet, Moscato). To aid readers in locating them, the following abbreviations for regions (in parentheses) have been used preceding the relevant page number(s).

Ab *Abruzzi*; Ap *Apulia*; Bas *Basilicata*; Cal *Calabria*; Cam *Campania*; E-R *Emilia-Romagna*; F-VG *Friuli-Venezia Giulia*; Lat *Latium*; Lig *Liguria*; Lom *Lombardy*; Mar *Marches*; Mol *Molise*; Pie *Piedmont*; Sar *Sardinia*; Si *Sicily*; T-AA *Trentino-Alto Adige*; Tus *Tuscany*; Umb *Umbria*; VdA *Valle d'Aosta*; Ven *Veneto*.